W9-CPB-568

Table For Six

The Extraordinary Tales of an Ordinary Family

By Katrina Anne Willis

Bradley United Methodist Church
PENNSYLVANIA AND MAIN STREETS
GREENFIELD, INDIANA 46140

Copyright © 2011 by Katrina Willis
All Rights Reserved

ISBN 978-1-4583-7151-5

Cover design by Nicole Ross
Author Photo by Christie Turnbull Photography

For My Tribe,

Chris, Sam, Gus, Mary Claire, and George

Special thanks to my first readers, my most dedicated blog followers, and my biggest cheerleaders:

Molly Faber, Liz Farrelly, Logan Fisher, Jenny Godby, Andi Jeffers, Sarah and Lynn Kissel, Andrea Maurer, Jeryl and Larry Mitsch, Dawn Pier, Mary and Scott Robison, Nicole Ross, Patsy See, Carrie Smith, Dave and Jean Willis, and Jody Zahn.

And a big kiss to my first and forever fan, Mom.

Prologue

It's All About Setting Expectations

The two most engaging powers of an author are to make new things familiar and familiar things new. ~ *Samuel Johnson*

Before we begin, let me make one thing perfectly clear. If you're in the mood for a novel, for a strong story arc, for a primary plot twist and a revealing climax, this is not the place for you.

If, however, you're looking for a quick fix, a lighthearted read, a good cry, a glimpse into another life, a recognition that makes you smile and say, "Oh, yes – I remember that happening to me," then sit down and stay a spell.

I feel compelled to explain exactly what you're getting within these pages because it's not your ordinary, expected read. *Table for Six* is a series of essays (or perhaps more accurately defined in today's vernacular as blog posts) gathered together and presented under a common heading – which could range anywhere from career musings to vomiting to family discord to canine gastrointestinal distress. This anthology was born out of life experiences, recorded for the sake of my own feeble memory, compiled for those who see their own stories within mine, and offered up as a handshake to humanity – as a means to acknowledge that in sharing our stories, we ultimately partake in each others' lives. And I relish the opportunity to serve as that conduit in my own little corner of the world.

These are the stories that everyone has, but the ones that not everyone is willing to share. As a storyteller, I offer them to you. Because it is my sincere belief that in sharing, we close those gaps that tend to separate one life from another. In humbling ourselves to the common experience, we erase colors and step over socioeconomic lines. You may sit down with a cup of tea (or a Scotch on the rocks) and find comfort in the experiences that help articulate what it means to be a parent, to be a child, to be a spouse, to be a friend, to be human, to be alive.

These stories could have been told in numerous ways. They could have been strung together chronologically, might have been weaved into a narrative tale with a definitive beginning, middle, and end. But ultimately, they felt most at home as snippets of a larger life lived. They stop and start unexpectedly. They jump from one idea to the next. The first might make you laugh and the next might make you weep. Such is life, especially a life filled with love, happiness, friends, children, pets, homes, tears, angst, and abundance.

And isn't that your life, too?

Welcome to our stories, Dear Reader.

The Insanity Plan

Four Kids in Five Years

When my kids become wild and unruly, I use a nice, safe playpen. When they're finished, I climb out. ~ Erma Bombeck

"The Secret (And Not the One Featured On Oprah)"

I have a secret.

When I was younger, I dreamed of boardrooms and power suits. I thought day and night about the career I would have, the people I would lead, the money that would inevitably result. The money, in fact, might have been my biggest driver. Having next to nothing as a child, I often imagined all the things I had yet to experience. Money, of course, would open all the doors to those things. Exotic trips, fine dining, designer clothes, high-powered friends.

I planned the decor for my condo in some fast-action town. New York? London, perhaps? My furniture was going to be sleek, angled, shiny. My closets would be crammed with swanky high-heeled shoes and a matching handbag for every evening gown.

So, what – you might ask – does that have to do with my secret?

In all my childhood, young adolescent, and college dreams, being a mother never factored in. It wasn't part of the future I'd planned, wasn't a natural step on the ladder I was envisioning.

But four short years out of college, I was happily married to my beloved high school sweetheart, and we were living in the middle of rural Indiana on the farm that had been in his family for over 100 years. There was nothing angular or edgy about any of our furnishings. The lace curtains blowing at our oversized windows were, in fact, the antithesis of urban hip.

Oh. And we had our first baby.

The first of four.

In five years.

"And So It Begins"

I was born into this world in 1970 to a breathtaking black-haired beauty who modeled as a teenager and longed for nothing more than to be a wife and mother – and to a father who was the life of the party. The party, however, wasn't with his family. It was in a dark, dreary bar where the drinks went down easily and everyone called him by name. ("Hey,

Bill!") It was in a faraway state where the Aces were wild and the bets steep. My dad was a dreamer, an achingly handsome face that we never saw, a man in search of something more than a family could offer him, and the root of all my angst and insecurity.

I hated being the product of a single-parent family. I loved my mother more than anything in my small world, but I yearned for the things that I thought would make me complete… the clothes that came from a store instead of a cousin, the house with a backyard, the security of a father's sure and constant embrace, the smile of a mother who had not been abandoned, whose dreams had not been casually tossed aside.

Perhaps it was the insecurity of my own childhood that made me search for fulfillment elsewhere. I wanted to win, to be the best at everything, to be noticed, appreciated, and loved. Who knew that a kind and faithful husband and four sets of sticky, warm hands would fill that emptiness inside me so completely? It wasn't money, things, or perceived success that made me whole. It was what I'd been missing all along – the adoration of a man who vowed to stay by my side forever, the unfailing love of four small souls who depended on me for nourishment, warmth, shelter, food, love, and belonging. In providing for their needs, I met my own.

Chris and I first crossed paths in high school at the height of my teenage insecurity and drama. We were at opposite ends of the high school spectrum. He, the swimmer, band geek, drama guy who enjoyed math more than a good movie. Me, the three-season athlete with short hair, joke-cracking, constantly-singing, surrounded-by-friends gal who loved to write an English essay even more than nailing a clutch three-pointer. (And I truly enjoyed nailing a clutch three-pointer.) I was a year older. He was not even on my radar.

But via the wily ways of fate, we landed in Pop/Swing Choir together under the instruction of our mutual friend and teacher, Gail. He asked me out. I refused. He asked me out again. I refused again. And so continued the cycle. Eventually, Gail talked me into auditioning for the high school musical, "Fiddler on the Roof." Under the magic of the stage lights, as we sang "Now I Have Everything" to each other, I fell. And the rest, as they say, is history. After being endlessly drawn to the bad boys and the ones outside my reach, I marveled at how it felt to be truly loved, respected, and cherished.

Of course, we fought. I was a screamer back then – I couldn't express myself adequately unless the entire neighborhood could hear me. Often, I brandished a red pen and wrote scathing letters. Chris knew them by sight. When the ink was red, he knew he was in trouble. Many of our arguments stemmed from our religious differences. He was a staunch Methodist. I had Catholicism coursing through my veins.

Through those early years, we learned how to dance together. We learned how to more gracefully two-step around our disagreements. We tripped sometimes, but we grew up together. We agreed to disagree sometimes. We understood each other. We were best friends and partners. We married on a beautiful October day when we were both fresh out of college and began our forever journey together.

Then one morning in the Willis family farmhouse before I left for work, the EPT stick came back with a plus sign.

"Holy shit," I said.

"Holy shit," he replied.

When I became a mother for the first time in 1996, I was as crazy as they come. Certifiable, even. Motherhood apparently tripped some latent insanity wire in my brain and caused me to join the ranks of overbearing, weepy, paranoid first time mothers. Don't get me wrong – I loved Sam with my whole heart and soul. I loved being a mother. But I also began to obsess about childhood germs; to cry when a car pulled into the driveway and I didn't feel like visiting; to scream at my dear, patient husband when he arrived home 32 seconds after he said he would. Maybe it was a touch of postpartum depression. Maybe it was a snippet of genuinely inherited insanity. Whatever the cause, motherhood was the catalyst that changed me. It turned me into a different person. I was a raving lunatic, a snarling mother bear, an emotional wreck, a heartsick teenager with a flabby middle – all rolled into one tired, fashion-challenged mess. Motherhood definitely changed me. It made me redefine myself and experience feelings that emanated from the very core of my soul. And it happened with all my other children, too. With Gus in 1999, Mary Claire in 2000, and George in 2002. I'd like to say that I regained some of my sanity; that I reclaimed some of the wisdom of my youth, but that would be untrue. With the births of my four children, I waved goodbye to the calm, controlled, OCD-driven days that I knew so well, I accepted that the fringe on the carpet wouldn't always be straight and untangled, and I peered curiously into my crazy, tumultuous future. But, oh, what a wonderful, magical ride it has been.

We enjoyed the two years we had alone with Sam. We marveled at his every coo, his first tentative steps, his unarguable brilliance. It seemed we had Sam for an eternity before Gus came into our lives 26 months later. And before our little deep soul was walking or talking, into our lives popped sweet Mary Claire. Less than two years later, we welcomed Baby George, the happy-go-lucky caboose. People used to look at me with wonder, awe, and pity when I visited the mall with my four little hooligans in the early days. George was strapped to my middle in his

Baby Bjorn, Gus and Mary Claire rode side by side in the double jogging stroller, and Sam had a birds-eye view of everything from his perch on my shoulders.

"Look Mom!" Sam noticed one afternoon as we were running errands in our maroon Suburban, passing a woman moving at warp speed with her own double jogging stroller. "That woman has a stroller just like yours. Only she runs a lot faster than you do." And indeed, she did. (I was never known for my speed.) But I wasn't racing through this life. Although at times it seemed that the frenzied cycle – diapers, laundry, meals, dishes, bottles, more diapers – never slowed down, I tried to soak in as many moments as I could.

Way back in high school when I was cracking jokes and crying at the drop of a hat (because that's what teenage girls do), I was voted "Best Sense of Humor" in the class of 1988. Chris often argues that he's wittier than I, but I always remind him that I have the award to prove it. It sits in a dusty, sealed box right next to the large bumblebee trophy I was awarded upon winning the Hancock County Spelling Bee in 1983. I never truly understand how funny and frightening and poignant and fulfilling life could be, though, until I had four little products forged from our DNA who changed me in ways I could never have imagined. I may have been funny when I was 18, but there's nothing funnier than a three-year-old who refers lovingly to his penis as "his magic wand."

For as long as I can remember, I've written. As a child, I never went anywhere without a pen and a notebook. I wrote stories, one-liners, songs, poems, books. Adult strangers would ask me what I was doing, and I would proudly reply, "I'm a writer. I'm writing." But as an adult, it was a difficult thing for me to say.

"I'm a writer."

Claiming I'm a writer always seemed presumptuous to me. Am I writer just because I write? Or do I need to be acknowledged with publication to truly earn that coveted title? Even now, after years of being paid to put my words on paper, I still find it difficult to say I'm a writer. But I know in my heart that's who I am. What I am. What I've always been destined to be.

In multiple moldy boxes in our attic and drawers in my desks and tucked away in forgotten hiding places, I've amassed a lifetime of words. Some are the recorded words of my favorite authors – a litany of quotes, songs, fragments. Most words are my own. Journals, notebooks, random pieces of paper – all contain the thoughts and ideas that flowed from my pen, my pencil, or my Brother word processor, depending on the year.

I've begun at least 50 books with at least 50 different story lines. Some are bad. Most are worse. I've completed two novels. And you'll have to trust my judgment when I assure you that they'll never see the light of day.

Many of my notebooks were ripped up and thrown away in a fit of writing angst when I was in my early 20s. I'm sad that what once was so important to me is lost forever. That I didn't do a better job of protecting and nurturing the young, inexperienced, fledgling caterpillar thoughts that were trying their damndest to become important, meaningful, beautiful butterflies.

But the great thing about words?

There are always more.

And this parenting gig?

No better inspiration.

"Small Goodbyes, Big Hellos"

A mother's life is, indeed, a roller-coaster of emotions. One day I want to hug those four creatures close to my heart, the next day I want to give them all a swift kick in the ass.

Some more than others.

Some more frequently than others.

But every time they walk out the door to begin a new phase of their lives, they take a little piece of my soul with them. At back-to-school time, I hear lots of keening about kids starting kindergarten for the first time, about kids sleepless over their first freshman class, about kids decorating their dorm rooms too many miles away. I talked with a young friend about the bittersweet act of moving her infant daughter from a bassinet to a crib. She cried. And I remembered.

I remembered those pivotal moments when each of my babies moved a step away from me. From cribs to big kid beds to school to cell phones.

And I realized that parenting is a series of small goodbyes.

You tidy them up, kiss their cheeks, wish them well, and send them on their next adventure.

Is it bittersweet? At times, yes. When I look at my almost-teenager and remember him spitting up on me violently and without fail, I can't believe how many years have passed. And as he reminds me, only three more years until he drives. Only six more until he's an adult.

Their little goodbyes may be heartbreaking in many ways, but exciting in so many more. Who in God's name knew that Chris and I were capable of creating four little *people*? People with individual ideas and thoughts, unique hearts and minds. Human beings. From us.

My mom never wanted me to leave. Softball scholarship in Arizona? Forget it. Job offer in St. Louis? Never. She begged me to stay nearby, and I complied. I don't regret, but sometimes I wonder. Who would I have been if I'd spread my wings and flown a little farther?

The greatest lesson her need taught me was not to need so much. To be able to let them go. To send them on their way with a warm meal, some change in their pockets, and love in their hearts. They're mine, but they're not mine.

They are Sam, Gus, Mary Claire, and George.

Perhaps they'll be doctors, teachers, writers, or bums. They will choose their own destinies. They will make the decisions that will shape their futures. And with every little goodbye, I'm teaching them how to fly.

Just a bit. Then a bit more.

I feel like I know these creatures so well – like I have to know them well because they are from me and of me. But yet, they are still such mysteries. When I look at them through others' eyes, a whole new world opens up to me. I'm always surprised when my best friend, Jackie, makes an observation about one of my own, and I'm taken aback by her accuracy and wisdom. I want to shout, "Yes! You're right! Why didn't I ever see that?" But that's the beauty of them, isn't it? They are such multi-faceted human beings that no pair of eyes can fully and adequately see them.

In so many ways, my kids are alike. And in so many ways, they're such unique, complex individuals. I suppose that's true of human beings in general, but it's never as obvious as it is when four mini-people are taking over the house that you live in and pay for. I watch Sam sometimes and see him morph into Chris – with his actions, his words, his mannerisms. I look at Gus crossing his legs and can only see Pappaw. Mary Claire's freckle-faced feistiness is a bit of a self-reincarnation. And George? Well, he's just got the piss and vinegar of all of us running through his veins. I marvel at the knowledge that each of our kids has his an unprecedented story to tell, a unique history to write.

Samuel Joseph

"The Firstborn"

11/06/1996

Having a child is surely the most beautifully irrational act that two people in love can commit. ~ Bill Cosby

"An Ode to Spit-Up and Unabashed Adoration"

Sam came first. He was our guinea pig baby. A beautiful, head-turning, blue-eyed ten-pound dream who arrived in this world via c-section after 36 hours of unsuccessful labor and unplanned vomiting. We lavished him with love and attention, but we also tested all our mistakes out on him. At 25 and 26, Chris and I were somewhat ill-equipped to be responsible for another human life, but we wholeheartedly threw ourselves into the task at hand. Sam was an easy baby – solemn and quiet, he cried only when he was hungry or tired.

And he was hungry all the time.

I decided long before he emerged from my grossly distended belly that I wouldn't breastfeed him. Despite the admonitions of the experts who staunchly argued that he would probably be stricken with rickets, grow a second head, and be subject to a life of abject poverty if I didn't breastfeed, I opted for formula. We were young, we were poor, we had a friend who kept us fully stocked in free Enfamil, and I was going back to work in eight short weeks. And besides, I was entirely uncomfortable with the idea of whipping my girls out in public and on demand.

Sam guzzled his formula like it was manna from heaven. And then he promptly spit it up with geyser-like force when he was finished. All over me, the couch, the carpet, the dogs, and whatever innocent bystander happened to be within ten feet of him. I went through the first year of Sam's life smelling like rotten eggs – and feeling very much the same way. Our trusted Dr. Andrews assured us that Sam would "spit up till he sits up." When he began sitting and still continued spewing, the good doctor changed his mantra to "he'll spit up till he stands." Then "he'll spit up till he walks." We were fairly convinced that Sam would spit up until he turned the tassel on his college graduation cap. Luckily, however, he stopped his projectile vomiting long before he started school, and we were able to discard most of the clothes that were permanently marked with stubborn, yellow formula stains.

We forgave Sam his insatiable need to drown us in baby vomit. Amazing what you can get used to when a fat, happy child is lying contentedly in your arms. Love is a word so overused that it seems strikingly inadequate to describe what I felt for this little stinky bundle of happiness. The thought of him growing inside of me, of being introduced to this world via little bits of both Chris and me, of watching him grow up and become an inimitable creature — it was all a little too much to swallow at times.

Chris and I fumbled through parenthood with false confidence and preconceived notions about how children should be raised. We believed in spanking — it was good enough for us, it would be good enough for our own kids. We believed in strict bedtimes, solid routines, high expectations, and a great deal of laughter. We adopted some things our parents suggested, but we rejected most. We lived happily, simply, and frugally in our little farmhouse in the middle of nowhere.

I took Sam for walks in his stroller along the bumpy, back-country roads. We'd stop and feed the cows, grunt at the pigs, watch the butterflies. When we returned home, we'd swing together under the shade of our side porch, endlessly picking white paint chips from our shorts. I'd feed Sam in our neon-bright, yellow kitchen while our dogs, Zebedee and Noah, waited patiently for something substantial to fall on the floor.

Returning to work after my maternity leave ended was a traumatic event for me. We needed the second income, but I couldn't bear the thought of leaving Sam every day. My mom agreed to watch him because there was a wait-list at my onsite daycare center. I was so grateful for her offer, so afraid, though, that she would undermine my authority. That Sam would love her more. That I would become the outsider.

"We need to set clear expectations," Chris proclaimed. "We need to tell your mom what we expect, what we want to happen during the day, what we think is important. We're his parents."

So, when Mom started calling Sam "my baby" (as in, "When are you bringing my baby over tomorrow?"), my husband's head nearly popped off. When we found out she'd been feeding him sips of Diet Coke at age six months, Chris nearly lost it.

"He's my grandson," Mom would argue dismissively. "I'm supposed to spoil him."

"But you're also his babysitter," we would respectfully counter. "We insisted on paying you so we could maintain a babysitter relationship. We need you to respect our wishes when it comes to Sam."

"Oh, pshh," was Mom's reply. "I raised two girls by myself. Certainly, I can take care of my grandson."

And so we danced that tenuous line between "Honoring thy Mother" and insisting upon her doing things our way. Chris had a great deal more trouble than I did keeping his opinions to himself. As is generally true in my life, I saw everything in shades of gray. Sure, Sam was eating cookies, and breathing secondhand smoke, and sleeping in my mom's arms instead of in his crib. But he was adored and showered with attention every minute of the day. Maybe both ends were a bit too extreme, but surely Sam would emerge from this experience with a balanced blend of all the best.

When the daycare spot opened shortly before Sam's first birthday, I feared for Mom's sanity and overall general health.

"How could you take him from me? Who will love him more than I do?"

We tried with great fervor to explain the benefits of having Sam with me every day. I could have lunch with him. I could take him for walks in his stroller. I could interact with his teachers. He would have friends his own age. He'd learn to socialize, to share, to interact.

And as I stared at his daycare building from my office window view, I was jolted with unexpected sadness. Why was he mere steps away from me, being raised by someone else? Why did his daycare providers spend more time with him than Chris and I did? Oh, wait – my income.

That was it. But as the days dragged on and Sam cried when I left him –
when they had to pry him from my arms and assure me that he was fine
the minute I left – I came to a crossroads. I couldn't do it anymore. I
couldn't leave him. I couldn't let someone else fill his days with love and
laughter. And I was feeling the need to give him a brother or a sister,
sooner rather than later. With two in daycare, would it really make sense
for me to work? Chris was finishing his Master's work in education, and I
was convinced he would soon land a higher-paying administrative job.
Armed with that faith, I gathered up the courage to write my letter of
resignation, steadied myself to give up the high-powered career I hoped to
someday have, read Iris Krasnow's "Surrendering to Motherhood" at least
five times, and quit my job.

I've never described myself as a stay-at-home-mom. First of all, I
like to believe that I'm a woman first, a wife next, and a mother after that.
And in those early days, I never stayed at home. I planned daily trips to
the park, to the mall, to lunch with my cousins and their kids. Sam and I
spent more time in our wood-paneled Buick RoadMaster station wagon
than we did in our house.

And in those glorious days, I became pregnant with Gus.

That initial discussion went something like this…

ME: Honey, I want to have another baby.

CHRIS: Well, then we better get to it!

And so it was. We talked about it, we did it, it took. A few short weeks later, the EPT stick showed positive again, and I was over the moon. I've had beloved friends who have battled infertility. I am not immune to the heartbreak, expense, frustration, self-doubt, and then more heartbreak that accompanies that particular journey. I would never for a minute take my fertility for granted. But God graced me with a body designed for babies. When Chris and I wanted to get pregnant, we did. He would argue that his virility was the reason. I would argue that my superior ovaries did the trick. Whatever the case, God granted us babies as quickly as we mentioned we wanted another one.

He obviously had a lot more faith in our ability to parent than most.

Augustus Charles

"The Sick One"

02/09/1999

Every child begins the world again. ~ *Henry David Thoreau*

"Life's Greatest Lesson"

Sweet, quiet Baby Gus with a cap of auburn curls and an innate flair for the dramatic made his way into our lives on a bitterly cold February day in 1999. He was a planned c-section. After battling for far too many hours to deliver Sam and eventually vomiting all over my freshly-scrubbed, surgery-prepped, overly-pregnant, non-dilating self, we decided to opt for the c-section without all the preceding drama.

I distinctly remember Dr. Jones proclaiming, "He's a boy!" as Gus was pulled from my belly.

Chris was distracted by the ability to see my internal organs. "What's that, Doc?" he asked whilst gazing at my intestines at least five or six times during the actual surgery.

When I glanced at Gus's sweet face and that mess of wet curls, all I could think about was my two sons growing up together. I was so grateful Sam had a brother. At that instant, I didn't know Gus well. I loved him with every ounce of my being, but I was so happy for Sam.

While I was in recovery, things took a turn for the worse. Like a play unfolding before our eyes, we didn't know how bad things were going to get. But our Gus was sick, sick, sick.

"What does that mean?" I kept asking. Before Gus, sick meant a sore throat, a high fever, an ear infection. I couldn't reconcile Gus's "sick" with my own limited knowledge of childhood illnesses.

Before he was 24 hours old, before I had a chance to hold or touch him, before his visitors had an opportunity to greet him, Gus was transferred to St. Vincent's NICU in critical condition. Both of his lungs had collapsed, he was intubated, and he was placed in a drug-induced coma. Every minute of his new life was touch and go. And I was stuck in a hospital bed an hour away with fresh abdominal stitches and an OB who refused to release me before he felt reasonably sure I wouldn't end up sick as well.

"Where my baby?" Sam asked as he trotted into my empty room. "Where my Baby Gus?" And I held him, and I stroked his soft, blonde head, and I cried hot, stinging tears that wet his upturned, questioning face. Visitors came to see our new addition before the word had spread. Uncomfortable silences filled the room as they arrived armed with blue balloons, blue outfits, blue bibs. I sobbed as Chris called me with updates. He took a Polaroid picture and brought it to me so I wouldn't be shocked when I saw Gus for the first time. I looked at his still little body, crossed with tubes and wires, spotted with blood, a machine taped to his face, and I knew that nothing could prepare me for that particular, horrifying sight.

When I was finally released from the hospital and able to make the drive to Indianapolis nearly 48 hours after Gus's birth, I was introduced to a world I never even knew existed. Funny how you can meander through life not understanding the gravity of another man's troubles until they become your own. The Neonatal Intensive Care Unit was a planet inhabited by devoted professionals, grief-stricken and stunned new parents, and critically ill babies. At seven pounds, Gus dwarfed his preemie neighbors. He looked so robust and healthy, but he resided in the corner of the NICU that was reserved for the sickest of its patients.

I sat in my wheelchair at his bedside watching the ventilator mechanically move his tiny, broken chest, and I willed the air from my own lungs into his. I glanced briefly at the other babies, at the other parents – careful not to invade their private heartbreak, always aware of the tenuous threads of life that kept these babies feebly tethered to our world.

"Gus is very, very sick," our nurse, Lynn, explained to us softly.

"Will he...die?" I dared to ask one day, choking on the word that had yet to be spoken.

She chose her words carefully.

"He is critically ill. But he's not as sick today as he was the night he came to us. He is still not out of the woods, though. Talk to him, sing to him, love him. Give him something to hold onto."

And so we did. We talked to him. We sang to him. We recorded a tape that the nurses played for him when we grabbed a few interrupted and restless hours of sleep in the waiting room. On that tape, I softly sang about "The Things We've Handed Down." And I cried as I recorded, "Don't know why you chose us. Were you watching from above? Is there someone there who knows us, said we've give you all our love?" I wondered what Gus heard through the fog and haze of his medication.

Lynn explained the various doses he received through the central line that was sewn into his chest. "This one is for pain. This one is for edema. This one is for infection. This one helps him forget."

Heartbreaking to think that Gus needed to forget before he even had a chance to remember.

Days in the NICU are measured in minutes, in seconds, in miniscule victories. His PEEP settings improved today. Victory! His oxygen saturation levels dropped. Two steps back. Leaving the NICU for food, for clothes, for Sam was like stepping into a bright, unfamiliar world. I squinted in the daylight like an animal coming out of hibernation. The noises were too loud, the cars too fast. Conversation was challenging, English seemed an unknown language during those days. I couldn't produce thoughts, couldn't form sentences. I had too many foreign words clogging up my mind. Vecuronium, Versed, pseudomonas, bronchopulmonary dysplasia, pulmonary interstitial emphysema. When contemplating these realities, there was little room left in my brain for subjects such as weather, politics, and grocery shopping.

Sweet Sam was jostled from home to home, always wrapped in the tender, loving care of our family and friends, but always fiercely clinging to me when it was time for us to part again.

"Come home, Mama," he'd beg. "Please come home."

And his pleas would tear my heart in two. Half would follow him to his next destination, his next sleepover. The other half stayed with my sick baby. I don't know which one needed me more during those horrible weeks, but I know there wasn't enough of me to give them both what they required.

Days turned to weeks, and still Gus struggled. I pumped milk for him in the nursing room and stored it in the freezer. Someday he would need it. Someday. Strapped like a cow to a high-powered milking machine, I produced more milk than most of the other mothers combined. Once when I pulled my overflowing tray of bagged and frozen breast milk from the freezer, another mother looked at me and said, "Oh, you're the one." And so I was. The milk producer with the overactive mammary glands. The wet nurse with no one to feed.

"You should open your own Milk Bank," Chris joked with me. "We could pay for these hospital bills with the profits." Dutifully, I kept pumping, kept bagging, kept freezing. It was the only measurable thing I could do for Gus. One day, I fell asleep with the machine turned on, and awoke with nipples stretched to three times their normal size. I laughed at the sight, and then cried at the absurdity of it all. For half an hour, I sat in that nursing room with my disfigured nipples exposed for all who cared to see, and I sobbed with the force of a breaking dam.

Such was life in the NICU.

Our lifelong best friends sustained us during those trying times. Brent and Jackie lived within walking distance of the hospital, and they opened their home to us. They sheltered us, fed us, cried with us, cared for us. They got up with us in the middle of the night when the doctors would call and tell us to come in right away – that this night might be Gus's last. We stumbled in and out of their home, we left their refrigerator door open in our tired stupor, we let them raise and nurture our healthy child while we whispered to and cajoled our sick one.

"Honey," Jackie questioned one morning as we clutched our coffee cups with desperation, "did you mean to park in the yard?" I looked out the window and saw Chris's blue truck sitting squarely in their front yard. In the wee hours of the morning, I'd arrived at their home and neglected to take the truck out of gear. In the night, it had made its way into the grass and had come to rest by their front door.

"No," I sighed. "No, I didn't mean to park in the yard." And then I chuckled. But the gesture felt so foreign, so wrong, that I burst into tears instead.

"Shh, shh," Jackie whispered, rubbing my back and smoothing my tangled hair. "It's just grass. It will grow back." And I knew she was right. Those blades of grass that had been crushed by the weight of my husband's work truck would spring right back to life. And still my baby couldn't take a breath on his own.

One miraculous day when I stumbled my sleep-deprived self into the NICU after the 7:00 AM shift change, Lynn greeted me in the hand sanitizing room with a playful smile.

"Looks like Gus decided today was a good day to be born."

When I approached his open-air bed in the sea of tiny incubators, I saw what she meant. There was my boy with his beautiful, soulful eyes wide open, staring in wonderment at his surroundings.

"Hello, little one," I cried as I gingerly held his tiny hand, battered with needle sticks. "Hello, precious baby boy," I sobbed. "Welcome to the world. Welcome, Gus, welcome."

Lynn explained that Gus had broken through his medication and that as long as his vital signs remained stable, they would let him wake up.

Perhaps the most heart-wrenching moments of those days were the times when Gus would cry – silenced by the tube that ran between his vocal cords, yet visibly upset with fat tears rolling down his puffy cheeks. Day after day, Gus's edema worsened. His little bloated body continued to swell and grow as the doctors battled to find the right combination of drugs to keep his lungs working without causing his kidneys to fail. Always a balancing act in the NICU, always a game of wait-and-see.

Chris and I learned about pacing, about celebrating the small victories and surviving the inevitable setbacks.

"This is a marathon, not a sprint," Dr. Tolliver informed us at the beginning. And so we trudged on, thirsty for water, in need of rest, desperately searching for the finish line. And Gus journeyed with us, fighting valiantly for his brand new life, courageously battling to draw an unassisted breath.

Twice, he failed extubation. Twice, we held our own breath as his mechanical support was removed. Twice, we watched his oxygen saturation levels plummet. Twice, we witnessed the doctors painfully inserting another tube into his lungs with heavy sighs and promises of "next time." Every day, I sobbed silently at his bedside, willing my own breath into his lungs, eager to give my own life if it would grant him his own. At night, I dreamed about him floating carelessly in the darkness of my womb where there were no harsh lights, no painful needle sticks, no mind-numbing medications. I wished him back inside me where I could feed and nurture him with my own body, where I could protect and sustain him.

One night, Dr. Andrews came to visit Gus in the NICU upon his return from vacation.

I cried at the sight of our healer. I begged him for information, for answers.

"Is he going to die?" I asked cautiously, stumbling over the very word.

"He's a very, very sick baby," he answered with frustration, raising his voice. "Yes, he might die. But you can't think that way. You have to be strong for him. He can hear you, feel you, draw strength from you. You can't stand at his bedside crying all the time. This is *not* about you!"

And as I stifled my sobs and choked back my tears, I wondered how it wasn't about me. How it wasn't about Chris. About Sam. Gus was a piece of us, a vital part of our family. Without him, we would not be complete. Without him, I would never again be whole.

The following night, we ventured home for an evening alone with Sam. Driving away from the hospital felt like a betrayal. If I looked back, I was sure I'd turn to stone. Sam jabbered in his carseat from St. Vincent's to our gravel driveway.

"And I had gum at Nanny's. And I played with Molly. And I read two books…"

We smothered him with kisses, tucked him into his big boy bed, read him as many stories as his sleepy voice could request, and closed his heavy, wooden door. Then I inched down the creaky hallway to the Paddington nursery that was anxiously awaiting a new inhabitant. The air that escaped from behind the door was stale, cold. We had closed the vents to save on our skyrocketing propane costs, and the room now felt like an unused refrigerator. Dead flies lined the freshly painted windowsills. I gathered a sky blue blanket from the crib, and I sat on the cold floor and cried. Hot tears warmed my chilled face until I had nothing left inside. I curled up on the floor, clung tightly to the blanket in my arms, and fell into a fitful sleep. I don't know how much time passed before Chris gently led me back to our bed. And there we curled up into each other, filling the empty gaps with our arms and legs. Filling the void in our hearts with whatever leftover feelings we could muster.

The phone jarred us out of a restless sleep early the next morning.

"Yes, Doctor?" Chris asked as I snapped instantly awake.

"We'll be right there."

"What?" I asked anxiously with dread filling my heart, angry that we'd chosen last night to drive so far away. "What did he say?"

A smile — so foreign, so unfamiliar — tugged at the corners of Chris's eyes.

"He's off the vent."

With frantic excitement, we woke Sam up, threw clothes on him and on ourselves, loaded up in the RoadMaster, and tempted fate with our careless speeding. The morning air was frigid, our happy tears froze instantly on our cheeks.

"We see my baby?" Sam asked over and over. "We see Baby Gus?"

"Yes, Sweetie," we replied again and again, without hesitation. "We're going to see Baby Gus."

"Hooray, Baby Gus!" he shouted from the backseat.

"Hooray, Baby Gus!" we agreed.

Hooray, Baby Gus.

After we'd sterilized our hands and arms and donned our masks and gowns, we raced back to Gus's bedside. And there, sitting in the ever-present rocking chair, was Lynn, holding our son.

"Would you like to hold your baby?" she smiled at me. "Come on, Mom, he's been waiting."

Lynn arranged his remaining tubes and wires and placed his swaddled body into my anxious arms. After four grueling weeks, after two surgeries and multiple extubation attempts, after a week in contact isolation, after discussions of transferring him to a hospital where he could be treated on a heart/lung bypass machine, after 28 heart-wrenchingly silent days and sleepless nights, I was able to hold my second son for the first time.

His serious, cerulean eyes gazed at me with wonder. Then he squeezed his tiny, bruised hands into fists and produced his elusive, throaty cry.

"That's it, Baby," I whispered in his ear. "You cry. You cry all you need. You deserve it. There you go. Let is out, Gus. Let it out." And he wiggled in my arms and fought my touch – unused to being held, to being cradled, to being awake. The harder he struggled, the tighter I clung to him.

"You're safe," I cried. "You're safe. I'm here, Baby. I'll take care of you."

All the while, Sam gently touched his mess of curly hair and whispered, "Hi, Baby Gus. It's okay, Baby Gus. I'm Sam. It's okay."

And that day, we truly knew that it was, indeed, going to be okay.

Later, when the threat of losing Gus was far enough behind us, I asked Dr. Tolliver how close we'd come to saying goodbye to him.

"Let me put it this way," our neonatologist said as he carefully considered his words. "Gus walked to the edge of a very tall cliff. And he looked over the side. Had he taken another step, there was nothing medically that we could have done to keep him from going over. But he's back now. He's safe. And he's all yours. That boy is one hell of a survivor."

My still water that runs deep. My enigma. My loving, responsible, sensitive, emotional boy. Augustus Charles will always be a bit of a mystery to me, but I think that's the way he wants it to be. I was never a loner. I don't understand the loner mentality. Surround me with friends and put me in the center of attention, and I'm a happy girl.

Not so for Gus. He relishes his solitude, languishes in the boisterous chaos of a room full of ten-year-olds. "Leave him alone," Chris instructs when I ask if Gus wants to join in the play of a neighborhood group of kids. "He's happy." Happy doing his own thing when he wants, where he prefers, and as he pleases. That's my Gus.

We often describe him as "slipping under our radar." When we think he's upstairs in his room, he's actually wafted past us on his silent trip to the basement. When we think he's outside playing, we instead find him curled up in a chair with a book. But when I hug him at night in his bed, I know just where he is. Because he clings to me with his skinny, gangly arms, making me think that he might never let go. Wrapped around me tightly, I can hear the staccato beat of his heart and feel the rise and fall of the breath passing in and out of his lungs. The breath we feared he would never take on his own.

He was in such a dark and unknown world his first five weeks of life. Sedated with Versed, we'll never really know the first impulses that lodged themselves in his baby brain. Did he hear our voices? We'd like to think he did. Did he feel our love and warmth surrounding him? God, I hope so. But what I do believe is that those five weeks changed Gus, molded him into the emotional, creative, thoughtful boy that he is.

Often a target for adolescent boys who don't know what to make of him, I know that someday he'll be a fine man that people will flock to. For companionship, for wisdom, for insight, for life. I'm eager to see what kind of intellectual and spiritual beauty this little cocoon of a boy — quiet, reserved, socially challenged, and easily brought to tears — will someday morph into.

Mary Claire

"The Girly Girl"

07/17/2000

A girl without freckles is like a night without stars. ~ Author Unknown

"More Pink than Pepto Bismol"

After six months of staying home with a two-year-old and an infant, the NICU bills were steadily crushing us with their egregious weight, and I was losing my nerve.

The Willis family farmstead had become our home. Owned by Chris's ancestors for over 100 years, we'd devoted our time and energy – and what little money we had – to making the farmhouse warm and habitable. The little white house (with a stairwell steep enough to be considered more of a slide than a set of stairs) sat in the middle of three acres of land and was surrounded by fields of corn and beans that were tended by neighbor farmers on a land lease contract. The floors were creaky, there wasn't a wall that was built on a 90-degree angle, and the wind whipped through the oversized windows like water through a sieve.

But we grew to love that house. We sponged paint-soaked rectangles on our bedroom floor to make it look like brick. Sam's bedroom floor was bright green and lined with football field numbers. A painted scoreboard served as his headboard. And Gus slept fitfully (as Gus always slept) in his bright, primary-colored Paddington Bear nursery. On the warmest summer days, I would take my boys outside and read to them on the peeling white porch swing. Zebedee and Noah would frolic in the yard and chase field mice. Sometimes they'd be joined by Esau, the little beagle who showed up more often than he stayed away. Our lives were good. Money was scarce, but happiness, abundant.

"Honey," I said one night after we finished a casserole dinner, the only thing our strained and struggling budget could afford, "I think we should have another baby now." I continued before he could respond. "You're done with your Master's work, I'm sure you'll get an administrative raise next year, and if we don't get pregnant soon, I'm going to lose my nerve."

"Katrina," Chris interjected carefully, "Gus is only six months old. We're drowning in debt, we're outgrowing this house, and we're trying to survive on a teacher's salary. What could possibly make you think this is the right time?"

Although Gus's lungs were healing with every passing day, and his hearing – which we were forewarned he'd lose – seemed to be normal, and the threat of RSV was slowly fading away, the memory of our five weeks in the NICU was still fresh in my mind. Was I brave enough to tempt fate again? Could we survive another sick baby? Was my body ready for another pregnancy? I wasn't sure of any of those answers, but I knew if we waited too long, my fears would prevent me from taking that next step. For me, it was now or never.

Chris was never one to argue with guaranteed sex, so we took our chances. In normal Willis fashion, I was pregnant within a month.

Those first few months of pregnancy quite nearly did me in. The bills mounted, Gus cried more than Sam ever even considered crying, Sam became more talkative and needy, and the constant fatigue trapped me in a foggy haze. Often, I found myself asleep in our La-Z-Boy recliner with a baby on my chest, a toddler by my side, and a looming pile of unpaid bills strewn across the floor. When Gus would whimper his preamble to a crying fit, I would cry with him – begging him to let me sleep, pleading with him to close his eyes. But six-month-olds aren't very negotiable.

We muddled through those days and nights with tired eyes, weary minds, and an overdrawn checking account. But still, somehow, we managed to be excited about our impending arrival. We considered names and room rearrangements. We opened our hearts and our heads to becoming a family of five. And we never looked back.

On July 17, 2000, our sweet Mary Claire made her way into the world and into our lives. A month before her arrival, Chris received the anticipated job promotion and raise we were banking on, and we began packing all of our belongings for a move to Muncie, home of Ball State University, our mutual alma mater. We said teary goodbyes to the only home we'd ever known, comforted somewhat by the knowledge that we would never really have to say goodbye – that the farmhouse would always be Willis owned. We rented a 3rd floor, three-bedroom apartment in Muncie to house our three children under the age of three amongst a horde of undergrads and began an adventure punctuated with postpartum tears and new career excitement.

Although I had an undeniable longing in my heart for a daughter, Mary Claire scared me to death. All those folds, all those creases, all those hormones. Because I was a female myself, I thought I'd know how to raise one. But she came out differently than me. She was a baby. And she was Mary Claire, not me.

As an infant, Mary Claire was the most content, well-mannered, bright-eyed baby imaginable. Swathed in every known shade of pink, Mary

Claire stole our hearts — and the hearts of everyone who knew her. From the moment she arrived in this world, she sucked the index and middle fingers on her right hand. When she had enough small motor mastery to add her pink blankie to the mix, she'd hold it with her left hand, directly under her nose, while she gently rubbed well-loved holes into it.

We called that pink lifeline the "Skanky Blankie." As she crawled and toddled her way through her earliest days, Mary Claire would go nowhere without it. She dragged it into movie theatres, dirty restrooms, overcrowded restaurants, hot gymnasiums. She couldn't sleep without it, always had to know where it was. When we pried it from her resistant fingers to wash it, she would sit beside the front-load washing machine and watch it spin around and around and around — big, fat tears sliding silently down her cheeks.

"My blankie," she wailed with her chubby little fingers splayed out on the washing machine glass like starfish. "My blankie!" Inevitably, we'd give it to her with a bit of dampness remaining. None of us could stand to hear her wail through the entire drying cycle.

Sam doted on his little sister. He sang to her, played with her, brought her highly anticipated snacks of cheese. Gus watched her silently from his own reverie. He preferred to be an observer, was content to operate alone.

While Sam and Mary Claire developed a definite bond, Gus created his own language. Instead of words, Gus preferred to hum. We'd ask him to say thank you, and with the proper inflection and intonation, he'd respond, "Hmm hmm." We'd require him to ask for something politely, and he'd say, "Hmm?" – the final sound rising at the end, his own version of "please?".

And throughout our little cocoon of chaos, our newest baby smiled as she sucked her fingers, cried only when she was hungry or tired, and was content to be a part of the pack. She constantly held her little mouth in a perfect "O" – the tip of her little pink tongue sitting softly in its circle. Her bright blue eyes charmed all who crossed her path, her rosebud lips greeted strangers with welcome smiles. She was an adored addition to the family.

As a young, emotional, and deep-thinking girl, there is very little in Mary Claire's life that doesn't hold meaning for her. From her Jonas Brothers posters to her story notebooks to her rock and bottle cap collections, she is a keeper of important things. Sometimes she'll come to me in tears, accusing, "Mama, did you throw my blue polka dot ribbon away? That was SPECIAL to me!" Her current bedroom is a shrine to her inability to part with anything. She sounds so much like her Nana on cleaning and purging day when she proclaims, "I CAN'T give that stuffed animal to Goodwill. I won it at the State Fair when I was three, and it's a very special memory for me. I CAN'T donate that shirt even though it's three sizes too small – Nana bought it for me at Cracker Barrel, and it's a very special memory for me."

She has an unrivaled affection for pigs. She loves the way they look, the way they feel, the fact that they're good mothers to their piglets. She feels so strongly about pigs that she won't eat pork. And she's pretty much given up on other foods that once lived and breathed as well. She likes to call herself a vegetarian, but because she doesn't eat veggies, she's more accurately classified as a carbetarian.

What Mary Claire would like most in this life is a sister. Her brothers – although she loves them fiercely at times – make her crazy. She craves a girl to giggle with, to tell secrets to, to plan her future with. We're not obliging her wishes for another baby (she missed her final chance for a sister when George came out with boy parts), but I hope that someday she'll fill her heart with the magic of brotherly love and the reliability of strong female friendships. She loves her best friends with true zest. "Julia is my best friend and always will be – no matter what happens between our families. I love Rebekah so much! I don't know exactly why, but I just love that girl!"

She can melt my heart with her gestures of kindness – the bouquets of dandelions she brings, the dead baby bird she wants to bury, the love letters she leaves in my office. And then, on a dime, she can cry and fuss and shout out life's iniquities – "You're so mean to me! You let the boys do EVERYTHING!" – before she slams the door like a hormonal teenager. She is, I must admit, probably a lot like me in many ways. My little freckle-faced love.

My girl.

George Anderson

"The Baby"

05/22/2002

You can learn many things from children. How much patience you have, for instance.

~ Franklin P. Jones

"He Prefers to Be Called Georgeous"

While we juggled diapers, potty training, and a steady stream of doctor's visits, Chris made his way through three job promotions. The final one was our manna from heaven – a job that allowed us to build our first home in a quaint, little town that boasted a brick main street. As the construction on our house neared completion, we temporarily moved in to the two extra bedrooms that were graciously offered to us by my Uncle Chuck and Aunt Marcia.

The kids loved their borrowed bedroom complete with bunk beds and a crib. They giggled into the night and told each other stories as they fell asleep. In the evenings while Chris worked late, I ran them through the bath brigade – scrubbing silky curls and chubby legs. One by one, I lifted them from the tub and wrapped them in cushy towels. The boys adored their Uncle Chuck and worked out with him in the morning. As I fed Mary Claire her morning oatmeal in the kitchen, I could hear them yelling, "You can DO it!" to the beat of the workout tape in Chuck's DVD player.

Chris worked crazy hours, and the kids and I explored Indianapolis and our new home of Zionsville. We visited Chris at work, hung out at the construction site where our new home was slowly emerging from the dirt, checked out all the local shops and restaurants, and played in the parks.

And in the midst of the crazy chaos, Chris and I conceived the final Willis. (Chuck and Marcia obviously made us feel very much at home.)

George Anderson was the first addition to arrive at our newly constructed house. His baby blue room was replete with dark blue moons and pale yellow stars – a soothing night sky to welcome him to his brand new life. His room was next to Mary Claire's (a purple, pink, and floral dollhouse of a room with enough gingham and lace to make Holly Hobbie jealous) and across from the boys' room, complete with bunk beds, blue walls, and big-boy plaids.

The baby of the family, George's status was confirmed from the beginning. We all doted on him, cooed at him, catered to him. His baby book was thinner than the others, not by choice but by necessity. As the fourth in five years, I didn't have the time to lounge with him lazily on the bed, examining and marveling over each of his perfect fingers and toes into the late afternoon. But the corner in my heart with his name on it was just as big, just as expansive.

I always wondered how I could love a baby as much as I loved Sam. But in turn, the answer was given to me by Gus, by Mary Claire, by George.

The Willis baby learned things differently in our home. At age three, when our other kids were cutting their teeth on Barney and Sesame Street, George was watching *Lord of the Rings*. By five, he was a Guitar Hero aficionado and could rock out to Led Zeppelin and Guns 'N Roses with the best of them. By ten, we expect him to be teaching the others how to smoke and top off the missing vodka with tap water.

He's precocious, smart as a whip, and formerly cuddly. Oh, that boy once loved to cuddle. But before he was four, he would no longer kiss me on the lips. He'd seen his big brothers refuse, had decided early on that he would not be the family sissy who still kissed his mother.

But George and I loved each other fiercely. Even though he wouldn't demonstrate his affection physically, he was never far from my side. I could always count on his little warm presence by my feet as I cooked dinner, by my side as I sorted laundry.

We call him the "Rain Man" of Legos. He can build anything with precision, symmetry, and speed. He has a freakish ability to construct complex creations far beyond his years. He'll open a new Lego set, spread out the instructions, color code his Lego piles, and get lost in another world for the next couple of hours – or minutes – depending on the resultant product. He's meticulous to a fault, unable to think about anything else until his latest masterpiece is finished. There are Lego displays all over his room. He becomes infuriated when I move them to dust his shelves, occasionally breaking off a piece that I can't put back. He'll sigh with the ennui of an old man as he instructs me how to rebuild what I broke.

He's the loudest of the Willis's – perhaps not by choice, but by necessity. Demanding to be heard, he makes noise endlessly. He sings to himself, talks to himself, whistles incessantly, hums and chatters to fill in any noise voids. When he wants to be heard, he yells. There is no "inside voice" for George. He has just one setting. And it's stuck on "loud."

He's ferociously committed to his best friend, Luke (Jackie's youngest), whom he's "known all my life except for three days because he wasn't born until three days after me." He and Luke have plans to move to Africa and "raise monkeys as their babies." Jackie and I have been granted visiting privileges, but only on the next hill over. We will not be allowed to have an integral part of raising our monkey-grandchildren.

George's imagination is boundless, but I often question his work ethic. Much like Sam, he prefers to have things handed to him, to only tackle those things that he's already good at. He's got an entrepreneurial spirit, though. Two of his ideas? Lickable meat wallpaper and a body zipper for easy surgical access. You have to give him points for creativity.

He's the last child I'll ever have. My OB informed me – in no uncertain terms – that "my uterus was tired." Although I would have liked a couple more kids, my uterus (and our income) cannot support that dream. The last of the Willis's, George Anderson is funny, aware of the world around him like none of my other kids, can guilt us into almost anything, is a tad bit spoiled, unrestricted, energetic. And loud. Did I mention loud? Because his volume level could break the sound barrier – and my nerves. He's always in trouble because he's always the one we hear above the rest. As smart as he is, you'd think he'd figure this out. The silent instigators are the ones who get away with it, Buddy.

My little caboose is the classic bittersweet combination. When he's bitter, I want to tune him out and sic him on his siblings. But when he's sweet, I could eat him whole. He continues to challenge me in every way. In the morning, when I wake him up for school, I breathe in his sleepy little-boy smell, the warmth of his body, his marshmallow cheeks. I whisper sweet nothings in his ear and admire the curl of his eyelashes until I elicit a sly little smile on his ruby red lips. He snuggles into my arms as he wakes up slowly. It's our stolen morning moment, the one point of the day when he and I are alone. And quiet.

And by the time I hustle him into that same bed at night, I'm usually ready to turn off his lights and shut his door for a long, long time. Inevitably, he's already fought with his siblings, argued a request to pick up his toys, tortured the dogs, ridden his bike without his helmet even though he knows it's strictly forbidden, presented me with a school paper that says, "I don't think George is working to his potential," burped at the dinner table, refused to eat his green beans, used all the hot water in the shower, trashed the basement, and talked back to me.

But in the morning when he's warm and soft and cuddly, he's always forgiven.

Family Ties

Insanity Really Is Hereditary

Life consists not simply in what heredity and environment do to us but in what we make out of what they do to us. ~ Harry Emerson Fosdick

"Running Through Our Veins"

The old adage "the apple doesn't fall too far from the tree" is the one that molds and shapes our lives on a day-to-day basis. As much as I hate to admit it, I'm slowly turning into bits and pieces of my own parents – and Chris, into his mom and dad. In many ways, that's a good thing. In other ways, not so much.

As I get older, I'm developing neuroses for my neuroses. That's how deep some of these issues run. I recognize that my thinking and reasoning isn't always rational. That doesn't always mean I have the means to change it, but admission is the first step, right?

The human condition is such a complex, multi-faceted, fragile thing. We are all made up of bits and pieces of our families – woven together into an entity that is unique to each one of us. I am not my mother, but I am pieces of her. I am not my father, but his blood courses through my veins. And then there are my grandparents, my aunts and uncles, my cousins, my niece and nephew, my sister. Add in Chris's family heritage, and our kids become these intricate mosaics of their ancestors – some pieces beautiful, shiny, sharp-edged; others dull and virtually unnoticeable. What will their final art project become?

The human condition is a wonderful thing, indeed.

"In Search of a Good Man"

Thinking back to my own youth – the one so different from my children's – it didn't make much sense that I wanted my father to love me. I didn't even know him, knew only that he broke my mother's heart, left his two young girls, and never looked back. But that innate human need to be unconditionally loved and accepted by the ones who brought you into this world – it took hold and wouldn't let go.

My father would send a check once in a while with a good-natured request not to cash it until he called. And my older sister, Carrie, and I would wait. And wait. And eventually, Carrie – always willing to accept her fate and move on – would shrug her shoulders, tear up her check, and return to the escape of her latest steamy romance novel. But I would carefully fold that check and place it at the bottom of my cedar jewelry box, along with my beloved turquoise horse earrings and the autobiography I penned when I was eight. It was only later – years later – in a fit of rage and defeat that I ripped those yellowing checks to shreds as if he could somehow feel the tearing in his very soul.

But in the mean time, I wanted him to love me. It wasn't that my mother's boundless love was not enough, but I needed my father – the other half of my genetic make-up – to see that I was smart, witty, athletic, and altogether loveable. I wanted it to hit him over the head like an anvil, the realization that he couldn't live without me, couldn't stand to miss another second of my childhood.

I pictured it all perfectly in my mind. Like the poor sap who should have had a V-8, he'd hit himself in the head, and he'd fly back to Indiana with a baseball glove in hand so we could play catch the minute he arrived at my doorstep. He'd look into my eyes and see the mirror reflection of his own, and he'd realize that he never should have walked away. My mom would fall in love again, would stop working three jobs to pay the rent on our two-bedroom apartment and keep Kraft macaroni with tuna on the table, and we'd be a family again. In my wildest of dreams, we'd buy a little pale yellow ranch home, move out of our second story apartment with the crumbling balcony and the hoodlum neighbors who taught me how to inhale my first cigarette, and we'd buy a puppy named "Buster."

But life has a way of moving on despite our deepest wishes and desires. Days turned into weeks, weeks into months, months into years. And my dad never came back. He wrote occasionally, visited less. We recognized his face, but we didn't really know him. When he said, "I love you," it made me uncomfortable. "How can you love me when you don't even know who I am?" I wanted to yell. But I remained silent, passive, agreeable. Conflict and confrontation was never one of my strong suits. I watched my mom work her fingers to the bone as I grew up, grew older.

Eventually, my mom remarried, and my stepfather brought a male presence into my life. I loved Bob – he was good to us, good to Mom – but I still fought him at every turn. Through my tumultuous teenage years, we had argument after argument. But he taught me how to perfect my off-hand layup, took me to the batting cage, instructed me on the golf course. And little by little, he became the father I never had.

When I see Bob wrestling with his grandkids and fulfilling their every whim, when I see Chris tuck our kids into bed each night and skewer worms onto their fishing poles, I now realize what fatherhood is supposed to be. Perhaps God didn't see fit to give me my own, but he made up for it later in so many wonderful ways.

"Granny's Fire"

After sledding with the kids on a bitter and blustery day, they begged for a fire to warm their toes. Chris loaded up the fireplace with wood, and we all enjoyed the quiet serenity that only crackling blue flames can bring. Well, we enjoyed a few minutes of bliss until the "he's touching me!" and "she's looking at me!" arguments began.

But in those quiet moments, I thought about Granny.

My great-grandmother was a four-time world champion bowler in her youth. When I knew her, Sally Twyford was simply "Granny" to Carrie and me. She lived in a cabin at the top of a hill on Clay Lick Road in Brown County, Indiana. She wore her white hair in long, tight braids and killed rattlesnakes with her shotgun. She taught my sister and me how to play blackjack and saved all her spare change in a giant Mason jar for us to divide when we came to visit.

We didn't have many material things when we were children. But we had our weekend trips to Granny's. Those were the highlights of our childhood.

Granny wasn't a warm, loving, grandmotherly type with a kitchen that smelled of cookies and a warm lap to lounge in. She cursed and drank with the best of them. She was fearless and wouldn't put up with sass from any of us – my mom included. She had a mean, old dog named Rusty who would bite us if we came too close. And we all knew that

Granny loved Rusty more than any of the rest of us. But when I was at Granny's house, I felt safe. I never questioned this gift. I just took it and held tightly for fear I might someday lose it.

When we visited Brown County, we hiked through the woods during the day. We tied red bandannas around our heads to keep the ticks out of our hair. Granny would bring her walking stick, and I knew there wasn't a rattlesnake that would dare show its scaly face in her presence. We spent afternoons skipping stones on Zack's Lake, and in the evenings, we'd sit at Granny's feet while she played her guitar and sang, "Please, Mr. Conductor." She didn't have a particularly good singing voice, but I loved to hear her sing, anyway. She often sang "Two Little Babes," which always made me cry. And made me a little nervous, too.

After an evening round of poker, Carrie and I would settle downstairs with our sleeping bags in front of the fire. It would pop and crackle and dance in the darkness, and although I was pretty sure there were monsters in the cold, damp basement laundry room, that fire always made me feel safe. Mom and Granny would stoke it throughout the night so it wouldn't burn out, and Carrie and I awoke in the mornings with the smell of campfire in our pajamas and in our hair.

I was eight when Granny died. She was the first person I had ever known and loved who left the world I inhabited. Cancer ravaged her body quickly and although her death came fast, it was laden with pain and suffering. I prayed for Granny with all my heart. I was afraid she wouldn't get into heaven because she drank, cursed, gambled, and wasn't particularly nice to our cousins.

At her funeral, I couldn't stop touching her. Her body was so cold, her face so still. My cousin, Ellen, and I were fascinated by the obvious fact that her nose hairs had been removed. We giggled about it in the funeral parlor, and I was sure that a mortal sin would reside in my soul forever. What good Catholic girl laughed at her dead grandmother's absent nose hairs?

When we lost Granny, I lost a part of my childhood. Our weekends seemed long and lonely without our road trip in the blue Chevette – sleeping bags positioned carefully in the hatchback area. When I attended CYO camp down the street from Granny's house, it felt lonely and strange. Foreign, almost.

I sing Granny's songs to my children now, but I change the songs so they're not quite as disturbing. The two little babes don't die in the woods in my altered rendition. The train conductor's young passenger's mother isn't on her deathbed, either; she's simply waiting for her son to arrive for a visit. My watered-down version of Granny's songs make my kids laugh and roll their eyes. They would have loved their Granny. They would have probably been a bit afraid of her, too. They would have laughed when she unknowingly passed gas because her hearing was gone. They would have been scared to sleep in the basement, but they would have loved the fire.

It's the one piece of Granny we can all share.

"Toughening Me Up"

When I was little, my older cousins, Carrie, and I used to play the "Tasting Game." As the youngest of the crew, I was typically the recipient of their most daring adventures. We'd sit on my aunt's gazebo steps, blindfolded, and the Food Chooser would place secret bites of food on our tongues. We would then have to attempt to identify the culinary delight.

One night while eating with my cousins, I refused to try the candied yams at the dinner table on the premise that they were unpalatable and disgusting to anyone human. When we played the "Tasting Game" later, guess what I got on my tongue?

Yup. Yams. And how did I respond? You guessed it — "Yuuummmm! What is this? I love it!" And did they let me live it down? Never.

Because I was the baby of the group, I was everyone's favorite guinea pig. And I cried a lot. And I held my breath until I passed out when I didn't get my way. I'm sure there was a great deal of satisfaction in tormenting me.

I distinctly remember a coffee ground/hot sauce combo that almost did me in.

But as Ellen would continually remind me, "We're just trying to toughen you up."

My cousins were an integral part of my childhood, of my identity, of the person I would someday become. As a child, I burned with envy at the "things" they had – the trips they were able to take, the clothes that were abundant and well-matched, the sparkling pool in their backyard. I loved them, envied them, wanted to be them. They were beautiful, accomplished, admired. Their financial futures were secure.

And I had a face that was covered with freckles, a school uniform blouse that was perpetually wrinkled, and a propensity toward athletic ass-kicking. I wanted my cousins' lives, but was stuck inside my own. It was only later – after I'd been awarded my college degree with summa cum laude honors, after I'd married the handsome and successful man of my dreams, after I'd given birth to my four beautiful children, after I'd learned to love my freckles and my athletic abilities – that I realized how much they'd unknowingly done to help chart my course in life. By wanting what they had, I chose it for myself and my kids. And now that I'm an adult, I can love and respect my cousins for who they are – imperfections and all. I no longer worship them, I am free to simply enjoy them.

They did, after all, "toughen me up."

"Shift"

One summer while I was busy transporting my kids to various and sundry extracurricular activities, my mom was subjected – against her will – to a home remodel. Now, in Bob's defense, the house needed a pick-me-up. And my mom needed to purge. But she was overwhelmed by the process – and by the amount of crap in her garage – so, like the good, compliant daughter I am, I hired a babysitter and went to Mom's to help her sort and purge.

The house looked really nice. Mom and Bob knocked out a wall separating the two bedrooms to make a large master bedroom instead. The entire house had been painted, the driveway had been resurfaced, and the landscaping spruced up. When I arrived with my trash bags in hand, there were dishes and knick-knacks littering the kitchen table and the sunroom table, but overall, the house looked bright, clean, and fairly well organized. The new bedroom was beautiful, and the closets were full of freshly washed and hung clothes.

Then I saw the garage.

It was filled to nearly overflowing with boxes, boxes, and more boxes. Apparently when the remodel began, Mom simply packed everything up, took it outside, and decided she'd go through it later. I, being an organizational junkie, agreed to help her sort through what was left. The first problem I noticed, though, was that the house already seemed reasonably full. There was no room for anything from the garage to make its way back in.

My niece, Amber, and I decided that the best approach would be to start in the kitchen and help Mom sort through her overstuffed cabinets and hutches to make room for things in the garage that she wanted to keep. Mom was not thrilled with this approach. "That was not on my to-do list," she argued. We had to strong-arm her a bit to convince her that nothing else could come in until some things went out.

As Amber and I began the cleaning process, we quickly realized we were in over our heads. We had Mom sit in a chair. She had three choices for every item we presented to her: keep, give away, or put in the "maybe" pile. After about ten minutes, we had moved everything from the cabinets into the "maybe" pile.

It was not a purge, it was simply a shift.

Mom's response to everything we held up to her was, "…but don't you think that's pretty? That was a gift from (fill in the name of the friend, relative, co-worker of your choice). I got it for my (fill in the appropriate holiday, birthday, etc.)." We finally had to remind her that we weren't making judgment calls; we simply needed one of the three acceptable responses. Inevitably, she'd look nervous and say, "maybe."

Here are a few of the more enjoyable finds from that adventure…

1. An unopened, unused food chopper. It had to have been in her cupboard for at least ten years; it was all the way in the dusty back corner under some cobwebs. She reasoned, however, that because it was brand new (albeit ten years ago), she couldn't possibly give it away.

2. Five calculators. They all worked. We encouraged her to pick one. She couldn't understand why she shouldn't keep all five if they were in good working order. We talked about all the underprivileged kids in Africa who didn't have any calculators. I pointed out that one of those calculators went through college

with me. She argued that it had to be a fine specimen if it was still working.

3. Fourteen decks of cards; eight complete sets. We let her keep all the sets of 52. It wasn't worth the fight.

4. An unused basket with a microwaveable pouch to keep rolls warm. Again, she argued that she needed it because it was brand new. I argued that she didn't need it because she doesn't even know how to work the microwave.

For two hours, it went on and on. Finally, she broke for a cigarette, and we never resumed the battle. I threw as many things into the "give away" pile as I could when she wasn't looking. She promptly took ¾ of it back out.

"666"

When I turned 37, I partied like a rock star. Why 37? Because as a kid, I frequently dreamed I would die at 36. I know, it's more than a little morbid and neurotic, but I truly believed that 36 was as good as it was going to get for me. That fear was probably born of some deep-seated Catholic belief in the evil power of the number six. After all, six is the devil's number. And six times six equals 36. Can there be a number more evil than one whose square root is six? It made perfect sense in my young mind. And as a kid, 36 was a million years away.

I believed so strongly in the curse of 36 that in the last few days before my 37th birthday, I avoided any unnecessary trips in the car believing that a Mack truck was waiting for me in the wings. It was good to turn 37. That feeling of impending doom was celebrated away with good friends, nasty and inappropriate talk, and far too much plum wine.

"Technologically Challenged"

In mid-winter of my 38th year, Justin the Garage Door Guy, visited us. Maggie wouldn't stop barking at him. Every time he started a new power tool, she'd bark. Every time she glimpsed the corner of the Overhead Garage Door truck in the driveway, she'd bark. Every time she'd look at me, she'd bark. I feel that she was trying to remind me that SOMEONE WAS IN THE HOUSE.

Just in case I'd forgotten.

You might wonder why we had a garage door repairman visit. And I'd assure you that it's a good story. One worth hearing.

Over the weekend, Mom and Bob came to watch the kids while we celebrated birthday number 5-0 with our dear friend, Scott. I asked my parents to arrive about 5:00 on Friday because Chris and I were both at work and the kids were attending their after-school activities.

They were in our driveway at 2:00.

They attempted to get into the house using our garage code, but they didn't have the code correct. They were SO CLOSE… but still a few numbers off.

The situation might have been easily resolved if, perchance, they had a cell phone. Instead, Bob walked around the house trying all of the doors. He then tried to manually lift the garage door. No luck.

So, they loaded up the car and drove to our local Marsh to find a pay phone. (Do pay phones even exist anymore?) They ended up using the manager's cell phone in the store office and called Chris at work to find out what the mysterious missing numbers of the code were.

They then drove back to our house and promptly punched the correct code in. The door lifted about an inch, made a scary grinding noise, and refused to go either up or down. Apparently, Bob had inadvertently locked the garage door when he attempted to open it manually.

And now the garage door was hopelessly stuck.

Bob walked to my neighbor's house to use her phone. He called Chris again, and Chris drove home to investigate the situation.

After an hour of finagling, Chris was able to get the door closed again. But it was seriously jammed and broken. The metal tracks were bent, the panels warped.

As a result, we had two rows of panels and a great deal of hardware replaced. Problem is that the Overhead Door panels are white and our panels are beige. Because it was nearly negative 136 degrees (almost), we couldn't paint the new panels until a warm front blew through. So, we were stuck with a white trash, two-toned garage until Easter.

Just one more thing to add to the neighborhood association's "Why I Hate the Willis's" list.

"Celebrating Mom"

When my mom turned 68, I decided to work on a special project for her birthday. She's the most impossible person in the universe to buy for. No, she doesn't want her own cell phone – they just annoy her. No, she doesn't want any books – she hasn't read the ones she already has. No, she doesn't want any clothes – she's got two closets full of things she never wears. And on it goes.

Anyway, I decided to do a little scrapbook/photo collage for her and asked each of the kids to finish this question for me:

"I love Nana because..."

(Before I give you their answers, let me stipulate that I asked each of them individually so they weren't listening to each others' answers.)

SAM: She used to take us to Zoobies before it closed.

GUS: She takes us to "That Fun Place."

MARY CLAIRE: She gives me cheese.

GEORGE: She has Odie.

I was looking for something a little more like, "She has the softest lap in the world," or "She always cuddles me before I go to bed," or "She loves me more than anybody else in the world."

Apparently, however, my children have no souls.

I tried to call my Mom on her 68th birthday. She's been my rock, my inspiration, my role model, my caregiver. I wanted to wish her a happy birthday, wanted the kids to sing an off-key birthday song to make her smile. Or cry. Either one would have been an expected response.

But I couldn't get anything other than a busy signal.

Oh, my mother. If only she had an Internet connection, or a cell phone, or voicemail, or something resembling an invention from beyond 1980…

But the busy signal.

Really? Do people still get busy signals?

"Table for Seven"

When the "baby" was six and the firstborn was 11, we had a bit of an awakening. I'd been nauseous, bone tired, sniffly, experiencing heartburn. What do all those add up to? Well, that's what we thought, too. Never mind the fact that we've done everything humanly possible to prevent such a feat from occurring. Stranger things have happened. As my obstetrician told us, "If your tubal ligation fails, it will fail at around ten years. Sometimes nature finds a way." So much for permanent solutions.

We talked about the possibilities at dinner. Chris chuckled about it for an hour or so. Finally, I had to buy a test.

And the result?

Negative.

That was the result we wanted, right? I'm on the fast track to 40. Our youngest is six. Our oldest is old enough to be embarrassed by an aging, pregnant mother. He's taken The Class. He understands how It happens. Our daughter would have been terrified of the prospect of ending up with another brother – elated at the possibility of her highly-coveted sister. And Gus? Well, he might not have even noticed another addition. He would have just continued on his solitary way, stopping occasionally for a large, carnivorous meal or a hug.

We can't afford another baby. We don't have room. I'd just returned to work. My body – according to my doctor – is unable to carry another baby without substantial risk. My uterus is tired.

But I wouldn't have cried if that second line had appeared. In fact, I was thinking a bit about names. I like Duke. And Hank. And Oliver. (Although Chris would have never agreed to the latter.) I got a little nervous about the fact that we used Maggie and Lucy on our dogs. We would have had to go back to the drawing board for a girl. I could have adjusted to late night feedings for a Betsy or a Ruby or a Cecelia.

It wasn't meant to be, though.

Instead, we continue on as a table for six. The Willis Tribe. A happy, healthy home filled with love and laughter and enough chaos to last a lifetime.

But we would have made room for one more.

"The Foreman"

I've read John Grisham. I know how these things go. And when Chris was called to jury duty to sit on a murder trial, I was less than pleased.

Disgruntled defendants go after jurors. How does that happen if they're incarcerated, you ask? Well, haven't you heard of the underground cigarette trade? What about jailhouse sexcapades in return for street favors?

Okay, maybe I haven't either. But I could imagine those things happening. John Grisham can imagine those things happening. Maybe they actually happen.

So, while my husband was sitting there in the juror box all decked out in his school colors (maybe not his wisest wardrobe decision), perhaps the alleged murderer was recording every line on Chris's face, every distinguishing scowl, every gray hair. And maybe that alleged murderer was planning to go after my husband next. It could happen. We all know it could. Paranoid or not.

I mean, really, who hasn't seen "Law and Order?"

He might have been stressed out about sitting on a murder trial and having to welcome 1,600 high school students back to school in less than two weeks, but I think my concerns more than trumped his.

"Trifecta"

Thanks to my dear friend, Mary, who nurtures and encourages my writing and is the #1 fan of the Soon-To-Be-Famous-Novelist, Katrina, I've been reading Stephen King's "On Writing." (The cover of which, by the way, Mary Claire finds "VERY CREE-PEE!") I can't read Stephen King novels. The book jackets are usually enough to give me nightmares. I mistakenly saw "Misery" because my mom said it wasn't scary. You'd think I'd stop listening to her blasé reviews of psychotic movies by now. Nothing scares that woman. After watching the movie, I had continual night sweats that were prompted by the word "cock-a-doody" and the sight of James Caan's hobbled ankles.

So, when Mary gave me "On Writing," she promised it was not Stephen King-ish. And because she's my #1 fan (Oooooh, that just made me think of Annie Bates, too!), I believed her. I read it voraciously over the span of a couple of days and loved every word of it.

Shortly thereafter, Chris rescued me from the cloffice for a quick lunch, and we found ourselves discussing the book. The conversation went like this:

ME: I really enjoyed that Stephen King writing book.

CHRIS: Oh, yeah? Why?

ME: Well, he's very funny, very irreverent, very convincing in his writing methodology. And he obviously adores his wife.

CHRIS: That doesn't surprise me. Horror and humor and love are all very closely related.

(Uncomfortable pause.)

Go back and read that quote again. "Horror and humor and love are all very closely related." That's my husband's perspective.

What do you suppose that might mean about our relationship?

He went on to explain that if you really love someone with your whole heart and soul, the worst thing you could imagine would be losing them. (Obviously to some mallet-wielding psychopath or a homicidal car.) Then that thought – taken a step further – could lead to some horrific "what ifs." And that a horror story twisted around a bit is not so far removed from a comedy.

Hmm.

My response, then, was that he should stop mocking me for imagining dark death scenarios. Because in his Horror/Humor/Love ideology, those visioning thoughts simply mean I love him deeply.

When I imagine a family of hungry grizzly bears hunting and eating my entire family when we're out for a hike in Yosemite, that's just my mother-love rising to the surface of my heart. Likewise, when I'm sure we're being circled by menacing sharks in the Atlantic. Or when we're all about topple down the side of a mountain like dominos on the Appalachian Trail. Or when the crazed psychopath disguised as the ice cream man snatches all my children away before he hands them their SpongeBob popsicles.

In my husband's strange and twisted trifecta, my psychological instability and irrational fears are simply a manifestation of my familial love. And in some strange and similarly twisted way, I find that comforting.

"His Body Is a Wonderland"

"Torn between two lovers, feeling like a fool. Loving both of you is breaking all the rules..." ~ Mary MacGregor, 1976.

Oh, Mary MacGregor, you knew, didn't you? Way back in 1976, you knew. I love my husband. He's the light of my life.

But.

There's another man.

I dream about him, grow Jell-O legs at the sound of his voice, marvel at his lyrical prowess. John Mayer, what is it about Jennifer Aniston that's more appealing than me? Sure, she's beautiful, thin, wealthy beyond belief, witty, successful, adored by millions.

But, really, what else is there?

I could make you happy, John. Chris would understand.

We went to see him in concert at Verizon – a traditional summer outing. It was a perfect evening. The weather was lovely, the beer was cold. John and I were in the same venue at the exact same time. It doesn't get much better than that.

Sitting in a sea of hot, young 20-somethings didn't unnerve me at all. They don't scare me. What John needs is a woman with a little history – with a little something to teach him.

My new BFF – the 20-something redhead dancing beside me – shared my affinity for John.

"I just want one night with him," she admitted to me.

"I just want to run away with him," I sighed. "Or I want my boys to grow up to be like him."

A bit twisted? Perhaps. But love is always complicated.

"Author Stalker"

One of my very favorite events of the year is the Christamore House Book and Author Luncheon. This is the annual fundraiser where authors come to the Indiana Roof Ballroom to talk about their recent publications, the writing process, and whatever else strikes their fancy. My sweet, generous, kind cousins always invite me to be their guest, and I always reply, "Yes! My God, what took you so long to ask?!"

Anyway, Sue Miller was an author who was there to talk about "The Senator's Wife," about being published for the first time at age 43, about her lifelong love of writing. I was sitting in the audience, jumping out of my skin, whispering to myself, "Yes! Yes! That's MY life!" Except I'm only 38, so I have five more years to write my breakout bestseller and pick out my Oprah outfit.

After the luncheon, the authors always make themselves available to sign books. I hastened my way over to Sue Miller to inform her of our parallel lives. She smiled kindly, wrote "Good Luck" on the title page of my book, and I was on my way. Anne told me I was a fool if I didn't give her my contact information, so I sidled back over to her table like a bit of a stalker, handed her my business card and my blog address, and incoherently mumbled something about her mentoring me as a new writer – if she was ever interested – blah, blah, blah. She smiled kindly again (albeit a bit warily), and before she could summon security, I thanked her and rushed away from the table.

That's how very cool I am.

Maybe when I'm a wildly famous author, she and I can laugh over a glass of Pinot at my sophomoric attempt to sound somewhat educated. Right now, though, I'm sure she's thinking, "Stalker." With a capital S. And I can't say I blame her.

Here's the thing about these authors – they're so eloquent. Hillary Jordan, author of "Mudbound," read an excerpt from her debut novel that took my breath away. I sat on the edge of my seat, afraid to breathe, scared to move because I didn't want to miss one "an" or "the" so beautifully strung into lyrical prose.

And here I am writing about dog farts.

If I'm ever blessed and lucky enough to be speaking in front of an audience of privileged, well-educated women about my recently published novel, I'm sure I'll say something punctuated with multiple "ummms" and "stuffs" and nervous, schoolgirl giggles. Impressive, indeed.

And on another note, I returned to the Indiana Roof Ballroom the following night for the prom, and I still wasn't crowned Queen. Maybe next year will be my year. Or five years after that. Because we'll be chaperoning for the rest of our lives. So there's always a chance.

"Move Over, Babs"

Before the Big School Budget Cuts hit, Chris's holiday work gathering took place at a hip, quaint little restaurant with best wine list in our hometown. Mary (my friend, not my daughter – it gets infinitely confusing, doesn't it?) was there looking stunning as ever. She'd just had her hair done, and it had turned out a bit darker than she'd hoped.

"I like it, Mary," I complimented. "I really do. It's beautiful with your blue eyes."

"Good God, Katrina," she replied with a heavy sigh, "I'm one black fingernail away from being Goth."

I all but fell to the floor laughing hysterically because she's so dramatically ridiculous. Her hair could be orange and purple and she'd still be the most beautiful woman in the room.

But I'm not sure if that was my favorite comment or if it was when she brushed by me on the way to the hors d'oeuvres and whispered nonchalantly, "I'm embarrassing myself with the cheese." Ah, dear Mary – biggest fan of goat cheese on the planet.

The party was nice, the ambiance warm, and the wine, red. There was an adorable 78-year-old woman playing piano like a virtuoso. She took a quick break and ended up talking to Chris, lamenting the fact that no one was singing along. Chris, having had a couple of drinks, declared that his wife would be happy to sing.

I, of course, willingly obliged.

After a rousing version of "The Christmas Song" and "Stille Nacht," Nancy the Pianist and I became fast friends. She told me of her colorful history, her vocal music instruction, her experience with opera, and her Butler University past. She then asked if I would consider being her voice student.

"Honey," she crooned, "I haven't wanted to teach anyone for 20 years, but I love your beautiful voice and I want you to be my student."

Umm. Okay.

After we closed with our final number, Nancy hugged me and told me she loved me. Apparently, I'm easy — and quick — to love.

"I think God brought us together for a reason," she said. "I want you to sing with me on Thursday and Saturday nights here. How do you feel about Gershwin and Cole Porter and show tunes?"

Show tunes? Me?

Umm. Yes.

"Will you sing with me?"

Umm. Me? A lounge singer? How could she possibly know that's my ultimate career goal? I'm all about Barbra Streisand — the Early Years.

As fate would have it, sweet Nancy fell ill shortly thereafter and had to retire her lounge-playing career. But every time Chris and I frequent that restaurant, I savor a creamy glass of Cabernet and think about what might have been.

"Death By Broken Heart"

Before I began working full-time and letting our home lives sink into a bottomless pit of stress, I was devoted to gathering my little chick-a-dees around me at bedtime and reading to them from a well-regarded young adult novel.

We had nearly finished "Where the Red Fern Grows" when all hell broke loose and I decided that we'd be better off as a two-income family.

Once I returned to my senses and began working in my PJs again, I decided it was time to finish reading about Old Dan and Little Ann.

So, I gathered all my munchkins around to finish the book.

And…

Did anyone know the dogs died?

Both of them?

One killed by a mountain lion? The other done in by nothing less than a broken heart?

I was sobbing as I read the final chapters – tears and snot streaming down my face – boys giggling under their breath at my unrestrained show of emotion.

During the scene that vividly described Old Dan's "entrails" spilling out after his fight with the mountain lion, Mary Claire ran up the stairs crying, "I can't do it! I can't stay here! I. Can't. Listen. Anymore. It's TOO SAD!!!" She was sobbing hysterically as she slammed her door and turned Bette Midler's "The Rose" on full-blast in her bedroom.

The boys wanted me to finish the story, so I muddled through, stopping from time to time to blow my nose and gather my wits while Mary Claire's sobs could be heard in the silences between "When the night has been too lonely, and the road has been too long," and "When you think that love is only for the lucky and the strong."

I'm not sure who will need the most therapy after those dual outbursts.

Me? Well, that goes without saying.

The boys? Quite likely.

Mary Claire? Undoubtedly.

I threw some extra cash into the "Future Psychotherapy Fund" just to be safe.

And for the record, we made a quick return back to "Captain Underpants."

"Making Memories (That I Can't Remember)"

A great gathering of friends and colleagues brought me out of my house, out of my jeans, and out with my hubby for a fundraising event. Much German beer was drunk, many meatballs eaten, and numerous conversations were held.

What they were all about, I couldn't tell you.

Now, rest assured that many of these conversations took place before the Drinking of the Beers. I can remember myself stumbling over word choice, repeating questions, asking about things I already knew the answers to.

My mind is going. I'm sure of it.

My grandmother died with a progressive, heart-wrenching, soul-stealing case of Alzheimer's. My mom is already struggling to put her sentences together cohesively. More often than not, she'll just shrug and say, "Oh, never mind," when the frustration becomes too much for her to grapple with.

I am following in their footsteps. And I haven't even crossed the threshold of 40 yet.

I need to get some damn books out of this head before they're locked away forever.

And to add to the mix, I danced like a 20-year-old, sweated like a teenage basketball player, and felt it in my right hip like a 90-year-old woman this morning.

My hip! I've been hobbling around like a granny all day – getting out of a seated position with great amounts of trepidation, grimacing, and under-my-breath profanities.

Only old people with feeble minds have hip problems. And I'm afraid to call Dr. Andrews for a diagnosis because he'll just tell me to lose weight. And he'll be spot on.

My self-diagnosis tells me it's something that ends in "itis." Arthritis, bursitis... take your pick. Oh, the travails of age.

"F11"

My beloved washing machine is broken.

She doesn't look sick. In fact, she looks stately and proud – almost regal in her orange home. But she's sick indeed. She's got the F11.

What is the F11? Alas, I cannot tell you. Chris was able to find remedies for F1 - F10 through various Whirlpool sources. But F11 - F23? Mysterious, third world ailments. Diseases you best not try to repair without assistance.

And so, the Whirlpool repairman is scheduled for a visit. Sometime between 8:00 AM and noon. While I write titillating copy about email marketing automation, I will be anxiously awaiting his arrival. Because, Dear Friends, life without a washing machine for a family of six is really no life at all.

We're drowning in stinky basketball jerseys, dirty socks, grass-stained jeans. God have mercy on us – two of the Willis's are still wipe-challenged. (I'll let you draw your own conclusions there. Suffice it to say Whirlpool didn't create the "Sanitary Cycle" for naught.)

With every passing day, the piles grow larger and hope grows dimmer. The only saving grace was my dear Mary who allowed me to bring a dripping wet load of darks to her home when the F11 first began showing symptoms. Together, we shared chocolate scones and chewy cashews – the perfect blend of salty and sweet – while we listened to the beautiful symphony of her chugging washing machine and talked about how much I am screwing up my kids on a daily basis.

But I digress.

My poor dryer is becoming lonely. No longer part of a Duet, he is weary of singing his solos. He needs his partner back.

If the Whirlpool repairman can breathe life into my sick friend, I will take his face between my hands and kiss him full on the lips.

And if he can work his magic for less than $200, I might even treat him to a romp through my night-sweat riddled pajamas and Chris's dirty undershirts.

Seriously, who can resist that?

Emil, my Ukranian ray of hope, arrived at the end of his scheduled time, fiddled with the girl for awhile, and came out of the laundry room grim-faced.

With a slight shake of his head at the mention of The F11, he erased any hope that my girl could be easily and inexpensively repaired. After much cajoling, whining, pleading, and sexual innuendo on my part, he slightly reduced the price and presented me with a bill for $562 for the washing machine repair.

And he promised me another week sans clean underwear while we anxiously awaited the arrival of the necessary 24-carat replacement part.

Damn.

But then you'll never guess what happened.

My husband – under the cloak of darkness – swooped in (wearing his new boxer briefs that we purchased to survive the upcoming washerless week) to save the day.

With mighty screwdriver in hand, he dismantled my girl, examined her innards with furrowed brow, plugged and unplugged some important looking wires, did a little voodoo dance, and put her back together.

And you know what?

It worked!

She's back! In all her sudsy glory, she's back! Today, I get to call the service repair company and cancel my order. Today, my bank account will be credited a large chunk of change instead of the usual, customary debit of a large chunk of change. Today, our underwear will sparkle.

But friends, that's not all...

He also fixed the Xbox.

He took that bad boy apart, too. He wrapped some towels around some important pieces (I'm not kidding) and intentionally overheated them to re-solder the joints. (Or something like that. My eyes glazed over a bit when he was explaining it to me.) And I'll be damned if those three Red Circles of Death weren't laid to rest.

The kids played Guitar Hero World Tour all weekend long. (Okay, okay! So, yes, I sang a few songs! I mean, "Livin' on a Prayer" is on the playlist. Of course, I sang! There was so much rejoicing to do.)

And the magic didn't stop there, my friends.

Fed up with the dirty, disgusting underground cave we call our basement – and the space the kids use as their personal trash pit – he decided it was time for an overhaul.

So, he spent a good deal of his weekend purging, dusting, moving furniture, and steam cleaning the carpet. Let me say that again. He steam cleaned the carpet.

God, that's such a turn on.

Handsome, witty, brilliant, crabby, sexy, and handy all rolled into one yummy package?

That makes me a lucky, lucky girl.

"A Play In One Act"

Cast of Characters:

CHRIS: A 30-something high school principal meeting the needs of 1,600+ local students and parents while working on his doctorate and simultaneously tending to his four children and his needy wife.

KATRINA: A semi-neurotic, 30-something freelance writer and mother of four who is working on a novel in the wee hours of the morning – and whenever else she can steal a few uninterrupted moments.

Curtain opens on Chris sprawled out in an antique rocker in his living room, suit jacket hanging loosely on his shoulders and tie loosened and askew. His wife, Katrina, slumps on the dog hair-lined couch with her laptop open. The four children can be heard in the basement arguing over the Xbox and who is going to be the Guitar Hero lead guitarist. The family's two dogs, Maggie and Lucy, are lounging on the floor. Lucy is snoring and farting in her sleep, and Maggie is noisily licking every inch of herself. It is 5:00 PM – the Witching Hour. The family has just arrived home from a long day of school/work and is preparing for the onslaught of the evening, including a Cub Scout meeting, play practice, basketball practice, homework, something resembling dinner, and showers.

CHRIS: Sometimes I wish I were a dog.

(Katrina stops typing and glances at him.)

CHRIS: I mean, they've got a pretty good life.

KATRINA: They do.

CHRIS: They sleep all day...someone brings them food...

KATRINA: They fart and no one really cares...

CHRIS: They can lick themselves whenever and wherever they want...

KATRINA: They can sniff each other's butts and no one thinks twice about it...

CHRIS: They eat poop...

(Katrina looks up, a bit startled.)

KATRINA: Do you think eating poop sounds appealing?

CHRIS: No, but I'm just saying – they have that option.

(Katrina shrugs her agreement and continues to type.)

CHRIS: There's no judgment in the dog world.

KATRINA: None.

(Maggie continues to lick herself as the room fades to black.)

"Secret Code"

My Christmas season online shopping began to pay off when the highly anticipated Christmas gifts started to arrive. (What can Brown do for you? Heh heh.)

So much excitement... with one minor glitch.

The previous year's secret hiding place has morphed into the cloffice, and I've been perplexed as to where I should discreetly stash this year's gifts until The Big Day.

And then it hit me like a bolt of lightening. Maybe it was a little too much email marketing copywriting. Perhaps an overdose of caffeine. Whatever the case, I've discovered the kid-proof solution.

I'm storing all the gifts in tightly sealed packing boxes – right out in the open – and I'm very cleverly labeling them so only I know what's inside.

Here's an example of the code for Box Number One: SONAIREADSGICMD.

You can't figure out what's in this box, can you? Neither can my kids. But I know what's in this box. I'll let you in on this one (but don't spill the beans):

SONAIREADSGICMD

SON = A present for George. His middle name is Anderson. SON is his secret code.

AIR = A present for Mary Claire. AIR is her secret code.

EADS - Short for melting bEADS sets.

GIC - Code for maGIC kits.

MD - Presents are from Mom and Dad. (SC = Santa Claus and SS = Stocking Stuffers.)

Clearly, this box contains the much coveted and top-of-the-list melting bead sets and two magic kits. These presents will be wrapped and signed from us versus being left under the tree or in a stocking from Santa.

The code does morph and change a bit as necessary. Sometimes I use a little Pig Latin just to spice things up.

Here's another one for you to cut your teeth on:

ABYAIROARSS

ABY = bABY doll clothes

AIR = Mary Claire (Come on, we've gone over that one!)

OAR = baby bOAR (Her 3rd grade specialty animal!)

SS = You guessed it! It's a Stocking Stuffer!

Do you see what I mean? It's foolproof.

Yes, Chris thinks I'm crazy. Indeed, I probably am. We laughed until we cried when I was explaining my very high-tech, intellectual system to him. Because in about 48 hours, I'll be scratching my head and pulling out the scissors to slice open these mystery boxes and find out what's inside.

Then we'll shove everything under our bed and lock the kids out.

But until then, you can bet your sweet ass that those kids of mine will never crack the code.

"You're As Cuddly As a Cactus, You're As Charming As an Eel..."

Despite the best efforts of my four cheerful cutie-patooties, I found myself in a foul Christmas funk. Tis the effing season.

I'm mad at everyone right now. I'm mad because I took on too much work and now I'm stressed beyond human endurance. I'm mad at my kids because I fold their clothes in the endless pursuit of Bureau Drawer Perfection only to find mismatched PJs wadded up between wrinkled t-shirts. How many times, really, do they need to be reminded that long sleeves and collared shirts are hung in the closet? (Ellen once told me that she believed claiming your laundry "was done" was a fallacy. "How can your laundry ever truly be done?" she asked. To which, I – standing in my dirty socks with four overflowing baskets of clean undies – had no good response.)

Now back to everyone I'm angry with...

I'm mad at my bank for jacking around with my weekend deposit so that my funds still aren't "available." I'm mad at my husband because I willingly enable him to do absolutely nothing to help prepare for our Christmas celebration. (Okay, he put the tree up. But he hasn't seen the inside of a Toys-R-Us for the last 12 years, nor can he distinguish Christmas wrapping paper from the Cinco de Mayo variety. And just because he hung some outside lights last night because I was screaming at him and slamming lots of doors doesn't really count.)

I'm mad at the mice because they poop too much. I'm mad at John because he swims around in his filthy fish bowl like the stench doesn't bother him in the least. I'm mad at my dogs because they have horrible breath. And because they can't bathe themselves. Or get their own damn food. And I'm especially mad at Lucy because she sheds so much that I always feel I'm wearing a Blonde Mutt Fur.

My wise and sagely friend, Patsy, assures me it's just the normal stress of the season – and that perhaps following her lead and eating raw cookie dough would assuage my imaginary pain and suffering. I'm sure she's right. But that still didn't stop me from drowning my petty sorrows in Ghirardelli squares of caramel-filled milk chocolate all day. With some Xanax chasers. And a heart-attack-inducing piece of meat-laden pizza that would have probably killed King Kong long before they shot him off of the Empire State Building.

My troubles are so very inconsequential, I know. (I know that, damn it!) In fact, they're probably all hormone-related. I'm trying to snap out of it, really I am. Perhaps if Santa brings me some vodka – lots of vodka – I can once again revert to my cheery, charming, glass-half-full self. Perhaps if I find some good Cabernet under the tree it will inspire me to climb out of the 12th Circle of Hell. The one exclusively reserved for the Whiny Asses Who Make Unreasonable Demands and Wallow in Stupid Self-Pity.

Are you listening, Santa?

"Social Graces"

When I was a little girl, I remember many nights out with my mom. She was (and still is) a beauty, my mom. A social butterfly. The life of the party. The center of a unique and eclectic group of friends. We spent many evenings at The Anchor Inn, at The Milano Inn, at Grindstone Charleys. Late into the evening, I'd be sprawled out on the booth with my head in her lap while another round of Manhattans was served.

And when my eyes were bleary and the smoke was thick, I'd beg to go home.

"Please, Mom, can we go?? Now??? Pleeeeeaassse?"

But the laughter was still strong and Mom would always say, "Just ten more minutes."

And I swore to myself that when I was an adult and had my own kids, I would never make them sit for hours in a restaurant and listen to boring adult banter.

Tonight, I met some friends from our stage production of "Dearly Beloved" for dinner and a couple of drinks at Red Robin. Having just seen "The Tale of Desperaux," Mary Claire and George attended with me.

After two and a half hours of dinner, wine, and laughter, the kids were sprawled out in my lap and begging to go home.

"Just ten more minutes," I'd promise.

And the world came full circle.

I truly have turned into my mother. And there is nothing else I'd rather be. I know now – at the ripe, old age of 38 – those years formed me and made me who I am. Conversation skills, a sense of humor, social graces, those were the gifts that were bestowed upon me during those late night dinners with my mom and her fabulous, loyal friends.

And these wonderfully interesting and entertaining people that my son and daughter were fortunate enough to mingle with tonight? That was a gift they'll someday thank me for.

Maybe not tonight as I drag their tired, whiny rears into bed... but someday.

"May Your Holidays Be Functional"

We gathered at 1509 to celebrate Christmas with Mom, Bob, Carrie, Kevin, Amber, and Andy. We feasted on a buffet of goodies –

from ham to chili to buffalo chicken dip to chocolate fudge. And we laughed. And then we laughed some more. And then we poured another round.

Mom (God love her) – in her infinitely practical way – bought Andy a new robe, socks, and slippers because he once mentioned that his bedroom was cold. So Andy – in his 16-year-old-way – sported the robe and slippers all day long and lounged around a la Hugh Heffner. He carried a brass reindeer in his pocket, too, and posed with it periodically. We inappropriately referred to it as his "strapping young buck."

Sam received his first round of knitting supplies from the Smiths. Just this week, he decided that he wants to join his 6th grade Sit-and-Knit group. We're not sure what his motivation is. Chris is convinced it's the male to female ratio. I think he might have a bit of a crush on his teacher. Whatever the reason, he's now equipped with knitting needles and green and white yarn. Currently, the extent of his knitting needle prowess, however, is limited to using them as substitute drum sticks and mercilessly poking his younger siblings. Because he's 12.

George received a K'nex electronic ferris wheel set that he promptly assembled with great tenacity and precision. He often brings us perfectly symmetrical and color-coded Lego creations and can build the

Taj Mahal out of Lincoln Logs. He may cry like a wild animal when he gets poked with a knitting needle, but damn, that boy can build things.

Today was our final family gathering before Amber journeys off to Alabama. Although we'll miss her sweet, smiling face, it will be so good to watch her spread her wings and discover worlds that she never even knew existed. We met her adorable friend, Steve, today, too. And we got to ogle his larger-than-life biceps. Wow. (And don't call me Mrs. Robinson, Chris! Just because I'm 38 doesn't mean I'm blind.)

Perhaps the best part of the afternoon was playing a rousing game of "Christmas Charades." I, for one, am very fond of the always-effective "sounds like" gesture so I can act out an array of rhyming words that leaves my fellow players either looking very confused or mocking me with great glee. Tonight, I very clearly held up my finger in the "number one" position. I then gave my infamous "sounds like" gesture and pointed to my toe. Then one more "sounds like," and I performed an unmistakable bell ringing. Crystal clear.

"ONE TOE BELL??" Andy screamed above the din.

Umm. That would be "The First Noel."

To everyone's great delight, Andy – aka Heff – gleefully sang "The first Toe-Bell, the angel did say..." for the remainder of the afternoon. Do you think Sam found that amusing? Have you ever met a middle school boy?

My family can make me crazy. They can get on my nerves. They can push all the right buttons. We have our own brand of dysfunction. But I love them. And being with them never fails to feel like home.

"Green Girls, Mean Girls"

The following January, we spent three, fun-filled, whirlwind days in Chicago. We visited the Star Wars exhibit at the Science and Industry Museum, ate fabulous Greek food with Mary, Greg, Jody, Jim, Jacob, Jordan, and Jackson. We shopped at Water Tower Place, and Mary Claire and I visited the American Girl Doll Store. We crammed four kids into a hotel room, spent way too much money, and had a blast.

The initial point of the trip was to see the musical, "Wicked." After listening to the soundtrack non-stop for the last few months, I was dying to see the stage show. Mary Claire asked to go for Christmas, and that sealed the deal. I'd heard nothing but glowing reviews from everyone until I talked to Anne. She hated it. Really hated it. Loathed it, in fact. She admittedly enjoyed the talents of the performers, but hated the whole "Mean Girls" underbelly of the story itself.

After seeing the show, this is the conclusion I arrived at:

I loved it. The whole darn thing. Every little piece of it.

And let me also say that I admire Anne so much – her brains, her spunk, her insight – everything about her. She's my parenting role model, a dear and trusted friend, and one of the smartest people I know. And I understand her viewpoint as well. I totally get the "Mean Girls" on stage review. But I still loved it.

Mentioning one of my favorite classics might shed a bit of light on my love for "Wicked." As a high school and college student, I couldn't get enough of Dante's "Inferno." I like the concept of getting what you deserve, of the karmic payback, of everything coming around full-circle. I believe life did come full-circle for both girls. Glinda became the "Good," but in her quest, lost her love and her best friend. Elphaba ended her sad and misunderstood youth by ending up with her true love – in his less handsome, more appealing form.

Anne didn't like the show because it glorified mean, nasty, catty girls and the damage they inflict on others. I liked the show because I think all girls have a bit of Elphaba in them. Which one of us hasn't felt picked on? Laughed at? Shunned? Who hasn't recognized the injustice of the "Galindas of the World" being loved and worshipped for their shallow and pointless hold on popularity?

It broke my heart to watch Elphaba dance her strange dance at the Oz Dust Ballroom. Which one of us hasn't wanted to be accepted? To be the trendsetter? To lead the dance? To simply fit in?

Mary Claire had so many questions about the show. And as I was trying to piece it together for her seven-year-old brain to absorb, it boiled down to this explanation: Elphaba was a good girl who was treated poorly all her life because she was different. And isn't that injustice a good lesson to teach our little girls? Shouldn't they be friends with the kind-hearted, green-skinned girls of the world as well as the blonde cuties? Better yet, shouldn't they learn early on to judge a person's character instead of her appearance? I think it's a good lesson for all of us.

Maybe I related strongly to Elphaba because my childhood was challenging – because I was poor and virtually fatherless and wore hand-me-down clothes and had to fight all my battles with my fists and my brain and my athletic ability. Couldn't I, too, have ended up being shunned and disgraced by the blonde-haired, blue-eyed beauties – the ones who had everything I did not? And wouldn't enough kicks while you're down cause you to stay down eventually? How often do misunderstandings and assumptions turn into tall tales on a daily basis? How much damage do lies and injustices do?

For me, this story was real. And as a huge "Wizard of Oz" fan, I loved the creativity of the back-story. The scarecrow and the Wicked Witch of the West running off to live together in secrecy? Love it! And sure, if they wanted to cast an overweight, 30-something Elphaba, I'd be first in line.

"The Name Game"

I'm not a big fan of the made-up name or the made-up spelling of a pre-existing name.   My apologies to all you Bleuellas and Jobobdaves. I'm sure there are many others who would never have named their boys something as crazy as George or Gus. To each his own, of course. Those made-up names, though, are just one of my pet peeves.

Problem is, I'm probably going to have grandchildren with the most outlandish names you could ever imaging… thanks to my darling daughter.

Four of her most recent flashes of brilliance include:

1.   An American Girl Bitty Baby named… Bitty.
2.   A stuffed moose named Moosey Moosey Moo Moo #2.
3.   A new stuffed pig named Terrace. (No, not Terrence. It's a girl. Terrace – as in Balcony.)

4. A pet mouse named Staluna. This, apparently, is a shortened version of Stellaluna. I suggested "Stella" or possibly even "Luna," but those names were quickly and wholeheartedly rejected.

I can't stop cringing at the thought of holding and cooing over my granddaughters, Allimohama, and her toddler brother, Jackamack the Second.

"This Now"

It was a book I didn't even think I was going to like. But it captured me instantly and didn't let go until the last page. "Still Alice" by Lisa Genova is about a brilliant woman with early onset Alzheimer's disease. It's the story of her quick, early, and cruel descent into dementia. It chronicles the heartbreaking stages of the disease's progression – the early signs, her embarrassment and despair, and the gradual slide into the unknowing.

It is my dear, sweet grandma's story.

I distinctly remember when Grandma's downward spiral began, at least in my mind. I'm sure my grandpa knew far before the rest of us. But what I remember is her embarrassment, her innate understanding that something was wrong, desperately wrong, and her noble attempts to hide it.

We were on a cruise ship together when Grandma got lost. We searched frantically for her, wondering whether she'd disembarked, worried that something had gone tragically amiss in a country that wasn't our own. And then a kind and compassionate crew member returned her to us, unscathed. In her confusion, she'd journeyed downstairs and ended up in the boiler room. There she sat, waiting for someone to come to her rescue. Her fear must have been overwhelming, but she smiled at us grandly and declared, "Thank goodness this fine, young man came to get me since none of you seemed to be concerned about me."

And for the rest of the trip, we never let her out of our collective sight.

My grandma was always a bit of an enigma to me. She loved us, but always at an arm's length. She'd borne eight children – eight siblings as different as night and day. My grandpa, on the other hand, was the one I felt close to. The one who threw a baseball to me in the summers, the one who made me feel special because I was a lefty, just like him.

We spent some summers visiting them in the cemetery they owned and lived in. Summers where I wandered through the gravesites, reading the names and dates, and wondering about the fates. Those summers were dreamy, distant, more than a little unnerving.

I loved my grandparents – as much as they would allow me to. I sat with my grandpa as he fought for every last breath, his lungs ravaged by years of abuse. He held my hand in the hospital and told me that he was afraid. This pillar of strength, of bigotry, this father of eight, grandfather to many more. I was with him when he died. We clasped our left hands until the very end.

Grandma's end, however, did not come so quickly. Instead, we watched her spiral into oblivion. I watched my own mother's weariness take hold as she fought to care for her ailing, beloved mother. I cried as my mom had to re-teach her own mother how to drink the chocolate shakes she so adored. Even the simplest of pleasures cruelly eluded her.

I remember singing at Grandma's funeral. Singing through tears about "Mary, Gentle Mother" while my husband sat in front of me in a blood-stained shirt, the result of a car accident he'd had on the way to the funeral. Such a sad, strange day. Such a long-awaited final goodbye to a woman whose mind had made its final exit many years before.

They say that Alzheimer's skips a generation. And so I wait. It is my silent, unspoken fear. Every time I read a book and forget the ending a week later, every time I forget to send a permission slip to school with my kids, every time a bill sits unpaid until the due date has long since passed. It is at these times that I wonder whether it's beginning, or whether my mind is just overloaded with four kids, two dogs, four mice, a freelance career, a house to clean, a husband to love.

But that book. Oh, that book.

I wept as I read into the wee hours of the morning. I cried as my sweet Mary Claire crept into my room, her sick eyes matted shut, her nighttime cough raspy and labored. I gently wiped her swollen eyes with a warm washcloth and tucked her in between Chris and me. I listened to her ragged breath, smoothed her sweaty curls, and thought to myself, this is it. This is what we are given, what we know is real. This is our only guarantee.

This hour, this moment, this now.

"Pacing Ourselves"

My mom and I have reached a crossroads. For the first time in her life, she called to ask if she could stay with me for a while. But it wasn't just for a visit. She needed to stay because Bob was going out of town – and she can no longer stay alone.

Difficult for me to hear; devastating, I'm sure, for her to admit. My beautiful mother who once took care of my every need, who raised my sister and me on her own, who has always been a pillar of strength and my biggest supporter and number one fan – my mom is now in need. With her stooped walk, her ever-present cane, and her array of daily medications, she came to stay with us for a week.

That mother of mine adores her grandchildren like nothing else in this world. She sometimes can't get out of bed in the morning, but she'd crawl on her fingernails to get to them. (She'd also crawl on her tongue to smoke her beloved cigarettes, but that's a different story...)

In true Nana fashion, she wanted to attend every lacrosse game, every softball game, every baseball game, every play rehearsal. And although I wanted her to experience our lives, our pace is not slow. Having my mom with us is like having another child in many ways – a child who can't walk very fast, who needs time to rest, who has to be assisted in and out of the car, who pushes my husband's buttons at every turn. An extra child who frustrates the daylights out of me even as I'd sacrifice anything to make her broken body whole again. Those who know us well know that we rarely build in any extra time for error. We push our time to the wire, rarely arriving anywhere early. This week was no exception. My dear mom tried her best to hold her ground, to keep up with our crazy pace, but by day two, we'd worn her down.

It's such a sad and humbling awakening to realize that life is coming full circle – that while I'm taking care of my children, I have to begin to consider how to take care of my mom, of Bob, of Chris's parents. Because inevitably, the ones who loved and nurtured us might someday need that care in return. By some cruel twist of nature, the ones who once did everything for us could soon need it all back.

Perhaps through a different lens, however, it's not a cruel twist of fate, but a blessing in disguise. Because when the games were over and the kids were in their PJs, they crawled in next to their Nana on the couch and played cards and listened to bedtime stories.

Her presence made us all slow down a bit – if only for a few fleeting moments.

"Brave Heart"

It's an interesting one, this game, full of twists and turns, isn't it? I'm sitting beside my mom's hospital bed watching her fitful sleep after she had four stents inserted into her carotid artery – aka, "The Widow Maker."

Farrah Fawcett died today. Michael Jackson, too. And here I sit at my mom's bedside, grateful that her heart – with a little surgical encouragement – opted to keep beating.

People all over the TV are mourning MJ. I've seen "Thriller" snippets played at least ten times in the last half hour. And my mom's IV beeps a steady rhythm beside me.

I used to watch Farrah on "Charlie's Angels." Used to love that famous 'do. But it was Mom's lap that I rested on as we watched TV together, the worn couch cushions familiarly settling into their known positions. It was my mom's smell I breathed, the leftover antiseptic soap from the doctor's office she worked in, the lingering scent of money from the final day's business deposit.

When I was older, I donned my prom dress and posed in front of the piano with my high school friends. We were venturing out to see MJ in concert at Market Square. My mom dutifully snapped pictures.

Today, the world mourns the loss of two of my childhood icons. And today, I celebrate my mother's tenacious grip on this world.

The mourning can wait. My personal, silent celebration has begun.

"Issues"

I was tuned into XM Oprah Radio the other day listening to Nancy Snyderman discuss the bane of being overweight. She stated her belief that most women who are overweight hide behind the pounds because they're hiding from other unresolved issues in their lives.

Okay, I'm overweight and I have a few issues. I'm irrationally afraid of spiders. If I watch a scary movie, I have to be escorted to the bathroom for a minimum of six months. I have a bit of an abandonment complex. I want everyone to love and accept me. Little things like that.

So, Dr. Snyderman continued to talk about how therapy was vital in confronting and overcoming things in life that keep us rooted in denial... and fat. A friend's doctor, however, once likened therapy to a pile of dog poo on the sidewalk. "When your dog poos on the sidewalk," she explained, "you don't go back and examine it, sniff it, sift through it... do you? So, why would you want to dig up the shit in your past and put it under a microscope?"

Interesting analogy.

I decided to take the conversation to my always objective and supportive spouse. "Chris," I began, "what do you think about extra weight being a cover for deeper issues?" He thought for a moment and then agreed that Dr. Snyderman might have a point.

Next, I explained the dog-poop-on-the-sidewalk therapy theory.

"So," I continued, "do you think I have unresolved issues?"

He looked at me like I was an unexpected visitor from another planet.

"YES."

And then I became defensive. "Like what?" I countered. "Name one!"

"One?" he laughed. "Do you have a notebook? I want to write them all down so I won't miss any."

When I regained my composure, I asked, "Do you think I should be in therapy? I mean, I've obviously already walked by the dog poo. Why would I want to go back?"

His response?

"Honey, you haven't walked *by* the shit. You're *wallowing* in it."

That is true love at its finest.

"Recognizing Her Worth"

For over three months, Mary Claire took part in an after-school gymnastics program. She begged and begged and begged for a leotard to wear (like the other girls), and I let her choose two new ones – one purple and shiny, one sleek and black.

A week later, when I put her leotard in her backpack, she said she wasn't feeling well and thought she might throw up. I felt her head, took her temperature, and deemed her healthy enough to go to school.

"I don't want to wear that leotard," she said, pointing to the purple one in her backpack. No problem – I pulled her black leotard out instead.

"I don't want to wear that one, either," she argued. "Can I please just wear some shorts and a t-shirt?"

"Why did I buy you new leotards if you're not going to wear them?" I argued because I was annoyed and distracted and it was early and we were rushing around like maniacs so we wouldn't be late – as usual.

"Please, Mom," she begged. "Please just let me wear some shorts."

I finally engaged a bit, listened, looked up at her, and saw that she had tears in her eyes.

When I asked her what was wrong, she broke down crying and told me that "Gracie" had told her she looked fat in her leotards.

"Can I please just stop going to gymnastics?" she asked. This from a girl who bounces around the house non-stop and begs for a trampoline at every possible occasion – birthdays, Christmas, Halloween, Our Lady of Guadalupe Day – you name it.

Those who've known me for a long time know that I had a slight problem with food during my teenage years that involved a lot of bingeing, purging, and nearly-lethal amounts of laxatives. I'll still argue that my food obsession began with a former coach of mine telling me that I'd "be much faster if I just lost twenty pounds." This comment came when I was a very athletic, very fit, very muscular, very lean, 16-year-old size eight.

The point of the story is that words can – and often do – change who you are and how you perceive yourself. Mary Claire is seven. Let me say that again.

Seven.

Since when do seven-year-olds worry and talk about being fat?

This one scares me. How do I convince my beautiful little girl that no one should be able to make her feel less worthy because of how she does or doesn't look? How do you get into that little girl psyche and strengthen her resolve so she's able to flip that gorgeous, auburn hair and roll those baby blues and walk away from those who might try to steal a tiny piece of her soul with their careless words?

It's a lesson I'm still learning myself.

"Birthday Chaos"

Sweet Gus turned ten during a harsh winter February. Our quirky, quiet, sensitive boy who fought so hard for life a decade ago celebrated a big move into the double-digits.

And to commemorate the angst and heartache of the first five weeks of his life, we surrounded him with some high-intensity family drama.

For a couple of weeks, we'd been planning a Sunday night dinner at the Hard Rock Café, the restaurant of choice for Gus. Because Monday night was already booked solid with lacrosse, eye doctor appointments, hair cuts, and a board meeting, we knew we'd be hard-pressed to do much more than cut a slab of cookie cake on his actual birthday.

The Smiths unexpectedly went to Alabama, so it was just going to be the Willis tribe and Mom and Bob. Sam's basketball game ended earlier than expected (with a 40 point defeat. Ouch.), so at 3:00, I called my parents and asked if they wanted to meet us at 5:00 instead of 6:00. They were thrilled and said they'd see us at the Hard Rock Cafe at 5:00. We then proceeded to kill a little time by sitting in the Mike's Car Wash line for 40 minutes.

We parked our freshly scrubbed Suburban at Circle Center Mall around 4:00, bought the kids some Keens, ran into my aunt and uncle, and proceeded to the Hard Rock Cafe around 4:40. After all, Mom and Bob are always early, so we assumed they'd already be sitting and enjoying a glass of Zinfandel and a Keoke coffee.

5:00 came and went and although we were a little surprised that Mom and Bob hadn't arrived, we weren't concerned. The kids took turns watching for them at the front windows.

Then 5:30 came. At this point, the kids were a little tired of waiting and more than a little hungry. I called our home number and checked our messages. Nothing. Then I called Mom and Bob's home. Nothing there, either. Then I called their cell phones.

Oh, wait! No, I didn't call their cell phones. Why? Because they refuse to have cell phones.

At 5:40, we let the kids order dinner. At this point, I was getting a little nervous, and Mary Claire was nearing her emotional breaking point.

"What if we NEVER find them?" she asked, her blue eyes filling with tears. "What if they're lost FOREVER?"

I had convinced myself that – in a fleeting Senior Moment – they'd forgotten the time switch. I was sure they'd stroll through the front doors at 6:00 and wonder why we'd already eaten.

At 6:15, I began to panic.

"Something's wrong." That was my text to Chris, my vain attempt to keep the mood light and preserve some celebratory birthday aura despite Mary Claire's audible sobbing.

"Why?" he texted back.

"They would have found a phone by now if they were lost or at the wrong place."

Although they didn't have cell phones of their own, my mom was definitely not too shy to borrow a stranger's phone to make a call. And they knew we carried our cell phones everywhere.

A little before 7:00, my panic was full-blown. I excused myself from the table, headed to the back room, and called Mom's neighbor and dear friend, Meredith.

"Meredith," I began... And as soon as I opened my mouth, I started crying. "Can you please, please run over to Mom's house and see if they're there? They were supposed to meet us at 5:00 and we don't know where they are."

Meredith knew of the dinner plans – she'd spoken with Mom earlier. She knew they were meeting us at 5:00 at Hard Rock. She assured us she'd check the house and call us right back.

"They're definitely not here," she reported a few minutes later. The van is gone, the lights are out, and the dog is barking at us. Why don't you call and check on traffic incidents, and we'll drive their intended route and see what we can find."

I hung up feeling nauseous. Call the State Police to check on traffic incidents? That was a first. So, I called the State Police. Only one interstate accident in the Northwest – not them. I called the Metropolitan Police. No major injury accidents. I called the local hospitals. No reports of Mom and Bob's admission.

At 7:15, we headed home. I was going to have Chris tuck the kids in, and I was going to drive to Greenfield. I wasn't sure what else to do.

Then Chris said, "What else sounds like 'Hard Rock Cafe'? What if they're at the wrong restaurant?"

"They would have called us," I argued, still crying. "If we didn't show and they thought they were at the right place, they would have been frantic."

"Just call Rock Bottom Brewery," Chris suggested.

And so I did.

When "Michelle" answered, I explained that I was looking for my parents, that they were supposed to meet us for dinner at the Hard Rock Cafe, that we couldn't figure out where they might be, and had she seen a bald man and a white-haired woman waiting for a party of six?

"Are you the Willis's?" she asked.

And the mystery was solved.

For three hours, they sat at the wrong restaurant – just a half a block from where we were. They hadn't brought Mom's address book with them, and they didn't have our numbers memorized. They, too, had been frantic, panicked, had stayed for three hours waiting for us to show up.

When they finally arrived home and called us, Mom was shaking, apologetic, a mess.

"I'm so sorry we ruined Gus's birthday," she cried. "I was so worried. I'm so sorry. You need to put us away. Our best years are obviously behind us."

And although I don't have any plans to put them away, I do have one plan.

A new cell phone plan. And an easy-to-use phone with our numbers pre-programmed into it.

Whether they like it or not.

"Bittersweet Goodbyes"

I adore the KD Lang remake of the classic Roy Orbison song, "Crying."

"I thought that I was over you, but it's true, so true. I love you even more than I did before, but darling, what can I do? For you don't love me, and I'll always be... cryiiiing over you, cryiiiing over you. Yes, now you're gone and from this moment on, I'll be crying."

The kids went back to school this morning, and I'm singing that song in my sad, empty heart.

Seventh grade...

(Imagine a picture of Sam here. He's begrudgingly holding up seven fingers to indicate his grade. You have to use your imagination because I dropped my camera in the driveway this morning, and now I'm getting a download error every time I try to transfer pictures to my Mac.)

Fifth grade...

(Here you'll have to envision a picture of Gus holding up five fingers and looking a little bit nervous about starting middle school. But the locker combination? He's got it down, baby!)

Fourth grade...

(Imagine Mary Claire here. She insisted on sleeping in braids last night — because she likes her hair to be "curly," — and because it's still so short on the heels of her "Locks of Love" donation, it looks more like "large helmet" than "curly." But she's still awfully cute. I do have to admit, though, that her experience with orthodontia can't come too soon.)

Second grade...

(A mind-picture of cute, rotten George holding up two fingers — or a peace sign — goes here. He was so excited about starting second grade. But I have to admit that after his abhorrent behavior yesterday, I was not sad to see him go. He needs school, and I need my sanity.)

Am I sad because they're back at school and I have some hard-earned peace and quiet?

No.

Fly little birds, fly! Flap your wings and find your way in the world.

Don't call me hard-hearted because I'm not sad they're gone. It's not healthy for us to be together all the time. They need their space, I need mine. It's all about growing up, growing older, growing wiser. For all of us.

And the one who pushes my buttons the hardest? The one who gets my head spinning like no one else? The one whose name begins with "G" and ends with "eorge?" Well, today was a good day. For both of us. I'm sure he'll look much sweeter to me when I tuck him into bed tonight, thanks to the six hours we've had to ourselves today.

The reason I'm crying is because I've had to say goodbye to the love of my life today.

Carbs.

Last week, I visited Dr. Andrews, and he told me I needed to lose 80 pounds. My heart is strong, my cholesterol is good, my blood pressure is perfect. But none of that is going to stick if I don't take some drastic measures soon. Genetics are not on my side. I have a father who is built like a brick and a mother with multiple stents in her arteries. I knew I needed to lose about 60 pounds, but 80? Wow.

Dr. Andrews prescribed the South Beach Diet for me, so today marks the beginning of the White Devil purge. No sugar, no bread, no cereal, no pasta, no giant bowls of ice cream at midnight.

Oh, my carbs. My beloved carbs.

When I look at the "approved" food list, I recognize a few items, such as meat, cheese, veggies, and milk. A few others – namely Mung beans, Chayote, Shoyu, and Yuba – have never been introduced to my kitchen. (I capitalized them all because I'm not sure what in the hell they are. Proper names? Foreign names? Your guess is as good as mine.)

But the "not approved" list? My lifeblood. Bacon, honey-baked ham, ice cream, frozen yogurt, beets, carrots, corn, potatoes, bread, (sigh, sniff), cereal, (sob), croutons, oatmeal, pasta, (Oh, the HUMANITY!), pastries and baked goods, rice.

Oh, and for the first two weeks? No alcohol or fruit. Let me just reiterate. No alcohol. None.

So, I'm going to be hungry *and* sober.

Go ahead, South Beach Diet, just take my first-born, too! And while you're at it, why not run my dogs over with a mail truck, send a plague of large arachnids to my bedside, and smite my family with some incurable, third world disease?

Yes, I'm bitter. But at the same time, I'm a teensy-weensy bit inspired. You know why? Because – at the urging of a very lean and mean friend – I decided to document my journey in photos. Last night, I had Chris take a picture of me in my sports bra and undies. And that picture? I can't even look at it. It's so horrific, so disheartening, so... gross. I can't believe what I have let myself become. The thighs, the stomach, the chins...

I am not a pear or an apple – I'm an entire fruit salad.

For the first time in a long, long time, I'm committed to undoing all the damage I've inflicted on myself in the last 12 years. Step by painful step.

Will there be crying? Of course.

Will there be bitching? You bet.

And the yelling? Louder than ever.

But Chris is doing it with me, and the kids are committed to overhauling their diets, too. (Well, until the Fruit Loops are actually gone and they're staring down their first serving of sauteed kohlrabi, that is.)

It will be better for all of us.

But I'm in a bit of mourning right now.

So nobody better fuck with me.

"Half Moon"

The mashed potatoes and noodles didn't do me in this Thanksgiving. I ate a very reasonable amount of turkey, sweet potatoes, and green beans and felt very satisfied and in control.

It was the alcohol that kicked me right in the ass.

The cabernet... the merlot... the Drumgray Highland cream liqueur... the Wild Turkey American Honey... the ChocoVine... the Bailey's Mint Chocolate Irish cream...

Oh, the Bailey's.

Damn you, Bailey's.

The net gain of my Thanksgiving weekend overindulgence? Three pounds. And believe me, it was not the mashed potatoes or noodles. It was pure alcohol.

From Thursday through Saturday night, we drank with reckless abandon. First, with the Willis family. Then with Molly, Jeff, and Brian. And it was well worth it. Such fun, such good conversation, so much to be thankful for. We drank and laughed and then laughed some more. And then we drank some more. And let me just state for the record that when Sam woke up on Sunday, I was definitely not laughing.

On the Friday morning following Thanksgiving, I did my first holiday penance by agreeing to an early morning jog with my sweet friend, Jen. She said she needed to do an "easy three to four miles." Right. Of course, there's nothing easy about three to four miles for me. But I did do one. Without stopping. And with very little breathing. (Which is a feat in and of itself.) It wasn't pretty, but I did it. Jen was gracious and encouraging as she picked up the snail's pace and finished the next three without me. I tried my hardest not to pass out in her driveway or back over her mailbox when I left.

By last night, I knew I needed to get my ass in gear again. So, I loaded up the iPod with some inspiring workout tunes. (Some of the more appropriate selections included Duncan Sheik's "Barely Breathing" and Maroon 5's "Harder to Breathe.") At 5:00 AM, I donned my running tights, my UnderArmour, and my sassy new reflective Brooks running jacket and headed out to conquer the neighborhood.

Apparently, my weight loss has affected the fit of my favorite running tights.

About halfway around the block, I felt a cool breeze on my backside and realized that my pants were falling down. With all the heavy breathing, loud music, and efforts focused on not breaking an ankle, I hadn't noticed that my pants were very gradually creeping downward.

Until it was too late.

Yes, friends, at the ass crack of dawn, my ass crack made an appearance. And not only did the pants go down, but they released the UnderArmour shirt that then rolled up under my boobs like a window shade. And I just want to apologize to all my neighbors who might have been groggily taking their trash to the curb, or faithfully picking up their dog's poop, or collecting the morning paper with their first cup of coffee in hand when the debacle ensued.

Because that is one sight that human eyes should never be subjected to.

And I'd really like to apologize to the group of women who had just finished their own run – the ones who got to witness me yanking my pants up and pulling my UnderArmour down while juggling my iPod that was blaring, "Holding Out for a Hero." I'm sure they're home right now washing their eyeballs with Lysol and adding another shot of vodka to their orange juice.

Sorry, neighbors.

Luckily, it was still dark and I tried not to make eye contact with those poor souls. As I very ungracefully attempted to prevent the full moon from occurring, I said a little prayer that my neighbors would not recognize me. Or my butt crack. Not that they'd have any reason to know my butt crack personally. Or any desire, either.

A class act. That's what I am.

This neighborhood will be sad to see me go someday.

"Barry, Bette, Barbra, and the Bee Gees"

I had the opportunity to travel to Ohio last week for a work gig. You may be thinking, "Ohio? Meh." But I was thinking, "Two hours in the car all by myself? Hot damn!"

Why do I love my alone time in the Suburban? Because I can listen to whatever I damn well please on my iPod. I don't have Chris rolling his eyes and being a general Song Ruiner. And the kids aren't yelling, "Mom! Turn off the Barry Manilow! YOU'RE KILLING US!"

And what did I choose to listen to? My very special playlist titled, "Sappy Love Songs." The very greatest love songs from the 70s and 80s as chosen by moi.

Oh, the memories! When I was about Sam's age, I carried around a big blue three-ring binder (probably a Trapper Keeper) in which I penned truly appalling original poetry and wrote out the lyrics to my favorite love songs. Page after page after page of sappy, angst-ridden, bad 70s and 80s tunes. Handwritten in loopy, teenage script.

It was glorious.

I'm not sure why I loved writing out song lyrics, but I did. There was something about the physical act, the ink color choice, the wasteful destruction of so many trees. (But trees sacrificed for the sake of art.) To imagine having that much free time on my hands today is mind-boggling. But such, I suppose, is the life of a 13-year-old girl. This was also right after the period of my life when I wrote Adam Ant a multitude of fan/love letters asking him to please stop singing about sex so much. I was sure – thanks to Sister Veronica Ann – he was going to burn in hell for his lust. And if he was burning in hell, I would have never been able to act upon my own lust for him. (Yes, it's a tricky circle.)

But the Blue Binder was an integral part of my young life. So integral, in fact, that all the songs that were once contained within it are now collected in my "Katrina's Sappy Love Songs" list. And I know every word to every single song. And I can sing them all at the top of my lungs.

And on the way to and from Ohio, that's just what I did.

Here's a sampling...

1. (Our Love) Don't Throw it All Away - The Bee Gees

"(You alone) You alone are the living thing that keeps me alive. And tomorrow (tomorrow) if I'm here without your love, you know I can't survive."

That's right, Gibb brothers. What woman (or man – whichever way you guys swing) wouldn't want to have those words sung to her?

2. Woman in Love - Barbra Streisand

"No truth is ever a lie. I stumble and fall, but I give you it aaaaaallllllll."

So enigmatic, Babs. Indeed, no truth is ever a lie.

3. Tryin' to Get the Feeling Again - Barry Manilow

"Doctor, my woman is coming back home late today. Could you maybe give me something? Cause the feeling is gone and I must get it back right away..."

Something to get the feeling back might – in today's world – be known as Viagra, Barry. Although Chris would argue that the feeling might be gone for you because the love interest in your song is undoubtedly female.

4. The Rose - Bette Midler

"Just remember in the winter far beneath the bitter snow lies a seed that with the sun's love in the spring becomes the rose."

A classic by any standard. And Mary Claire would most definitely agree. I think this one even made an appearance as a "Nightlight Love Songs" radio dedication from yours truly.

5. Seeing You Again - Dan Fogelberg

"Running for your train, you smiled back through the doorway like you used to when our hearts still beat as one. And as I turned away, I knew the lonely days had just begun."

The haunting melody, the emotion in your voice, the sappiest of sappy lyrics – you capture my heart, Dan. Even beyond the grave, you can still move me.

6. Sometimes When We Touch - Dan Hill

"I'm just another writer still trapped within my truth; a hesitant prizefighter still trapped within my youth."

Aren't we all, Dan? Aren't we all?

7. Please Come to Boston - Dave Loggins

"Please come to Boston for the spring time. I'm staying here with some friends and they've got lots of room. You can sell your paintings on the sidewalk by a cafe where I hope to be working soon."

As good as hanging out with your unemployed self and sponging off your friends for an entire season sounds, Dave, I can't paint. But I'll still listen to your song over and over and over again.

8. I'd Really Love to See You Tonight - England Dan and John Ford Coley

"And I was thinking maybe later on, we could get together for awhile. It's been such a long time, and I really do miss your smile."

Although this song is nothing but a glorified booty call, it still gets me every time.

9. Bluer than Blue - Michael Johnson

"After you go, I can catch up on my reading. And after you go, I'll have a lot more time for sleeping."

Sounds like a good plan, Michael. Less sex does indeed mean more sleeping. But you sound a bit "sour grapes" to me if I do say so myself.

10. September Morn - Neil Diamond

"Look at what you've done. Why, you've become a grown-up girl. I still can hear your crying in the corner of your room."

I have to admit that as much as I love this song, it always tends to disturb me a bit. Neil, you kind of sound like the Father's-Friend-Who-Has-An-Inappropriate-Attraction-to-His-Daughter in that line. I mean, why were you listening to her crying? And in the corner of her bedroom? A wee bit creepy, but it does make me love a good September morning.

11. Baby, Come Back - Player

"Baby, come back. You can blame it all on me. I was wrong, and I just can't live without you."

Although I tend to doubt the sincerity of those lyrics from band members who thought their perfect name would be "Player," what teenage girl wouldn't want to hear that from the football star who dumped her?

12. Sara - Starship

"I'll never find another girl like you. For happy endings, it takes two. With fire and ice, the dream won't come true. Sara, Sara, storms are brewing in your eyes. Sara, Sara, no time is a good time for goodbye."

This, friends, is probably my all-time favorite. I spent many years trying to figure out how to look like I had storms brewing in my eyes.

13. Hello, It's Me - Todd Rundgren

"I take for granted that you're always there. I take for granted that you just don't care. Sometimes I can't help seeing all the way through. It's important to me that you know you are free cause I never want to make you change for me."

Okay, this is a tight contender for the number one spot. The horn, the melody line, the lyrics. Think of me, Todd. Indeed.

14. Against All Odds - Phil Collins

"How can I just let you walk away — just let you leave without a trace — when I stand here taking every breath with you. You're the only one who really knew me at all."

Phil, you're a master of the broken heart. But I'm with you, brother. Her coming back to you may be against all odds, but it is definitely the chance you've got to take.

15. I'll Be Over You - Toto

"Some people live their dreams. Some people close their eyes. Some people's destiny passes by. There are no guarantees. There are no alibis. That's how our love must be. Don't ask why."

Okay, Toto, I won't ask. There are a lot of people doing a lot of things early on in this heart-wrenching tearjerker of a song, but I'm not going to ask about them. Promise. And just for the record, when you're not a Christian singer and God makes it into your song, it really packs a punch. Well done.

16. After the Love Has Gone - Earth, Wind, and Fire

"And oh! After the love has gone, how could you lead me on and not let me stay around?"

I feel your pain, brothas. That's a dirty, rotten, nasty trick.

17. Sara Smile - Hall and Oates

"Baby hair with a woman's eyes – I can feel you're watching in the night."

Again, a little on the creepy side. But not enough for this one to be left off of my Top Twenty.

18. Into the Night - Benny Mardones

"She's just 16 years old. 'Leave her alone,' they say. Separated by fools who don't know what love is yet."

When I was 16, I wanted an older man to sing this to me. Now that I have a daughter who will someday be 16, I'm pretty sure I want Benny Mardones to go to jail. But the song itself? Seared into my mind as one of the classic sappy love songs of all time.

19. I Don't Have the Heart - James Ingram

"I don't have the heart to hurt you. It's the last thing I want to do. But I don't have the heart to love you — not the way you want me to."

Oh, James, I used to think this was the Best Play On Words EVER. And you seemed so sensitive, so stuck in the middle of an impossible situation. All the assholes I dated when I was 16 had the heart to do a great deal of hurting. Thanks for being one of the good guys.

20. How Do You Keep the Music Playing - James Ingram and Patti Austin

"How do you lose yourself to someone and never lose your way? How do you not run out of new things to say?"

There's no song on this list that lends itself more to dramatic, loud, over-the-top car-singing than this one. I harbor secret fantasies of someday singing a kick-ass karaoke rendition of this classic with Chris. Except, of course, that he refuses to perform anymore. And that he wouldn't listen to this song from beginning to end — let alone sacrifice the space in his brain to memorize all the lyrics — even if I held his beloved Bruce Springsteen collection over the fire.

And so, my friends, as I wrap up this version of Katrina's Top Twenty Sappy Love Songs, it's apparent that my Blue Binder days are truly not in the past. Because I would have willingly spent THE ENTIRE DAY listening to, singing, and writing about all the favorites from my angst-ridden youth.

The Blue Binder has simply gone digital.

"Fear Factor"

Do you remember the "Bloody Mary" legend from our youth? I do. It was a terrifying slumber party ritual for my Catholic school friends and me. We'd torture ourselves in a darkened bathroom for hours whilst summoning the face of Bloody Mary in the mirror. If she'd actually appeared, we would probably all be in some kind of institution yet today.

Apparently, Mary Claire's 2nd grade classmates know the story, too. Her friend, Brooke, told her about it at school. When Mary Claire came home, her loving brother, Gus, graciously Googled the Urban Legend (against all our computer usage rules) and gave her even more gory details.

At dinner, Mary Claire started telling us about it, started to get a little nervous and visibly upset, and promptly told us she didn't want to talk about it anymore. When it was time for her to take her shower, she reluctantly went upstairs and immediately started screaming, "Mommy, I'm scared! I'm scared!" And I'm not exaggerating when I say she was SCREAMING.

She ran crying back downstairs where Chris – in his infinitely gentle, quiet, nurturing, and understanding way – ordered her to stop crying and get in the shower. NOW!

As an irrationally fearful child myself, I can empathize with poor Mary Mac's fears. I remember that unsettled anxiety in the pit of your stomach, that hair-raising tingle on the back of your neck, that quickening heartbeat.

Okay, okay, so I'm experiencing it right now as I sit with my back to the window. I'm still irrationally fearful – I'm just nearing 40 now.

My mom was never afraid of anything. She watched every horror show known to man and never batted an eye. I sat with my face wrapped tightly in one of Granny's protective afghans peeking occasionally out one of the holes with my fingers solidly plugging my ears, and I still had to be walked to the bathroom for at least six months following every scary show. My mom never understood that paralyzing fear, and therefore, didn't have much tolerance for it. Needless to say, my husband is much like her in that regard.

He swept a crying Mary Claire up in his arms and began carrying her back upstairs. He walked her by a mirror and said, "Look. No one is there but you and me." She responded by squeezing her eyes shut, screaming louder, and crying frantically for me. She actually grabbed the banister as he was trying to take her upstairs in an attempt to stop their movement.

We finally got her in the shower, and Chris went into the bedroom to read while he waited for her. Halfway through, she began yelling in a panicked voice, "I'm starting to get scared! I'm scared! I'm SCARED!" She then ran downstairs naked and crying with shampoo still lathered in her hair.

Before bed, we talked about ways she could calm herself down and think good thoughts. I reminded her that when she was afraid, she should always remember that Jesus is with her, protecting her. I forgot that I gave her that advice a couple of years ago and she admitted to being thoroughly freaked out by the prospect of Jesus hanging out in her room at night.

Anyway, guess who snuck into our bed for the next six months? Even George joined her periodically until the Bloody Mary furor died down. And I have to admit that I didn't mind. Those damn ghost stories kind of freaked me out, too.

"Spiders and Snakes"

As I'm writing this, I can hear "The Rose" blasting in Mary Claire's room. And we all know what that means.

Angst. Because I'm the meanest mother in the world. Because she never gets to see her friends. Because life as an eight-year-old is hard.

But really, she's upstairs crying because she's exhausted. And that, my friends, is where this story begins.

The previous evening was the girls' high school basketball sectional, and we spent a little time noshing in the hospitality room. (Have I mentioned that my kids are bottomless pits when it comes to foods of the snacking variety?)

It just so happens that the hospitality room was set up in a health classroom containing various project posters on the walls. We saw skin disorders, CPR instructions, broken limbs — the educational experience was second to none.

Mary Claire was drawn — like an unwitting observer of some catastrophic train wreck — to a poster depicting various and sundry wounds resulting from spider and snake bites. Most disturbing of all was a bloody, pus-filled finger that had survived (but apparently, just barely) a brown recluse bite.

Remember that song from the 70s? "I don't like spiders and snakes. And that ain't what it takes to love me. You fool, you fool!" Corny, irritating, badly performed — and one of my all-time favorites.

Also Mary Claire's theme song.

When we got home, she asked me about brown recluse spiders and whether or not they lived in Indiana. Much to her father's dismay, I told her the truth. I told her that yes, indeed, they do live in Indiana. But I assured her that in all my years of Hoosier living, I'd never seen one in the wild. And I convinced her that none of them live in Zionsville.

(I refrained, however, from telling her about my Mom's Brown County artist friend who — legend has it — died from a brown recluse bite after putting her spider-infested slipper on.)

About ten minutes after I put her to bed, Mary Claire came downstairs all wide-eyed and teary.

"I can't stop thinking about those brown recluse spiders," she cried. "I'm afraid they're in my room. I can't sleep. I'm scared."

So we snuggled on the couch for a bit, I convinced her that our house was a safe, poisonous-spider-free zone, and that she needed to get some sleep.

And then.

She came into our room and woke us up three times. At midnight, at 2:30 AM, and at 4:00 AM.

"I'm having nightmares about spiders!" she cried. "I can't sleep!"

At first I was patient. Sort of. By the third visit, I was done. I ordered her back into bed with threats of punishment while Chris rolled over and resumed his snoring.

The next morning – over my third cup of coffee – I told Chris I wanted to put a fake spider in her bed. Just to get her back. He didn't think that was very mature or parental.

Whatever. He's the one who slept through all the drama.

Salty and Sweet

Little Stories of Youthful Incorrigibility

Even when freshly washed and relieved of all obvious confections, children tend to be sticky. ~ Fran Lebowitz

"The Garbage Men"

As I was preparing to pick Mary Claire up from a Monday afternoon Brownies meeting, George came running excitedly into the house.

"Come see what we found!" he shouted.

By the sound of his voice, I was expecting a frog or a turtle or a really cool spider. Instead, I found a large pile of trash in my garage.

"We went dumpster diving," Gus explained.

"You did WHAT?"

After a series of questions, I found out that Gus and George had revved up the old kid-sized John Deere tractor, hooked up the trailer, and proceeded to drive from house to house looking through our neighbors' recycling bins. I was mortified.

And more than a little grossed out.

"Where exactly did you go?" I questioned.

"Just to the Christopher's," Gus admitted sheepishly, sensing my displeasure. "And to their neighbors'. And their neighbors'."

"We went almost all the way around the block!" George confirmed with excitement.

"Gus..." I began, but he interrupted me.

"What?! George pulled me in! I couldn't help it!"

I then proceeded to explain to the boys that going through our neighbors' trash was:

A. Unacceptable

B. Gross

C. An Invasion of Privacy

D. A Punishable Offense

E. Gross

"But we found some pizza coupons," George argued as he dug out a Papa John's flyer.

"Put it all in the trash," I instructed. "And wash your hands. Twice."

"Even the coupon?" George sighed.

"Even the coupon."

I had clearly dashed their dreams of finding treasure in our neighbors' waste, but I was embarrassed and appalled. Imagine who saw them rummaging through recycling bins and throwing empty milk jugs into the back of their tractor. I called Chris to tell him what happened while the boys were cleaning up their mess. He was laughing so vehemently, I could barely finish telling him the story.

"Can you imagine their conversation?" he snorted. He then proceeded to make John Deere tractor noises. "Hey, Gus, let's have a look here! Oh! It's an empty baked bean can! We can use that for something cool." More John Deere tractor noises, followed by a squeaking brake sound. "Doesn't look like there's much here. Let's move on." More tractor noises. You get the idea.

I could tell by now that he had tears running down his face because he was laughing so hard. Then he began to sing the "Sanford and Son" theme song. I know there aren't any lyrics. Chris doesn't need lyrics. Just fill in the sounds with "waana, waana." Loudly. And you can imagine how his rendition went.

"Don't you dare let them know that you think this is funny," I warned.

"Oh, come on, Kat, you have to admit it's pretty ingenious! Did Gus really say that George 'pulled him in?' Ha! Which one should we call Fred and which one Lamont?"

These boys (the biggest one included) are going to do me in.

"Do you hear that, Elizabeth? I'm coming to join you, Honey!"

"The Mother of Invention"

My youngest is what we like to call "a piece of work." He's so sassy and so irreverent – a somewhat lethal combination – but that boy is smart. Scary smart in many ways. I can almost see the wheels turning in that little blonde head at times.

When he was five, I asked George what he wanted to be when he grew up. Apparently, he'd been thinking about it because his answer was completely prepared and well-rehearsed.

"I'm going to be an inventor," he said.

"I think that's a great idea, George," I encouraged, like a good mother should. "What do you think you might invent?"

"The Body Zipper."

"Hmmm," I replied, anxious for him to elaborate. "Tell me about that." (For those of you without children, let me explain that that's also the standard line to use when your child brings you a drawing and you can't quite determine whether it's a rendering of a fiery airplane crash, a mutant rainbow, or a dirty giraffe tongue.)

"Well, it's a zipper for your body so when you have to have surgery – like Nana – the doctors can just unzip you. And when you're done, they just zip you back up."

Okay, there are some details to be hashed out. But in the big scheme of things, I think that's a pretty damn good idea for a five-year-old. I would have loved a Body Zipper while I was having back-to-back c-sections. And with the Body Zipper, I bet you don't even have to fart before they'll let you go home. You can just unzip a tad, let a little compressed air out, and be on your way.

I thus continued my quest for information from the inventor.

"Have you thought about how the zippers might be made?"

"Well," he replied with conviction, "I think I'll just take the zippers off of old coats and use those. That way, I'll have lots of different colors and sizes for people to choose from."

And I say, why the hell not? I mean, a good, strong Clorox wiping and those puppies will be good as new!

Now I think we need to start working on a patent.

"Politically Incorrect"

Driving home from lacrosse one evening and simultaneously trying to plan a Spring Break getaway, I asked the kids if they'd be interested in vacationing in Mexico. George was adamant about not wanting to go.

"Why don't you want to go to Mexico, George?" I asked.

"Because I'm afraid they won't speak human there."

We need to get that kid out of Zionsville more often.

"Not of the Chicken Variety"

Lucy is our bad dog. She's our sweet, over-affectionate dog, but she has a lot of bad habits. Farting and chewing top the list – not necessarily in that order. She's eaten more bike helmets than she has Iams. George's helmet was the latest victim.

After purchasing a new one for him, we decided to take a family bike ride. We stopped at Pleasant Place to play, visited the Middle School Spring Fling, and enjoyed a beautiful spring evening on the Rail Trail.

When we arrived home, George got off his bike and proudly proclaimed, "Whew! My nuggets hurt!"

"Exclusive Membership"

Because we spend nearly half our lives in the Suburban on our way to one kid event or another, we have the opportunity for a lot of in-car conversation (unless, of course, we pop a DVD in for a little peace and quiet or unless we're all rocking out to Springsteen or DMB). On one such journey, George announced to the rest of us that he had a fan club.

"That's very interesting, George," I commented. "Who's in your club?"

"Well, lots of people," George explained. "Like Sam and his friends, and Gus, and Mary Claire, and some of my friends, and a few of my classmates."

"That sounds like quite a club. Are you a fan of anyone's?"

"No!" he yelled adamantly. "I'm not a fan of anyone else's. This is MY fan club! Everyone in it is MY fan!"

Mary Claire interjected, "What?! No one ever asked me to be in that club! Did you just add me to the club, George? You have to ASK me first! I am definitely NOT in THAT club!"

"Quotable George"

George has a difficult time keeping his mouth shut for more than two consecutive seconds. He's constantly talking, singing, humming, or yelling. All the time. Dinner time at our house is never a quiet affair.

And my favorite George Willis dinner quote of all time?

"My tongue is playing soccer with a piece of meat."

"Winter Wonder"

I tend to say rude and inappropriate things at times. I'm short with my kids and snippy with my husband. I begrudge having to feed all the family pets all the time. And the laundry? Don't even get me started.

But on an early December morning, my sweet George came stumbling downstairs at the break of dawn with his hair standing every which way and pillowcase lines still etched on his face.

"Did you see outside?" he asked with hushed, almost reverent excitement. During the night, we had our first snow of the season – a good couple of inches blanketed everything in sight. And it was still silently falling in that every-creature-is-sleeping-but-us kind of way when George woke up and took notice.

"I saw it, Doodybug," I whispered back. He climbed on my lap, and together we watched the snow fall in the delicately fragile space between the night and the day. His warm, flushed, cotton candy cheeks nuzzled my chest, and I was reminded of how good this life of mine truly is.

"Give Me Breakfast Or Give Me Death"

The good news is that our house didn't blow up.

The bad news is that my six-year-old needs to start filling out applications for military school.

I smelled natural gas in the garage when I woke up, so I immediately called Vectren to come check on the situation. They said they'd be out ASAP and ran through the litany of things I shouldn't do... like turn on the oven, pick up the phone, turn on my computer, run any appliances, brush the dogs, blink my eyes too quickly, breathe deeply...

So I announced to George (who was rummaging through the oatmeal box) that he'd have to eat cereal for breakfast because I couldn't turn on the microwave.

He instantly threw himself to the pantry floor in a sobbing heap of tears because HE. WANTED. OATMEAL.

I told him to march his skinny little ass (Yes, I actually said "behind." But I wanted to say "ass!") upstairs and come back down when he was ready to begin his day the right way.

After a few minutes, he came downstairs and ate his cereal in sulking silence. In the mean time, the Vectren man declared our house safe and gas-free and released us to our usual before school routine.

I hugged George goodbye (because he doesn't kiss anymore. Ewww.) before sending him to the bus stop, and he mumbled under his breath, "So, you made me NOT have oatmeal for NO good reason."

It took everything I had not to smack him right out of the center of the universe he's re-directed around himself.

We're seriously going wrong with that kid. The table-belching, butt-joking, tantrum-throwing baby of the house is going to be the first one in jail.

Mark my words.

"More Grounding, Less Spanking"

My youngest has been testing his limits. I know that his face looks sweet. But I have to admit that as of late, it's only sweet in slumber.

I love this kid, but he's pushing my buttons. He turned seven at the end of May. Some days, we're not sure he's going to make it to eight.

Maybe it's because he's the youngest and we've been a little more lax with him. Maybe he wants to impress his older siblings with his sassy mouth and his uncontrolled behavior. They certainly make a good audience for him at the dinner table. Maybe he just enjoys being in trouble All. The. Time.

Yesterday, I lost my shit with him again. He can't keep his hands off of things that don't belong to him. I'd taken the kids to McDonald's for a McFlurry before play practice so we could rehearse lines over some ice cream. We ordered – and I discovered that my billfold wasn't in my purse. Damn. So, I called Chris to see if he'd bring my billfold to me, but I'd forgotten that his car keys were currently MIA and that he, therefore, had no mode of transportation. I ushered everyone out to the car to head home for the cash.

But George's door wouldn't shut.

"What did you do to this door, George?" I demanded, my patience wearing thin.

"Whaaat?" He said with a sassy shrug of his shoulders. That's his favorite response to every question I ask him. If you state it like you would say, "Duh, you stupid effing moron," then you'd have the correct tenor.

"I know you did something to this door. Now tell me what you did."

"Whaaat? I just pushed this thingy." And he pointed to the door lock. He'd somehow jammed the door into a locked position, so it continually bounced open when I tried to shut it.

After finagling with it for a few minutes, I called Chris for auto-tech support. Sam held the phone and walked me through various and sundry scenarios until – about ten minutes later – we'd unlatched the lock. I was fuming.

Let me also explain that just one day prior, I had discovered the carpet in my basement was ripped to shreds in the TV area because of a "roller coaster game" George and his buddy had invented that involved pushing the top of the papasan chair all over the floor until the berber snagged and ripped beyond repair. And no one had bothered to tell me about it. In fact, I blamed the carpet debacle on poor Maggie who will probably never step foot in the basement again.

We seriously need to get that dog on some Prozac.

So, I was beyond angry by now. Over the past few weeks, this kid has repeatedly been told to keep his hands off of things that don't belong to him.

"George Willis!" I yelled. "What do I have to do to make you behave?"

He was crying now. "I'm soooorrry!"

"Are you sorry you jacked around with the door, or are you sorry you're in trouble?"

"I'm sorry I'm in trouble!"

Wrong answer.

"What should I do with you, George?" I continued yelling. (The other kids, by the way, were sitting silently in their seats like little, scared-shitless angels.)

Then I began the rhetorical questions.

"Do I need to spank you more? Do I need to ground you more?"

A big snot trail ran out of his nose as he sobbed, "I think it should be more grounding and less spanking!"

"Summer Conversations"

I adore the long, lazy days of summer – working until noon, heading to the pool until 5:00, eating dinner at 8:00, sitting on the patio with a glass of wine, and reading until bedtime. I love tucking my sun-kissed kids into bed at night while admiring their fresh new smattering of freckles. Love, love, love it.

Working full-time last summer darn near did me in. This is a much better fit for me. And because I'm home now, I don't have to miss poolside conversations like this:

GEORGE: What are we doing for Christmas break? (This question was posed a full forty-eight hours post our DC trip.)

ME: I have no idea, George.

GEORGE: I think we should go to Disney.

ME: You do? Why?

GEORGE: Because the last time we went to Disney, I was a baby and I didn't get to ride the teacups. Luke has ridden the teacups. I want to ride the teacups.

ME: The teacups make me vomit.

GEORGE: I want to ride the teacups.

ME: Would you be willing to give up a few Christmas presents to go to Disney?

(A pause.)

GEORGE: I think summer would be the best time to go to Disney. What are we doing for summer break?

At the next swim break, he sat beside me – all wrapped up in his striped towel with both of his front teeth missing – and said:

GEORGE: You know, Dad threw away my Moon Sand without even asking me. And there was nothing wrong with it. It was perfectly good.

ME: Didn't Dad ask you about throwing it away first?

GEORGE: Nope. He just threw it away. And it was perfectly good. Perfectly good.

ME: Maybe it was hardening up.

GEORGE: Moon Sand never gets hard.

ME: How do you know?

GEORGE: Because the TV says so. And so does the box.

(My little marketer's dream.)

ME: Then I bet it was moldy and yucky.

GEORGE: Nope. Perfectly good.

ME: If I called Dad, would he agree with you?

(A pause.)

GEORGE: Let's not call Dad. How about you just buy me some more?
And while you're at Target, I'd also like some Dominos and another
Legos set.

"Coloring Outside the Lines"

It's no secret that the youngest one challenges me.

He's sassy, he's irreverent, he's obnoxious, he's loud.

But the thing that really perplexes me?

His brain.

That's one smart little shit.

But day after day, he brings home school papers marked "Re-do," and "-20" and "George, you didn't follow directions," and "George, did you study for this test?"

Every day.

When he "fixes" his "re-dos," he never asks us for help. He knows how to do the work. He just chooses not to put forth the effort. He understands the math, the reading, the directions.

He. Just. Doesn't. Care.

But his latest project? Dismantling the broken Xbox. Why? Because he wants to figure out how it works. For hours, he's stood at the kitchen table with screwdrivers saying things like, "circuit board" and "power supply" and "microchip." He's cut himself with sharp metal parts multiple times – his little hands are covered with Hot Wheels Band-Aids – but he doesn't stop. Every day after school, he takes another piece apart, examines it, carries it around, studies it. Next, he wants to dissect the broken TV.

I realize there's a fundamental disconnect happening here. Traditional school is not meeting his needs. And conversely, he's not pulling his weight. I want him to be challenged, but I also want him to realize that every assignment he receives is not going to necessarily interest him. To understand that sometimes you have to do something right because it's the right thing to do.

I sat down to pay bills the other night and explained to him that although I didn't really enjoy paying bills, I did it because it was a necessary part of life and because it was part of my contribution to our family. (Okay, maybe the household finances are a contribution that should be shifted to Chris. And perhaps if I were being graded on my bill-paying skills, my checkbook would be marked with notes that read, "This is not your best effort. Please re-do." But that's another subject entirely.)

I feel badly that he's not challenged at school. But I get angry when he refuses to put forth any effort. I want him to take Xboxes apart and figure out how things work. But when he brings home papers on which he's received a 2 out of 30, I want to shove the Xbox pieces... well...you know...

There has to be a happy medium.

And it's not home-schooling. So don't even go there.

He's a lot like Sam. But as a Firstborn, Sam has a teensy bit more drive and ambition. A TEENSY bit. Enough to make me not want to strangle him on a daily basis.

But that George.

Oh, I love that kid. I love his sparkling eyes, his infectious laugh, his witty humor, his bone-crushing hugs.

He's going to grow up to do great things.

But I hope none of them requires him to spell the word "feast" correctly on a written test. Sans spellcheck. Because if they do, he'd prefer to live on a street corner with a sign that reads, "Will explain quantum physics for food. Just don't make me add 2+2."

"Jekyll and Hyde"

When Mary Claire arrived with her mysterious folds and creases, I was scared beyond belief. Sure, I was a girl, but I'd never HAD a girl. Before my daughter was born, I secretly found out her sex. Chris didn't want to know, but I had a feeling. And that feeling turned out to be a great deal of sassy, sweet girl growing inside of me.

I stocked up on enough pink to put Pepto-Bismol to shame. I hid pink onesies, pink sheets, and frilly dresses all over the house. I dreamt about taking her to the American Girl doll store and to Mother/Daughter teas.

What I didn't prepare for was how the extremes of her personality would constantly surprise me. One minute, this girl of mine wants to be a girly girl. "Put a pretty in my hair, Mama," she'd instruct. And I'd snap a barrette – known universally in our world as a "Pretty" – into her auburn curls. The next minute, she'd come to me with skinned-up knees, disheveled hair, and a Pretty that was MIA. George would tail her, screaming his lungs out as he tattled, "Mary punched me! Mary punched me!"

And he was usually telling the truth.

"Hocking a Loogie"

We have a spitter at our house. Most of you would probably guess that it's one of the boys. Maybe Sam. Probably George. And those would be very good guesses. But they'd be wrong. The boys might be nose pickers and nail chewers, but they're not spitters.

It's sweet Mary Claire, my eight-year-old daughter.

At one of Sam's football games, I watched her prance across the sidelines with her orange Gatorade. She smiled at me as she got closer and then promptly turned her head and hawked into the grass like a dirty, old baseball player.

She very nearly missed the shoe of an innocent bystander who looked at my girl as if she had three heads. I felt my face turn fourteen shades of red as I called Mary Claire to my side with that teeth-clenching-get-over-here-right-now-before-I-lose-my-cool voice.

"Whaaaat?" she replied in her nonchalant, snotty way as she chugged her Gatorade – obviously refueling for her next mucous launch.

"Spitting, Mary Claire, is a dirty, nasty habit. I don't want to ever see you doing it again. I don't want to see your brothers doing it, and I especially don't want to see you doing it. It is very unladylike."

She rolled her eyes at me, and it took every ounce of strength in my body to keep myself from throwing her over my shoulder and marching her to the car where I planned to lock her up for, say… the next 15 years.

"Young lady, don't you EVER respond to me that way," I hissed. "Do you understand?"

"Yes, Mom," she muttered with all the enthusiasm of a root canal patient.

"She spits all the time," George chimed in as he sidled up the scene, nibbling on his stale nachos. "She does it on the playground at school, in the yard, and in the basement."

"The basement?!" I yelled. "You don't spit on our carpet, do you?!"

"Yes, she does," George continued as he stuffed another nacho chip into his mouth. "She spits behind the toy box all the time."

I envisioned the wet, musty puddle of germ-filled, third-grader spit on my basement carpet, and I nearly lost my lunch.

"Mary Claire Willis," I launched, "if I ever catch you spitting again, you are going to be in BIG TROUBLE."

"Okay, okay," she shrugged as she moved on – giving George the Stink Eye.

I thought, perhaps, my words had been enough to make her rethink her spitting habit, but found out the next day that they'd been nothing more than my usual hot air.

"Mom, Mary is spitting behind your back," Sam confessed. "She started spitting when she got off the bus, she spit all the way home, and she's been spitting in the yard all afternoon."

My boys may not spit, but they're damn good tattlers.

And not only does my daughter spit, but she has the mouth of a sailor.

At the dinner table, Mary Claire was telling us about a "Calvin and Hobbes" comic she'd read earlier in the day.

"And then," she said with great excitement, "that guy…he said he was going to kick Calvin's ass!"

Chris and I choked on our garlic bread simultaneously.

"His assets?" I asked, hoping that she was repeating some play on words.

"No, Mom, his ass," she said with a flip of her head as she took another bite of spaghetti.

Because Mary Claire struggles with a bit of a lisp, her original statement sounded a lot like this, "He thaid he wath gonna kick Calvin'th ath!"

Definitely funny, but entirely inappropriate.

And yes, we have her in speech therapy.

"Is that what the book said?" Chris asked as took another necessary pull of Heineken.

"No," Mary Claire replied, "the book said something like 'kick his butt.'"

Hmm. Let me get this straight. So, the book said "butt," and my eight-year-old daughter decided to substitute the more benign "butt" with the stronger, more colorful "ass." Perfect.

"Honey," I said as Sam snorted and laughed into his spaghetti bowl, "you may have heard Daddy say that word…"

"Daddy?!" Chris interrupted. "I'm sure she learned that one directly from her Mother's mouth!"

Whatever.

"Anyway, Honey, that's not a word that you should be using."

She shrugged her agreement and went about the business of finishing her dinner.

And later that night, I kicked Chris's lily-white ass for throwing me under the damn bus.

"Pieces of Her"

Recently, Mary Claire picked out a little horse figurine to give to my friend, Nicole. Nicole rode horses as a child, was obsessed with horses as a child, and Mary Claire thought she'd enjoy this little token, this shared interest.

I've noticed that Mary Claire gives a lot of her treasured things away to people she truly cares about. I mentioned it to my friend, Mary, who – in her ever-eloquent and insightful way – said, "It's like she's giving away little pieces of herself to the people she loves most in the world."

Indeed, it is. And I would add that I think she's creating a bread crumb trail from her loved ones back to herself so they can always find her.

That sweet girl can be a nasty, sassy pain in my ass sometimes, but underneath all her eight-year-old angst and drama, she has a heart of gold.

"Just the Way You Are"

On the day it was released, Carrie, Mary Claire, and I went to see "Penelope," the movie about a girl who's cursed with the face of a pig. Mary Claire has a bit of an obsession with pigs, and we waited anxiously for the release of this particular show.

As one might guess, the moral of the story is learning to love yourself for who you are, not for what you look like. When we were leaving the theatre, I asked Mary Claire is she enjoyed it, and she shrugged her shoulders. I asked her if she understood what it was about, hoping to open the door for some engaging, deep, meaningful mother/daughter dialogue about the merits of a person's soul versus his or her physical appearance.

She looked at me like I'd just grown a second head and replied, "It was about a girl who looked like a pig."

Duh.

"Of Pigs and Penises"

"George! Stop touching my pig with your penis!!"

When your eight-year-old daughter is playing with plastic pigs in the bathtub and you hear her yell this at your six-year-old son, it's probably time for them to stop bathing together.

"A Style All Her Own"

My volatile, over-emotional nine-year-old is trying to make her way in this world. And my heart overflows with love for her even when I want to smack her in the head with a hairbrush. (For the record, I didn't.)

Today was picture day at school and Little Miss Thing would not let me touch her hair. I suggested a little side braid and that particular suggestion was met with a sigh that said, "OMG, you are the DUMBEST Mom that ever walked the face of the earth."

I then asked if I could straighten her part and brush out the bedhead in the back. She promptly burst into tears and claimed that I was "ruining her style."

And the tirade went a bit like this:

"You always want me to look NICE and that's not my look! I'm kind of messy, kind of fun. Not NICE! I don't want my hair to be perfect — I want it to look like ME! If you brush it, I'll just mess it up because I don't want to look NICE!"

And so I set the brush down and let her walk out the door with bedhead and cowlicks in abundance.

Oh, and did I mention the necklace? The double-stranded shell necklace that she chose for the occasion? Because, apparently, her style also includes some form of tropical island expression. And I think that's pretty appropriate since we live smack-dab in the heart of the Midwest.

Glad I didn't choose the "autumn" background for her picture setting. Fall foliage and Jimmy Buffett don't typically go hand-in-hand.

Tastes Like Chicken

Food Adventures

As a child my family's menu consisted of two choices: take it or leave it. ~ Buddy

Hackett

"Cross-Contamination"

When Sam was a baby, we didn't stay home much. I loved toting him from place to place, packing his suitcase-sized diaper bag with every essential we could possibly want or need in the next seven to ten days, and jetting off the in RoadMaster station wagon with The Cranberries blasting in the CD player.

The grocery store was one of our favorite haunts. Now, understand that I'm not a cook by any stretch of the imagination. But the lure of endless aisles of exotic food choices and preservative-laden snacks? Too much to resist.

One warm summer afternoon when Sam was around seven months old, he and I were perusing the cool, refreshing meat choices at our local Marsh while Chris was sent back to Aisle One for a forgotten gallon of skim milk. Sam was strapped into the front of the cart in all his chunky glory, his blankie was tucked safely by his side, and a colorful Discovery Toy was secured to the handle for his pleasure and entertainment.

But it wasn't the toy he was interested in.

I hummed contentedly as I checked prices and fat content on the packages of lean ground chuck. Satisfied with my choice, I turned back to the cart and found Sam happily gnawing on a raw pork chop. He'd stealthily turned around in his seat to find a package of pork chops, picked a hole in the plastic, pulled a pork chop out, and was gumming it with a big, drooling smile.

I was fairly certain he might die on the spot.

"Chris!" I yelled, my voice rising frantically into the higher decibel range. "Come here NOW."

"What's wrong?" he asked as he lumbered back with two gallons of milk.

He stopped when he saw Sam. And then he burst out laughing.

"Why are you laughing?" I shouted. "Get the Lysol wipes! He's going to get some third world, undercooked pork disease!"

"Honey, you can't use a Lysol wipe on his tongue," Chris reminded me as he took the wet pork chop from Sam amidst grunts of protest.

"It's got to be safer than the pork chop!" I yelled as I nearly scrubbed the first layer of skin off his chubby hands with Lysol.

"Give me a baby wipe!" I ordered. "That's just soap. It won't hurt him. My mom washed my mouth out with soap all the time when I was little."

"Katrina, calm down," Chris instructed patronizingly – which only served to escalate my anxiety.

"I've watched Oprah!" I yelled. "I know about cross-contamination! GIVE ME THE WIPES!"

And there, in the middle of the grocery store, I proceeded to scrub raw pork remnants from our baby's tongue with a soapy wipe, thereby choosing to inflict the lesser of the two evils on his virgin tongue. Sam screamed in protest while I assured him that he would be fine.

Chris – choosing not to take part in the scene I was creating – found his sanctuary in between the Fruit Loops and the Frosted Flakes.

"Picky"

From the beginning, we had issues with food. First, there was Sam's incessant baby vomiting. Then there was Sam's unwillingness to eat anything other than a peanut butter and jelly sandwich, a dry pancake, or a goldfish cracker. His finicky tastes made cooking dinner The Ultimate Challenge and eating dinner The Ultimate Test in Patience. Chris and I typically failed both.

"I refuse to be a short-order cook," I declared to Chris early on in our battle.

"Completely agreed," Chris replied. "He eats what you cook, or he doesn't eat at all."

According to the baby books that I read religiously when Sam was an infant and had chucked by the time Mary Claire arrived, a child has to taste an unfamiliar food 17 times before he begins to acquire a taste for it. And based upon that knowledge, we established our dinnertime rules.

1. You have to try at least one bite of everything on your plate.
2. You don't have to clean your plate, but if you don't, there is nothing else until breakfast.

Seemed simple enough.

We quickly learned differently.

Sam ate everything in sight when he was a baby. We fed him cold, mushy carrots, grainy green beans right out of the jar, and pureed macaroni and cheese that looked alarmingly like many of his post-dinner diapers. He gobbled everything greedily, then spit it back up down my back, in my hair, all over my clothes. We draped ourselves with burp cloths, loaded him down with plastic-backed bibs, set him on layers of sheets on the floor for easy cleaning. Everyone who knew Sam well knew to hold him facing outward. Those who didn't know him well ended up with putrid smelling stains down their backs. The kid was an eating – and barfing – machine. Until we introduced solid foods.

Meat proved to be challenging for Sam. We'd dice his hotdogs up into tiny, unrecognizable pieces. The chicken pieces we served him were smaller than the individual peas on his plate. But try as he might, Sam could not stomach any meat. He cried when we served it to him, made horrible faces when we tried to force a loaded fork into his mouth.

"He won't starve," Dr. Andrews assured us. "Kids in other countries survive on rice and fish eyeballs. Let him be. Offer him dinner and nothing else. He'll eat when he's hungry."

So that's what we did.

For the next ten years.

When Dr. Andrews suggested that Sam would grow out of his meat aversion, we thought for sure it would happen when he was no longer a toddler. Then we were convinced he'd eat meat in the public school cafeteria. Of course, he'd eat meat at a baseball cookout. The peer pressure would be too much. We continued to be impressed with his tenacity.

At the dinner table, we'd force him to take a bite.

"You don't have to eat it if you don't like it, but you have to try it," I'd coax. Sam would sit and stare at his plate until the rest of us were done eating, the table was cleared, and the dishes done. He'd sit and stare at his plate until it was time for bed. Chris would fuss and fume in the living room, unable to comprehend why his son didn't inherit his carnivorous tendencies.

As the sun lowered in the sky, Sam would sadly sigh his required lines, "Thank you for this wonderful dinner. May I be excused, please?" And he'd go to bed hungry. Night after night after night. With two uneaten peas and a fingernail-sized piece of chicken left on his plate – the same portion he'd begun with three hours earlier.

One night, out of frustration and anger, we forced Sam to take a bite of a hamburger.

"You don't know whether or not you like it if you don't try it," I begged.

"Samuel Joseph," Chris hollered, "put that bite in your mouth, chew it, and swallow it. NOW."

Seven-year-old Sam cried as he put a miniscule bite of cheeseburger in his mouth, closed his eyes, and began gagging.

"If you throw up at this table, so help me, Sam…" Chris threatened.

"I can't help it, Dad!" Sam sobbed.

"Swallow it. NOW."

Sam retched and gagged and cried as he forced down a piece of meat that was so small it merely required one chew.

After that, we never required him to try anything else. He went to bed hungry most nights. By age 11, he'd developed a taste for hotdogs, McDonalds chicken nuggets, and flank steak. I consider that a victory.

"A Vegetarian Prayer"

"Dear God," seven-year-old Mary Claire began as we all bowed our heads at the dinner table. "Thank you for my family and our food. And please help my mom and my dad and my brothers understand that they don't need to eat meat to survive, and that they should all become vegetarians. Amen."

We all stared silently at the slabs of grilled pork loin on the plates before us. That's a prayer that can certainly put a damper on a nice summer meat and potatoes meal. I saw a well-marinated piece of perfectly grilled meat. Mary Claire saw bits and pieces of Wilbur all over our plates.

I thought of Charlotte spelling out "Some Pig" on her intricately weaved web, and suddenly, my green beans looked better than ever.

"Foodie"

Even though two of our kids have some serious food aversions, we have one who makes up for their culinary shortcomings in his sheer and unfettered love of food. Gus eats anything we put in front of him. But he doesn't just eat it, he experiences it. Meal time is sacrosanct for Gus. Fingers covered with BBQ sauce? Heaven. A medium rare piece of steak? Manna from the gods. But Gus never comes right out and asks for something that he wants. He prefers skirting around the issue – dropping subtle hints and expecting us to read between his funny little lines.

A typical food request conversation with Gus is a merry-go-round of intimations and insinuations, much like when he was six and the following dialogue ensued:

GUS: Remember that really hot day last summer?

ME (distracted with something else): Well, Gus, there were lots of hot days last summer.

GUS (slowly and deliberately): I mean that one day when it was really, really hot.

ME (playing along): Yes, I remember.

GUS: Remember that we had popsicles on that hot day?

ME: Yes, I remember.

GUS: Don't you think it's really, really hot today? I know I'm really, really hot.

And that, my friends, was Gus's request for a popsicle.

Jackie's favorite food story was similar, but with a twist. We were at the park together one summer day and we'd both brought snacks and drinks along for the kids. All seven of our offspring were catching tadpoles, throwing rocks into the water, and running along the trails when Gus broke away and sauntered over to where Jackie and I were sitting.

JACKIE: Hi, Gus.

ME: Do you need something, Honey?

GUS: No. I just wanted to tell Jackie that I reaaaalllly like Doritos.

JACKIE: I really like Doritos, too. They're my favorites.

GUS: No, I mean I reeeeaaaallllly like them.

ME: Okay, Gus, why don't you go back and play with the kids.

GUS: I just want to make sure Aunt Jackie knows how much I like Doritos.

It was then that we both noticed the Cool Ranch Doritos sticking ever-so-slightly out of Jackie's bag of treats. And before she could get the words, "Would you like some Doritos?" formed, he'd already ripped the bag open and stuffed a handful into his mouth.

"Chicken Paper"

As a first time mother, I had my share of issues. I carried a diaper bag the size of a suitcase – packed to the hilt with diapers, extra clothes, toys, wipes, baby food, bottles, burp cloths, small appliances, and an extra couple of kids. (Well, most of those things at least.) I never wanted to be unprepared or in need of something that I didn't have. But my biggest fear?

Germs.

Those little invisible, omnipresent bastards.

At every turn, they threatened the health of my brand new, beautiful boy. Every grocery cart, every tabletop, every well-meaning grandmotherly type who couldn't keep her hands off of my smiling, barfing baby. The world was fraught with impending disease.

Gus's illness and subsequent battle with a compromised immune system didn't help that little quirk at all.

So imagine my horror when Jackie called me hysterical one evening during the dinner prep hour. When I answered the phone, I heard her wail, "She's going to DIIIIEEE!"

"Jackie," I insisted, "slow down! What? Who? What is happening?"

"It's Allie!" she cried. "I was making chicken for dinner and she toddled over to me with something in her mouth. She was chewing it and smiling and babbling and I asked her what she had. She just kept chewing, so I reached into her mouth and pulled out a giant wad of wet, papery mess."

"I don't think paper will hurt her," I encouraged. "I'm sure she'll be okay."

"No!" Jackie wailed. "It wasn't just paper! She'd gotten into the trash. You know the paper that sits under the chicken inside the package? The paper that soaks up all the chicken blood and juices?"

I felt my stomach turn.

"That's what she had!" Jackie yelled. "She was chewing on CHICKEN PAPER!"

I was well aware of the dangers of uncooked chicken.

"Oh, my God, Jackie," I gasped. "What are you going to do?"

"Do you think I should take her to the emergency room?

"Does she seem sick?" I asked.

"No, she's playing and watching TV."

"Did you clean her mouth out?"

"Well, I wiped it out with a baby wipe," Jackie said.

"A baby wipe?"

"Yeah, do you think that's okay?"

"I'm just wondering if it's strong enough," I replied. "I mean, do you think it's got enough germ killing agents in it?"

"Well, what would you recommend?" she asked.

"I was thinking about Lysol."

"In her MOUTH?"

"Well, yeah," I admitted. "It can't be worse than chicken paper, can it?"

"Well, if it POISONS her, it can be," Jackie argued.

I admit it was a good point.

But I still would have considered the Lysol if Brent hadn't arrived home and talked us both off the ledge.

Luckily, that experience prepared us both for the day just a few short months later when Jackie turned her back for one second at WalMart and found Allie drinking an open bottle of lamp oil.

LAMP OIL.

Apparently, she needed something to wash down the chicken paper.

And I can't even get my kids to eat a damn green bean.

"John Lee Supertaster"

"They Might Be Giants" has a song about a man named John Lee Supertaster. It begins like this:

"When I was 39 years old, I heard a story. I found out that there are people walking among us who have superpowers. These people are called Supertasters. To a Supertaster, bitter fruits taste far more bitter, and sweets far more sweet."

When we first heard of John Lee Supertaster, it was like a light from the heavens illuminating the answer to all the angst and frustration that Sam's eating (or lack thereof) caused us. Of course! He's a Supertaster! If only we'd realized that ten years ago, our paths would have been so much smoother.

The rest of the song sheds more light on Sam's obviously inborn issue.

> *"Nothing tastes the same to a Supertaster.*
>
> *When he tastes a pear, it's like a hundred pears (like a million pears).*
>
> *He's got superpowers. He is a Supertaster.*
>
> *Every flavor explodes. Explodes and explodes."*

Sam is not flawed in some fundamental way. He's got Superpowers, for God's sake! Every pear is like a million pears. (And that's a lot of pears.)

Knowing that Sam has Superpowers makes me a little less inclined to smack him when he gags on a bite of meat or refuses to touch a green bean to the end of his fork. I mean, who knows what a green bean tastes like to a Supertaster? Perhaps it evokes the essence of the dirt from whence it came. In that case, we really should cut him some slack. Even I wouldn't want to eat dirt.

And the pork chops that he wouldn't eat because they were too "spicy?" The ones that were seasoned with a mere hint of salt and pepper? Who knows what kind of barnyard taste he was experiencing on his supercharged tastebuds.

It's all so much easier to digest (no pun intended) now that we truly understand the root of his displeasure.

"The Pepper Mill"

Life with four active kids often requires us to dine outside our home. We're regulars at our local Subway, the Starbucks baristas know my tea order before I speak it, and we frequent our favorite pizza joints pretty regularly.

On the way home from an out-of-town basketball game, we decided to make a stop at a Ruby Tuesdays restaurant. Seven-year-old Gus discovered the pepper mill that was conveniently sitting in front of him.

"What's this?" he asked Chris as our server brought our salads.

"It's a pepper mill," Chris answered. "Here. Let me show you how it works." He then proceeded – in true Chris-fashion – to explain the inner mechanics of a pepper mill in elaborate, long-winded detail. (At moments such as these, my dear friend, Jody, likes to call him a Puffer Talker.) When he was done with his diatribe, he asked Gus if he'd like to try it out.

"Here, buddy," he said as he pushed his salad in front of Gus. "Why don't you grind some pepper on my salad?"

"Oooh, Daddy!" Six-year-old Mary Claire chimed in. "Can I grind for you?"

And at that precise moment, a vision of a tall metal pole popped into my head and I had to all but scrape my eyeballs with my fork to rid myself of the thought of Mary Claire in her stilettos onstage. If I live to be 179, I never ever need to hear those words out of my daughter's mouth again. Especially paired with "Daddy."

Now excuse me while I get my Rosary. I've got some serious praying to do.

"Hunters and Gatherers"

No childhood question has ever unnerved me quite like five-year-old Mary Claire's exploration of my youth – and the source of our bodily sustenance.

"Mom?" she began inquisitively, her angelic face turned toward mine with earnest interest. "Were there grocery stores when you were a little girl, or did you have to hunt for your food?"

"Meat Wallpaper"

Following is a transcript of a highly intellectual dinner conversation that took place before my kids' rehearsal for "The Best Christmas Pageant Ever:"

GUS: Can I have some gum for rehearsal tonight?

ME: No.

GUS: Why? It fits with my character.

CHRIS: Because it's hard to understand you with gum in your mouth. You can't enunciate very well.

MARY CLAIRE: You mean like when you try to talk with food in your mouth?

CHRIS: Yes.

GEORGE: What if...

(That's the way most of George's thought-provoking sentences begin...)

GEORGE: What if someone was chewing meat? And they started to talk with chewed up meat in their mouth? And they spit the meat out in little pieces? And it stuck to the wall? And then we could lick the wall and eat the meat?

(Pause.)

CHRIS: Well, George, that was very descriptive.

SAM (laughing): The schnozberries taste like schnozberries!

GUS: Things you lick? Things you don't lick!

(That was an obscure reference to one of our favorite "B" comedies – "Big Man on Campus." In short, a hunchback lived in a college bell tower and came down to become civilized. While watching the "$100,000 Pyramid" on TV, the contestant describes a fish. Gus's quote was the hunchback's – aka Bob Malooka Looka Looka Looka Looka's – guess. Trust me, it's funny.)

MARY CLAIRE: That's DISGUSTING, George! No one wants to eat your chewed up meat!

GEORGE (proudly): Meat wallpaper. It's my new invention.

If privy to our family dinner conversation, I'm not sure the world of academia will let my husband in.

An Apple a Day

Isn't There a Pill For That?

A good laugh and a long sleep are the best cures in the doctor's book. ~ *Irish Proverb*

"The Pox"

My true introduction to parenting came when Sam was three, Gus was two, and Mary Claire was six months. We were living in a three-bedroom, second floor apartment far from our family and friends. It was a transitory spot for us – a quick little side trip on our journey of life. One that just happened to land us in the armpit of the Midwest. And while we were there trying to enjoy the scenery, the spots began appearing. First on Sam. A week later on Gus. One more week, Mary Claire.

Chicken pox.

Three kids under the age of three. Three-bedroom apartment. Three weeks in confinement. Three times the amount of Prozac normally needed. What do they say about threes? That good things come in them? That the third time's the charm? That two out of three ain't bad? Three strikes and you're out?

Here's my favorite three-ism – three sheets to the wind.

Because if I could have been drunk throughout the nightmare known as chicken pox; if I could have avoided being sober when I was applying vats of itch-relief cream on three cranky, tired, fevered kids; if I could have hobbled with my vodka crutch through the pounds of laundry caked with the aforementioned itch-relief cream; I would have gladly hunkered down with Jim, Jack, and Johnny and let nature take its course.

That's the only trio that would have made those three weeks of my life somewhere close to bearable.

"Peanut Free"

Gus has always been our eater. Once he actually started breathing on his own, he also began eating. And he never looked back. But when he was a toddler, he began dissecting his peanut butter and jelly sandwiches and only ingesting the jelly half.

"Gus," I'd warn, "you have to eat your entire sandwich. The peanut butter gives you protein, and the jelly is too full of sugar to eat by itself."

His big, alien eyes would well up with tears as he reluctantly reassembled his sandwich and chewed with sad resignation.

Day after day, we went through the same routine. He'd ask for a peanut butter and jelly sandwich, he'd ignore the peanut butter side, I'd order him to eat the peanut butter side, he'd cry. And obey. Because that's what Gus does best. Cry and obey.

When Gus was five, the kids spent some time at my Mom's house. I arrived to pick them up on the designated day, and Mom greeted me with some anecdotal stories.

"…And the strangest thing happened on Sunday."

"What was that?" I asked.

"Well, Aunt Sally came over and we baked some peanut butter cookies. When we were finished and the kids had eaten their fill, Gus's hands swelled up and began itching. Then he broke out in red welts. But I soaked his hands and he seems much better now."

I glanced over at Gus who was still scratching his right hand with his left hand (and vice versa), and I could quite nearly see the light bulb illuminating over my head. That's probably because it was a blinking neon sign that read, "Dumb Ass. Dumb Ass. Dumb Ass."

Within 48 hours, we had an appointment with an allergist, and Gus settled in for his "prick test." We popped a movie into the office DVD, Gus stretched out on his stomach, and the allergens were poked into his soft, milky white back.

198

Then we waited.

And the welts began appearing.

"Oh, yes!" the doctor exclaimed in her broken English as she reentered the room. "You see those red? That mean he allergic. He allergic to…" she paused while she tallied Gus's welts. "He allergic to wheat, raw egg, and peanut."

And that, Mr. Obvious, explained Gus's aversion to peanut butter and jelly sandwiches.

The good doctor continued, "Kids usually know first. They self-diagnose. The peanut butter, it make they mouth feel funny, and they know. This what happen with Gus?"

I didn't want to nod my head. I didn't want to admit that Gus had been trying to tell us – through his normal communication mode of crying and obeying – that his tongue was swelling and his throat was closing and that every time I force fed him a PB&J, I was inviting an anaphylactic reaction to our dining table. I didn't want to nod. But I had to. And at that precise moment, I was eliminated from the potential pool of Mother of the Year nominees.

Again.

My poor, sweet boy was allergic to peanuts, wheat, and raw eggs. What kind of cruel twist of fate was that? I mean, hadn't he suffered enough already? Now he had to be subjected to a life of EpiPens and food avoidance with the very people who threatened to do him in with a jar of Extra Creamy Jiffy? Sheesh.

Truly, I am the worst parent an allergic child could have. I don't cook. I don't read labels. I have no interest in healthy choices. Well, at least I didn't then. It became a learning process for all of us – once again, Gus became our teacher.

I did fail one exam, however, on the day I made Chris an angel food cake for his birthday. See, all I had to do was write "angel food cake," and you all know what's coming, right? Not me. It was a pre-packaged mix. Who knew that angel food cakes contain about a thousand eggs? And not only was Gus allergic to raw eggs, he was also allergic to large quantities of eggs. I was able to avoid making him drink raw egg protein shakes to kick-start his morning workouts, but the lure of the angel food cake was apparently too much for me.

Thank God we never had to use the EpiPen with Gus. His reactions were always more topical than internal. Obviously, Someone knows that we can only handle so much. The thought of plunging a needle full of epinephrine into my young son's skinny, veiny thigh? Not so appealing.

Gus was nine when we returned to the allergist for another round of tests. And beyond all our wildest hopes and dreams, his testing came back negative. Every single test. Against the odds, Gus outgrew his allergies and now enjoys a benign world of whole wheat pasta and Reeses Cups.

But bug spray? Apparently, they didn't test for that. Because on our next camping trip, we doused the kids with Deep Woods Off to ward off the blood-sucking vampire mosquitoes. After about ten minutes, Gus came over to me scratching welts into his arms.

"Soooo…" he began in his deep, no-affect voice as he scratched welts into his bony arms, "…I guess the mosquitoes don't like this spray because it makes them itch, huh?"

And within two minutes, we had him in the shower scrubbing himself down with a full bar of soap. That poor boy is sentenced to a life of mosquito-bite covered skin. We're anxious to see what he ends up being allergic to next.

I'm betting on air.

"Sneak Attack"

Although it may be incriminating to admit, I will confess that when my kids were little, if they fell asleep in the car, we let them stay there. Of course, there were parameters. The car had to be safely parked in our own garage, the weather had to be just so, and the kid in question had to be in desperate need of an extended nap. (We just assumed Parameter #3 had to be met all the time.) When they were too little to unstrap themselves from their five-point harnesses, we would check on them every ten minutes. When they could unstrap themselves, we'd smile as they'd stumble into the house with tired eyes and tousled hair.

But we didn't smile the day three-year-old Gus toddled in with a stream of excrement trailing behind him.

"Tummy hurts!" he cried as he made his way toward us in the family room, leaving a fetid trail of diarrhea in his wake.

Chris and I jumped up simultaneously and rushed toward him. Not necessarily to ease his pain, but to stop the malodorous assault on our home.

"What's wrong, baby?" I asked as I led him to the laundry room, although the cause of his distress was clearly apparent.

"My tummy!" he wailed. "My tummy!"

I stripped him down, threw his wet, stinking clothes into the laundry tub to be dealt with later, cleaned him up as best I could with a paper towel, and took him to a warm bathtub.

Once I had Gus calmed down, cleaned up, and into some fresh pajamas, Chris came in from the garage with a ghostly pallor to his face.

"The car."

Those were the only words he spoke.

Those were the only words that could be spoken.

The car.

I made my way out to the garage while Chris followed silently behind. When I opened the driver's door to the Suburban, an offensive and eye-watering cloud of noxious fumes rolled out toward me.

It was clear from the trail of poop exactly what Gus's path had been. From his third-row car seat position, he had unbuckled himself, crawled to the front row, crawled over the console, and exited from the front passenger's side door. The car looked like it had been poop-bombed by a marauding raid of digestively-challenged toddlers.

And the smell. Oh, the smell.

"Go to Ziebarts. Right now." Those were the only instructions I could mutter.

"Why do I have to drive?" Chris asked.

"Because if I have to sit in that car, I'll vomit all the way there. And then they'll charge us double. I'm sure there's a surcharge for shit *and* vomit."

So Chris practiced his mouth-breathing exercises and drove the car in for a precision detailing. I'm not sure what the Ziebart employees who actually had to do the work thought of that particular job. I'm fairly convinced that it caused a few of them to quit on the spot. Or at least go out and slam some after-work Budweisers to attempt to erase the scarring memory from their brains. I have a feeling The Maroon Suburban has gone down in history as the Worst Job Ever.

But it was the best damn $100 we'd ever spent.

"False Alarm"

I have to admit that I've never actually called 911. That doesn't mean, however, that I haven't made my fair share of speed-limit-exceeding driving trips to the ER. With four kids, I think I've actually achieved "frequent flyer" status and hope to someday have a wing (or at least a waiting room chair) named after me.

After 11-year-old Sam ran a fever for three days – and we subsequently denied anything was wrong by pumping him full of Tylenol and Motrin – we decided to take another journey. I was putting clothes away in Mary Claire's room when he came staggering up the stairs declaring that he wasn't feeling very well, that he had a horrible headache, and that he was going to lie down in his bed. I hung up a couple more pairs of pants and went to check his temperature.

It registered at 106 degrees.

And what did I immediately think? What did I self-diagnose? What horrible disease was already percolating in my brain?

Meningitis, of course.

In a semi-controlled state of panic, I called Chris, ordered him home ASAP, and loaded Sam into the car.

When we got to the ER, we had to wait behind a teenager who had apparently choked on a piece of turkey three hours earlier. I thought a 106-degree fever trumped a three-hour-old choking incident, but no one asked my opinion. When the nurse finally took Sam back, she took his temperature.

101 degrees.

This is the moment that presents a great conundrum for a mother. You certainly don't want your child to be sick, don't want to confirm your deep-seeded meningitis fears, but you also don't want to look like a complete and total ass for rushing him to the hospital with a 101-degree fever.

I fumbled around and blathered on about my ear thermometer and how it probably needed new batteries. Blah, blah, blah. The nurse never actually said, "You're a complete and total idiot, and you should know better because you have four kids and have been at this for 11 years," but I know she wanted to.

"From Illness to Injury"

During my tenuous and challenging year of attempting to return to the work force full-time before any of us were truly ready, we were smote with a barrage of random, long-lasting, debilitating illnesses. The kind that forced me to call in day after day after day to inform my boss that kid #3 now had the swine flu and had to be taken care of by none other than Yours Truly. That's the thing about returning to work. Your career – which was on hold while you were raising your brood – cannot become the Alpha career. Your husband has held that position for too long and is unwilling to give it up. So, instead, you're the one to call in sick, the one who races home early because he has a late-afternoon meeting and the kids all have to be driven to 647 different after-school activities.

Needless to say, my novel attempt to rejuvenate a near-dead career was a dismal failure. In a corporate world that is ruled by young 20-somethings without kids, husbands, or anything else that might require them to work less than 80 hours a week, we mothers cannot compete. No matter how smart, successful, and upwardly mobile we used to be, there's an entire new generation of successful, smart, and upwardly mobile young women ready to push us back into our homes.

So, after the cloud of illness decided to mercifully move away from our home, we decided to take up random injuries.

On Day One, Mary Claire fell down the basement stairs – all 15 of them – with her beloved Christmas Nutcracker in her grip. Her stomach was scraped and gouged and looked like what I would imagine a tiger attack might look.

On Day Two, Sam trumped her with a driveway basketball injury. I'm not sure how he managed to only injure his left index finger, but injure it he did. And when I say "injure," I mean "mangle."

Truly, I had never seen anything like it. Leprosy comes to mind, though. It was the most sickening, most disgusting, horror-movie inspired digit I have ever seen.

Before I had kids and completely lost all my cerebral capacity, I had dreams of going to medical school. The sight of Sam's FrankenFinger would have stopped me in my tracks.

If that pesky Organic Chemistry class hadn't done it first.

"The Boy Who Didn't Cry Wolf"

Just when I thought we were wrapping up the final chapter of the Return-to-Work Plague, George decided to add an epilogue.

I had arisen at 5:00 AM to run (shuffle), shower, and enjoy an uninterrupted cup of coffee. As I was making the 6:30 AM morning wake-up rounds, I heard George moan, "It hurts! It hurts!"

I went into his room, turned the lights on, briefly took note of his pale baby face, and asked him what was wrong.

"My tummy!" he cried as big, fat tears rolled down his cheeks. "My tummy hurts! It hurts so much!"

Immediately, I was convinced that this was some sort of five-year-old ploy to stay home for one more day. I mean, really, who wouldn't want to stay another day in the God-forsaken nest of vomit germs that we lovingly call home?

"Okay, Honey," I said dismissively. "Go ahead and get dressed, and as soon as you get a little food in your tummy, I'm sure you'll feel better. Now hurry up! Mommy has a meeting this morning."

And like the good, obedient boy he is (occasionally), he crawled out of bed and got himself dressed. I found him in jeans and a t-shirt, curled up in the fetal position on the floor, with big crocodile tears running down his face.

"Now, George," I said less than lovingly, "is it really THAT bad?"

"Yes!" he cried.

Then Gus came in and said his tummy hurt a little, too. I reminded him that there were donuts downstairs, and he made a full and immediate recovery.

George, however, was not swayed by the lure of sweet, fried breakfast food.

"Honey, are you really feeling badly?" I finally asked with an ounce of sympathy.

He nodded slightly and continued crying. I started to panic. I had already arranged to drop The Middles off with Chris and head into the office early. This was really throwing my game plan off.

"Can you go to school today?"

He shook his head sadly. Then I said what definitely took me out of the running for the "Mother of the Year" award.

"George, you are the most important thing to me. If you really are sick, I will stay home with you. You come first. Always. But if you're faking it, you're going to be in BIG TROUBLE."

I proceeded to load everybody into the car as I was concocting a Plan B in my under-caffeinated brain. I decided I'd take Sam to school, drop The Middles off as planned, and head into the office with George where I'd pick up hard copy edits and attend my 9:00 meeting before heading home to work.

When we arrived at Chris's office, George was looking a little green and acting very listless. I called work as I was driving downtown, and they advised me NOT to come in. (Perhaps the fear of The Willis Plague is stronger than the need for a copywriter to attend a team meeting.) Reluctantly, I changed direction, hopped on 70-E, and headed to Dr. Andrews' office.

By the time we got to the office, George was so white he was nearly transparent. He fell asleep in my lap in the waiting room. When the nurse took his temperature, it was 103 degrees.

I didn't even know he was running a fever.

Dr. Andrews came into the examining room to see him and shone a light into his throat.

"Honey, come over here and look at this," he instructed.

I looked into George's illuminated mouth and saw all the very visible pustules on his tonsils and in his throat. Strep. According to the doctor, bad cases of strep can cause stomachaches and be totally void of throat symptoms.

He put George on a high-powered dose of Keflex and sent us on our way. I took George to Mom's while I filled his prescription. By the time I got back, he was raging with fever and lethargically fading in and out of sleep on Mom's bed.

I am truly the Worst Mother in the World. I'm sure I will burn in hell for passive-aggressively accusing my five-year-old of lying about being sick. I think I might be the devil. Someone please check my scalp for the telltale 666.

Mom asked George is he wanted to stay with her for a few days. My mom with her bleeding ulcers and her bad back and her general inability to move more than five feet at a time offered to take care of my sick boy so I could take care of the healthy ones and return to work.

George was a little worried about not having his blankie with him, but was comforted by the thought of watching "Mr. Bean's Holiday" with Nana at least 23 times.

"Shoe Casualty"

For months, I'd been looking forward to a trip to the Windy City for a copywriting seminar. A fun trip, a worry-free overnight sans kids, and some solid copywriting instruction. Well, that was the idea, anyway.

My poor, patient co-worker and friend, Nicole, stood hopelessly by after I pushed her out of the cab and tossed my cookies all over the sidewalk across the street from the Theatre Building in Chicago. (She later admitted that she was standing guard in case anyone tried to jump me while I was down. And I believe her. She's a kickboxer – and she has the knife to back it up. I've seen it. Very Crocodile Dundee.) Various pedestrians looked at me like I was some cheap drunk, but we all know it was the remnants of that Damn Willis Plague. Because when I left for

Chicago, George was walking around with a trash can under his face, crying that his tummy hurt.

So, who actually gets to experience the vomiting? Me. On my employer's dime. In Chicago. Not so neat. We stayed for a little over half the class. Thank goodness it wasn't very good, or I would have felt guilty leaving even though the chills were setting in and my kicky new black boots were splattered with vomit.

"Party Animal"

On a warm May day, my baby turned six. Yes, that sounds obnoxious. Yes, I still call him The Baby. Yes, he's much too old to be called The Baby. Yes, I'm going to stop that indulgent, child-worshipping madness. Someday.

Six!

On that May day, we officially became a school-age family. No more sissy little kids around here. We've moved on. We partied like rock stars to commemorate the occasion. We had ten six-year-olds dancing to "George's Jungle Rock" CD which included such fine hits as "Jungle Boogie," "Welcome to the Jungle," "Eye of the Tiger," "Bungle in the Jungle," and "Jungle Love." (We opted to leave "Jungle Fever" out of the mix. Chris thought it a bit inappropriate. Although I'm not exactly sure how Axl Rose singing about "his serpentine" is appropriate on any level.)

The kids went on a safari, pummeled a zebra piñata beyond recognition, had a jungle boogie dance contest, and ate the coolest snake cake ever! I couldn't have done it without Pam and Nicole, my trusty party helpers extraordinaire. And my house hadn't been as clean since when we moved in – thanks to Pam, The White Tornado. She actually cleaned my oven, my microwave, my glass patio door (who knew you could actually see through it when you wiped all the dog slobber off?), and the dirty fingerprints around my garage door entrance. Some of those aforementioned areas hadn't seen a Lysol spray bottle in far too many months – or years. Pammy asked if I was going to tire of her incessant cleaning. Let me think for a minute. No.

I love that OCD side of her.

After a few hours of post-party clean-up, we started Party Phase Two with our movie night crew. After a rousing game of Parents vs. Kids kickball (during whence we showed no mercy – just think for a brief second about Chris beaning the birthday boy in the head on his way to second base), we ordered pizza and waited for night to fall. (Which incidentally, didn't happen until nearly 10:00 PM. Thanks, Daylight Savings Time, for kicking movie night in the ass.)

At around 8:00, I began feeling a little clammy, a lot wheezy, and more than under-the-weather. I took my temperature — which registered a hearty 102 degrees — and then had to decide whether to be the Really Bad Hostess Who Abandons All Her Invited Guests or the Really Crappy Friend Who Infects All Her Friends and Their Children With Bronchitis. I opted for Choice A and excused myself to bed.

But the happy ending to this story — despite the antibiotics that ensued — was that George had a fabulous weekend. He partied at Luke's birthday party yesterday and had a late-night sleepover. He got a marshmallow bow from Pam. Enough said.

And let me just say that there's nothing quite like watching a group of six-year-olds wearing jungle animal noses and getting down in the backyard to an ear-splitting rendition of "Jungle Boogie."

A perfect way to welcome the sixth year, indeed.

"Quarantine"

Blog Post During The Willis Plague:

Screw spring cleaning. We need something more powerful over here. Like an atomic bomb. Since the Windy City Adventure, our home has turned into Vomitpalooza. All six of us. Every. Last. One. And should I even mention the explosive diarrhea all over my couch? No, probably not. My poor child would never recover if I embarrassed him/her on the Internet in such a way. Suffice it to say that we'll be buying a new couch soon. And maybe a new house.

Comment from Jackie:

We are probably not interested in a play date at your house anytime soon.

"Why We Don't Co-Sleep, Reason #486"

Q: What do you get when you let your sick kid sleep with you?

A: The same damn thing she has.

"Chicken Soup for My Soul"

My dear friend, Mary, brought me homemade chicken soup when I was down and out with the flu. It was like manna from heaven – the soup and the visit. She informed me that flu germs can infect people within a ten-foot radius. And then she positioned herself as far away on the other end of the couch as she possibly could – with her turtleneck discreetly pulled over her mouth and nose. I'm pretty sure that's what saved her.

But I must admit that there's nothing more special than a friend who braves the confines of the Willis Sanatorium. And who doesn't say anything about me not looking my personal best. And who ignores the dog hair rolling around on the kitchen floor instead of harvesting it to knit a sweater. Or an entire wardrobe for the inhabitants of a small Alaskan town.

"My Much Older Sister"

My big sister just spent the last two days jetting back and forth to NYC to be on the Rachael Ray show.

How did this come to be, you ask? Well, sit back, relax, and let me enlighten you.

On the previous Friday, Carrie was watching the Rachael Ray talk show while preparing her resume for her impending job search. (Okay, I have to admit – I didn't even know Rachael Ray had a talk show. But in my defense, I don't watch TV.) Anyway, at the end of the show, they ran a little teaser that went something like this, "Does everyone think you look older than you really are?"

Having been mistaken for my sister's daughter more than once (and let me clarify that she's actually only six years older than me), she decided to drop them an email.

Within ten minutes, they requested a picture. So she sent them a shot of the two of us from Christmas. And the producer replied, "No offense, but you're only six years older? Wow."

Saturday morning, there was a film crew at Carrie's house interviewing the entire family. Monday morning, she was scheduled for her flight to NYC.

She asked the producer if I could get a ticket to the show and sit in the audience. But alas! All tickets were sold out months in advance. And my sweet Aunt Sally (former Delta employee) had even offered me a "Buddy Pass" because a ticket to NYC would have cost me $905. Nine hundred and five dollars! Good God. Those are some damn expensive peanuts.

Monday morning, the producer called Carrie back and said that a ticket had opened up in the audience. And I would have jumped on a plane immediately except for one small detail.

I was drowning in kid vomit and diarrhea at the time.

Poor Gus. Sunday night, he came into our room telling tales of late night vomiting. And true to his word, there was a telltale trail of vileness leading to the bathroom. Let's just say – for the sake of discretion – that he had the "all orifices" flu.

Only a truly bad mother would have abandoned her young child in his hour of need. But don't you think for a minute that I didn't consider it. I wasn't sure, however, how to find a friend willing to watch him until Chris got home from work. I mean, I have fabulous friends, but that's pushing the boundaries a bit.

And so, I spent the last two days stripping sheets, using an entire bottle of Lysol, running the sanitary cycle on the washing machine over and over and over, and wiping my poor boy's fevered brow. And Chris had the steam cleaner working overtime.

Meanwhile, in NYC, my sister was staying on the 33rd floor of the Millenium Plaza, dining on herb crusted red snapper, and receiving a head-to-toe makeover so she could show off her sassy new look on national television.

Was I wallowing in self-pity? Oh, you bet I was.

I'm so excited for Carrie, though. I really am. What a fantastic experience during a pretty crappy segment of her life. And according to Amber (who received a picture via mobile phone), Carrie looked "HOT." (Direct quote from her daughter.) I can't wait to see it for myself when the show airs on Friday.

And she said she'd let me borrow the five-inch stiletto heels, so I really can't complain.

"Medicinal Entertainment"

This kid can't catch a break. For overall health and wellness, Mary Claire can rate her ninth year as a two on a scale of 1-10. At best.

I'm home with her today. She was up all night coughing and complaining of a sore throat. I was sure she had strep, but the diagnosis is two whopping ear infections. Again. Poor kid has had so many, they don't even bother her anymore. Apparently, three sets of tubes and a tonsillectomy/adenoidectomy aren't quite taking care of the issue for her.

Tuesday, she had a scheduled procedure at St. Vincent's that she was more than a little nervous about. (And although I write about a lot of things that embarrass my kids, I'm going to refrain from describing her health issues in detail here. You can thank me when you're 23, Mare-Bear.) Suffice it to say that although Tuesday's test came out well, we still don't know what the underlying issue is. Next step: urologist and geneticist.

Because of her general angst regarding medicine, thunderstorms, spiders, lightening, and the dark, we thought it would be in her best interest to opt for the sedation medication. So, she took oral Versed before the procedure.

And then the party began.

Seriously, I've never seen anything quite as funny as a nine-year-old drunk version of myself. She was slurring her words, slumping over on her pillow, giggling uncontrollably. She didn't have random sex with any frat boys or subject herself to highly competitive upside-down margaritas, though, so that was a bonus.

"I waaahn to plaaay Haaanghmaaann...," was her continual request. Never mind that she couldn't hold her head up, let alone hold a pencil.

Instead of encouraging her to rest, I asked her a litany of questions instead.

Just so I could hear her talk.

It was the most entertainment I've had in a long time.

My only regret is that I didn't have the video camera.

When she finally came out of her medically-induced haze, I did a re-enactment for her and for the boys.

The boys, of course, were rolling on the floor and wishing they hadn't been stuck studying algebra and learning cursive while the show was taking place on the opposite side of town.

Mary Claire laughed for awhile and then proclaimed, "You better not write about this!"

Shhh. Don't tell.

"Sour Spray"

I took the boys to the pool today because Mary Claire was at camp and it was at least one hundred and sixty-four degrees outside. We packed sandwiches and chips, and I promised each of them a dollar for a treat at the confession stand after lunch. (Even though none of my kids actually calls the concession stand the confession stand anymore, Chris and I still opt to use it. That little mix of Catholicism and mispronunciation never ceases to crack us up.)

Gus bought a frozen Twix, Sam bought a Drumstick, and George bought the most repulsive new "candy" known to man. Sour Spray. That's right. It's not even real candy. It's just compressed air laced with dangerous chemicals that are ingested into unsuspecting young stomachs. Gross. I mean, really, what's wrong with a good, old-fashioned ice cream cone? It's probably the pre-cursor to huffing or crack pipe smoking. You start with Sour Spray, and it's all downhill from there.

George spent the day spritzing this nasty concoction into his mouth while simultaneously making horrid faces at the taste. Enjoyable? You tell me.

Then my brilliant boy decided to spray it all over his chest. Just because he could.

Tonight when he stripped for his shower, I noticed that he had a bright red rash where the Sour Spray hit his skin. He told me it hurt so much that he had to sleep on his back. I wanted to be sympathetic, I really did. But he chose that stupid ass candy. And he chose to spray it on his bare chest. I know he's only seven, but he's not dumb.

So, I gave him my best, "Okay, Honey, we'll keep an eye on it," and kissed him goodnight. Now I must disclose that the last three times I ignored one of my children's medical concerns and faked sympathy with the "We'll keep an eye on it" line, we ended up with:

A. A broken collarbone (Sam)

B. Shingles (Gus)

C. A right tibial stress fracture (Mary Claire)

Which means I'm pretty sure something bad is going to happen to George's health during the night. I fully expect to see some kind of Sigourney Weaver-inspired alien emerging from his chest at the first light of day.

"Vocabulary Lesson"

Since we've had kids, we've learned a lot of Big Words and Scary Phrases.

With Gus, we learned Pseudomonas, Double Pneumothorax, Brochopulmonary Dysplasia, Pyloric Interstitial Emphysema, and Oscillating Ventilator.

Recently, Mary Claire has taught us Hemihypertrophy, Voiding Cystogram, and Wilm's Tumor.

Big, scary strings of letters, indeed.

Today, we took Mary Claire to the geneticist for a long-awaited appointment. The diagnosis? She does have hemihypertrophy. Her right side is asymmetrical enough to be deemed a medical anomaly. But her hemihypertrophy is very mild. At age nine, she's past the point of being at risk for kidney tumors. We have to keep an eye on certain things. She needs to be checked annually for blood pressure changes, kidney function, and eyesight issues, but in general, the doc sees no need for great concern. The urologist may throw a few more things into the mix when we see him in October, but our biggest health fears for her have been alleviated.

Interestingly enough, Dr. Eaton asked if she had trouble with math. (She does.) He indicated that kids with hemi often find the two sides of their brains developing differently. Poor kid may always struggle a bit with math, but now we know that she'll need some extra support and encouragement to keep up.

We'll teach our kids and they'll continue to teach us.

You know what some of my favorite words and phrases are?

"Out of the woods."

As in, "Gus is out of the woods. Now he just has to heal."

And okay.

As in, "Mary Claire is okay. I see no need to schedule a follow-up unless you have new concerns."

And healthy.

As in, "Your kids are all healthy."

And blessed.

As in, we are truly blessed.

With a Little Help From Our Friends

There's Nothing a Good Friend and a Good Cabernet Can't Fix

"Friendship is unnecessary, like philosophy, like art...it has no survival value; rather it is one of those things that gives value to survival." ~ *C.S. Lewis*

"Pennsylvania Double Pump"

When Sam was one and Allie was an infant, we trekked cross-country to attend the wedding of my dear childhood friend, Andi, on the Cornell University campus. We hired our niece, Amanda, to babysit the kids while we attended the ceremony, loaded all seven people up in a rented minivan, turned The Cranberries on full blast, and headed east.

I sang at the wedding, watched my beautiful friend walk down the aisle in her stunning gown, and we partied like rock stars at the reception. Jackie made friends with all the Hispanic waiters and flirted with them in the kitchen throughout the night. She danced like a maniac with Andi's best gay friend who was also serving as her event planner. We all drank like there was no tomorrow and paid for it the next day.

But the best part of the trip took place at a gas station in Erie, Pennsylvania.

We'd stopped to stretch our legs, take a quick bathroom break, and load up on some caffeine and sugar. Jackie stayed behind with the kids while we made our way through the mini-mart.

When Chris and I emerged from the store with Diet Cokes in hand, we stopped short in our tracks.

"What the... ?" he muttered as we approached the minivan.

Because there, in broad daylight, in the front seat of the car was Jackie – hooked up to an electric double-breast pump that was plugged into the lighter. In Erie, PA, we all watched in wonder – with the rest of the gas station patrons – as Jackie nonchalantly pumped, bagged, and stored the next day's meals for her new baby.

It's a sight none of us will soon forget.

"Boy Friends"

Chris, Brent, and Brian have been friends since middle school. They've known each other through puberty, first loves, bad high school teachers, and Ball State parties. That gives us a great deal of fodder for stories involving high levels of embarrassment and mockery.

Take, for instance, Brent's affinity for cheese. He's so enamored with cheese, we're pretty sure he's part rat. When we go to Steak and

Shake, we always know what Brent's order will be: double cheeseburger, cheese fries, and cottage cheese. Always. Without fail.

And although none of us will deny that Brent's a pretty smart cookie, we would never admit it to his face. When we had just graduated from college, he joined an online MENSA community. The conversation between Chris and Brent went something like this:

BRENT: I joined MENSA.

CHRIS: You WHAT?

BRENT: I joined MENSA.

CHRIS (laughing hysterically and falling to the floor): You're such a fag.

I'm not sure what binds these boys to each other, but whatever it is, it's strong. They don't discuss their feelings or their ambitions or their dreams like we girls do, they don't need to talk on a daily basis, and they'd rather chew their own arms off than go shopping together. But whatever they have is lasting.

At one point – perplexed by their relationship – I inquired about their conversations.

"What do you talk about when you go fishing?" I asked my husband.

"Fishing."

"What else?"

"Sports. Maybe beer."

"Do you ever talk about your relationships or your feelings?"

"No."

"What do you talk about when you're on the golf course all day?"

"Golf."

And thus, their relationship maintains its own aura of mystery to me.

And Brian lends us his own brand of mockery fodder on a daily basis. As our token single friend, we can't help but question whether he's gay (even though we're all pretty sure he's not). But it gives us great pleasure to number all the reasons why we think he might be.

Reason #283:

Brian enjoys preparing for our camping trips more than any human being should. He cleans and lays out all his goods, takes pictures of them, and emails them to us with a detailed listing so we can ensure we're taking everything we need.

Reason #170:

Brian has a standard appointment for eyebrow waxing at David and Mary's. He takes better care of his facial hair than I do. And the hair product? Don't even get me started.

Reason #485:

Recently he asked me what I thought about him wearing boot-cut jeans. He specifically called me on the phone to inquire about the cut of his jeans. And the truly humorous part of that story is that I'm still most comfortable in baggy sweatpants and oversized sweatshirts. The cut of his jeans? That's definitely Jackie's forte.

Reason #751:

"That bitch can cook." That's a phrase we all end many Brian-centered sentences with. For example, "Brian may be a little crotchety and set in his ways, but that bitch can cook." Or, "Brian really pissed me off last week, but it doesn't matter because that bitch can cook." And his cooking prowess is right on par with his decorating style sense. His house is definitely more put-together than mine can ever aspire to be.

When Chris, Brent, and Brian get together, there's always lots of beer drinking, laughing, and reminiscing. Add in a dose of Jeff, and the real entertainment begins. These boys alternately make me mad as hell and make me grateful as anything for the love and support that they give to our family. When the chips are down, they're there. When Gus was in the hospital, they were ever-present. When our lives are unraveling – as lives will sometimes do – they're the first ones to respond.

I wouldn't want anyone else in my corner.

"The Rewards of Eavesdropping"

When the Archers, the Fabers, the Willis's, and the Hendershot gather together, there is no shortage of foul language. Inevitably, little ears hear things they shouldn't, and occasionally, little mouths repeat things they've heard in drunken conversations.

Sam was four, Maddie was two, Allie was one, and Johnny and Gus were infants when we made a pilgrimage to Fort Wayne to spend some time re-connecting. The kids laughed and played like old friends, and the parents drank and cursed like old times. At one juncture in the evening, we went to check on the kids and heard Maddie talking to her baby doll.

"Time a go sleep, baby," she cooed. Jackie, Molly, and I peeked inside her room and watched her put her baby to bed. "Go sleep, baby," she repeated sweetly. She then covered her baby with a blanket and yelled, "I say go sleep, you fucking baby!"

The shock of hearing that word come out of that sweet two-year-old's mouth was enough to send the three of us into fits of hysteria.

"I can't believe she said that!" Molly gasped as we ran laughing back to the kitchen. "I've never heard her say that word!"

"But what's really impressive," I added, "is that she used it in the proper context."

That evening, we threw Sam and Maddie into the bathtub together before we put them to bed. Again, we watched the two of them play and talk until Maddie pointed to Sam's boy parts and said, "I like your... I like your..." It was obvious that she didn't quite know what she was looking at.

"I like your butt."

"Surrey with the Fringe on Top"

George and Luke were born three days apart. Luke is the only Archer baby I didn't get to welcome in the hospital because I was across town in another hospital with George. Jackie and I always talked about how fun it would be to be pregnant together, to have kids at the same time. And now we have the Bad Boys. Thick as thieves, friends forever – someday they plan to move to Africa, eschew wives, and remain together indefinitely.

When these babies of ours were six months old, the Fabers came to visit with Maddie and Elise. Never ones to sit around and do nothing, we planned a trip to Indy, a walk around the canal, and a visit to the zoo. When we got to the canal on that beautiful autumn day, however, we saw them.

The bicycle surreys.

Like the fabled sirens, they called to us. And so, we rented two eight-person surreys, we strapped our infants into their Baby Bjorns, loaded our littlest kids – including Mary Claire, Elise, Johnny, and Gus – into the front baskets, strapped Maddie, Sam, and Allie into their own seats, and set out on a grand adventure powered by Brent, Chris, and Jeff.

The air was crisp and the view was beautiful. The kids were having the time of their lives.

And then.

We came upon a downhill stretch of canal that didn't look too steep from the top. We paused briefly to assess the terrain, and Jackie yelled, "Let's turn these mothers out!"

With that, the boys began pedaling like mad and we raced down the incline.

I can't fully describe the feeling of being out of control in a bicycle surrey with all of our children screaming at the top of their lungs, so you're just going to have to use your imagination. For a few harrowing seconds – as we tipped and turned precariously on two wheels – we were pretty convinced we were going to end up in the icy canal. I began calculating in my head how I was going to keep George's head afloat in the Baby Bjorn while I plucked my other three kids out of the water and back to dry land. And as I was making my grand plan, every one of those kids (at least those who had already learned to talk) was screaming hysterically, "We're going to DIE!"

The headlines were playing themselves out in my head: "Multiple-Family Outing Turns Tragic When Surreys Plunge Into Canal."

And as we careened around the corner and skidded to a stop, all the kids began to cry. And all the adults – once we'd regained our composure – began to laugh hysterically.

"Let's turn this mother out!" is a phrase that has gone down in history.

"Through Thick and Thin…and Barbeque Chips"

I've been reflecting a great deal on what it means to be a friend. And what it means to have a friend. Having recently been burned by someone I thought was a friend (and when I say burned, I mean fried to a crisp. But that's another book in and of itself. You can find it in the creative non-fiction section of your local bookstore someday.), I've had lots to think about. And here are a few of my conclusions. I don't really have any words of wisdom – just a multitude of observations…

1. I love my friends dearly and trust them fully and without question.

2. Once you've lost my trust, it's all but impossible to gain it back. Fool me once, shame on you. Fool me twice, shame on me. (I get that grudge-holding gene from my maternal side.)

3. I'm not perfect and my true friends forgive my faults. I, in return, strive to give them the same courtesy.

4. My friends add joy and depth to my life; they do not suck the life from me.

5. I like for my friends to need me, but I can't be friends with those who are needy. There's a vast difference.

6. I can argue with my friends, we can get on each other's nerves, we can even come to a stand-off over barbeque chips. But in the end, true friendship always prevails.

7. My friends and I might parent our kids differently, but we love each other's kids as our own and respect the choices we all make as parents.

8. Not one of us is a perfect friend, but my real friends realize that those who live in glass houses shouldn't throw stones.

9. My friends celebrate my successes and support my through my failures. They don't celebrate my failures and sabotage my successes.

I love each and every one of you, my true friends – the ones who have weathered the good and the bad beside me. Thanks for the happiness you've brought to my life. Thanks for making me a better person than I was before I knew you.

"Indispensable"

"You've begun to feel like home…" is one of my favorite lines from The Fray. And when my dear Jody was moving to Chicago, it resonated in my sad head day after day after day. And I cried a lot before she moved. Couldn't stop crying. I had a dream about lost friendship that settled deeply into my bones. Yes, it was just a dream, but so vividly real. Sometimes I take my friends for granted. Our lives become too busy to stop, our days fill with errands and to-do lists that don't really matter in the long run. But I know that if I ever lost my friends, I would be lost. Jackie, Molly, Jody, Andi, Pam, Mary. When they are far from my heart, my world is not right.

Chris doesn't understand, and I don't expect him to. There is something between women that I don't believe men necessarily share. I love my girls like no one else. I need them like I need my own breath. That love doesn't lessen or negate the love I feel for my children, my husband, my family. It is a different kind of love – one that completes the circle within my soul. No one knows me like they do. No one understands my needs and my neuroses with such clarity.

Near the time of Jody's move, I was scheduled for a minor surgery. Nothing earth-shattering or of great magnitude, but enough to have to undergo general anesthesia. My underlying, unspoken, and all-encompassing fear during the days preceding my surgery – no matter how irrational – was not waking up.

What a loss it would be to miss out on what life has left to offer. Jackie, Andi, and I often joke about outliving our husbands and moving to Boca Raton as sassy, old women together. We know that we'll bicker and fight and probably have enough cats to keep us on the Humane Society watch list, but we'll love each other with a bond that can only be created through a lifetime of shared memories, laughter, and tears. And that outweighs everything else.

My dear, dear friends, "You've begun to feel like home."

"It Takes a Village"

On a balmy 60-degree March day in Indiana, I decided to clean out closets, wash winter coats, and look at new cars. A bit premature in Indiana – in fact, the snow returned three short days later – but worth it, nonetheless.

In honor of Spring, we decided to attend the Flower and Patio show. All six of us. I had an idyllic view of what a great bonding experience it would be.

That lasted all of three minutes.

Then Gus was starving, Mary Claire's feet hurt, and George was all but backstroking in the hot tub displays. I took them home to play outside, and we all were much happier.

The following day, George had the Mother of All Tantrums. He had pajama day at school (which he was extremely excited about), and I picked him up early to go visit Jackie, Jody, Luke, and Jackson. When we got to Jackie's house, he decided he wanted to go home and change his clothes first. I told him that wasn't an option, but that I was sure Jackie would loan him an outfit of Luke's to wear.

That sent him into a complete and total breakdown.

He sat in the back of the Suburban we were test-driving for the night and screamed like a banshee. I left him in the car, took the keys, and told him to come into Jackie's house when he was done with his fit.

Jody, however, was very concerned about him being in the car by himself.

"I'm not worried about him," she explained. "I'm concerned about the safety of the $50,000 car that's not yet yours."

So she went outside to persuade him to come in and ended up forcefully removing him from the car.

Now, let me explain that George isn't a small four-year-old. He outweighs his six-year-old sister by a good ten pounds and is solid as a brick. Jody, on the other hand, is a wiry little redhead who was clearly overpowered by my demonic, screaming son.

Jackie and I stood at the window with glasses of wine and laughed our asses off as she dragged him inside to continue his tantrum in the relative safety of Jackie's office. If I hadn't laughed, I'm sure I would have spanked the daylights out of him.

It was not one his (or my) better moments.

"Middle School Stakeout"

Returning to work was a strong consideration after spending an entire afternoon behind a bush in Jackie's neighbor's yard. In the midst of a giant cobweb. With mulch digging into my knees. And a cell phone camera at the ready.

It was a noble cause, though.

Sweet Allie had been inappropriately addressed by a much older boy at the bus stop the day before. And when I say inappropriately, I mean in both word and deed. So, Jackie decided to catch him in the act – with a borrowed video camera. She wanted to make sure she had hard evidence to back her claims because the young perp's parents have been less than concerned with all the other numerous neighborhood complaints. (Apparently, all of this young boy's lewd behavior has been provoked. As if riding a bus to the middle school is such a sex-filled adventure fraught with blossoming boobs and raging hormones that this poor young fella couldn't help but proposition his much younger classmates with inappropriate suggestions and gestures.)

And because the thought of returning to my roots and kicking the ass of some middle school derelict was so compelling, I agreed to join her in her quest for justice.

"I'm going to position myself behind my neighbor's tree. They won't be able to see me from the corner. And you go across the street and behind that row of shrubs," Jackie instructed.

"You mean the ones right in front of their living room windows?" I asked.

"Yes."

"What if they're home?"

"They're not. And if they are, they don't have guns."

Fantastic.

Jackie – cleverly disguised in sunglasses, black hat, and a great deal of foliage – hid on one side of the street with video camera in hand. I (sans disguise) crouched in some unsuspecting neighbor's yard, praying the entire time that they wouldn't call the local police on the deranged woman who was balled up behind their shrubbery with a Blackberry camera aimed at the bus stop.

The headlines played themselves out in my mind: "Local Principal's Wife Arrested on Trespassing Charges."

Finally, the moment of truth arrived.

The bus pulled to a stop, the doors opened, and two young girls (including Allie) walked down the steps and onto the sidewalk. No menacing boys followed, and the bus continued on its way.

Mission thwarted. That damn kid was probably sneaking into an X-rated, after-school peep show.

But don't think we won't assume the same stance in the future. Same time, same place, same mission. I'll even wear my fancy-schmancy, ass-kicking shoes in the name of middle school justice. Mission Mama Bear…take two.

Game on, Eighth Grader. Game on.

"Drunken Debacle"

When you reach a certain point in your life, you should probably have learned a lesson or two. By the time you're 38, you should be aware that life isn't always fair, you should understand your own stance on the existence of a higher power, you should have a firm grasp on the difference between right and wrong, and you should probably be intimately familiar with the Golden Rule and all its intricacies.

Most importantly, though, by the time you're 38, you should be fully aware that consuming two bottles of red wine within a five-hour time frame will leave you clutching the toilet and barely clinging to life. And knowing that should, in all likelihood, prevent you from entertaining that level of overindulgence.

Theoretically speaking.

Alas, when you're enjoying a long-overdue evening out with your best friends, the bisque is creamy and hot, the steaks are tender, the conversation is engaging, and the wine is flowing freely, sometimes it's difficult to remember all those life lessons.

And so, dear friends, let's just say I took one for the team. Jackie, you said it most eloquently: "The price of good times with good friends is sometimes high." And because I was still in bed at 1:30 PM on the most beautiful day of the year, I will wholeheartedly agree with you.

"Picking Up My Slack"

"Did you ever know that you're my hero? And everything I wish I could be? I can fly higher than an eagle, for you are the wind beneath my wings. Thank you, thank you, thank God for you, the wind beneath my wiiiingggsss…" ~ Bette Midler

Yes, it's one of my favorite songs. I don't care how sappy or contrived it is. I also love the movie "Beaches." And I don't care how sappy or contrived it is, either. What I do care about, however, is when my irreverent husband calls my favorite movie "Bitches." Just to make me mad.

But my girlfriends, have indeed, saved my life – on more than one occasion. Consider the morning that I was short of breath and wheezing with alarming force. Being the stubborn and pig-headed nuisance that I normally am, I planned to drive myself to Greenfield to see Dr. Andrews for a quick steroid prescription to alleviate the symptoms.

After talking to me on the phone for two minutes, however, Jackie heard my raspy, breathless voice, and proclaimed, "Absolutely not!"

"I'm picking you up right now and we're going straight to the hospital. Now shut up, get outside, and wait for me!"

And because I don't want to be on the wrong end of her business, I did as I was told.

When we got to the ER, they took me straight back, gave me a breathing treatment, and then proceeded to give me five more. Plus a whopping dose of steroids. Apparently, my airway was nearly closed thanks to a virus that was wreaking havoc on my ability to get oxygen to my lungs. After a spot of pneumonia was detected on my right lung x-ray, they admitted me for the night where I received round-the-clock breathing treatments and a few more steroid injections. I came home the following night with a nebulizer, an antibiotic, another round of steroids, and enough albuterol to keep me jittery for at least five years.

Am I grateful to my best friend? Absolutely. Is she still the bossiest girl I know? Without a doubt. But she stayed right by my side through my ER visit, she called everyone who needed to be called, she made me laugh and cry with her dirty, inappropriate talk until I was wheezing, wetting myself, and begging for mercy.

And then she took my kids to her house for the night. She fed them, oversaw homework, and kept them safe and sound while Chris conducted teacher interviews. (He was busy entertaining the Governor during the day, so he wasn't available to hang out in the ER with me.)

The following day, sweet Pammy picked George up from kindergarten and took him to her house for the afternoon. By the time I returned from the hospital the next day, she had prepared two complete meals for my family and delivered them to my home with a big McDonalds Diet Coke. One of the meals included grapes and strawberries – ones that she had already cleaned and cut for us. Cleaned and cut! Do you know how decadent that is to me? Fruit that is already cleaned, sliced, and ready to be popped directly into my house – without even a dirty cutting board to show for it?

And this on the heels of scrubbing my oven and my sliding glass door and meticulously icing – and re-icing – George's birthday snake cake.

I truly have the best friends in the world. One who can flawlessly sing every word of every 80s song that was ever recorded, and one who can bring my to my knees with her dirty, raunchy, and often unexpected potty mouth.

As my heartfelt thank you, I refrained from kissing either of them on the lips until every trace of my hacking, wheezing cough was completely gone.

"Birthday Bliss"

For my 38th birthday, Brian sent me a picture of a shirtless John Mayer flaunting his perfect boobs. It was the Best. Present. Ever. Because it's commonly known that if Johnny Boy came knocking on my door tomorrow and asked me to run off with him, I would do it. Chris knows it, and he's okay with it. He just gets the same consideration when Halle Berry shows up. Whatever. Like *that's* going to happen.

I posted John's boob picture right on my desktop right next to my favorite shot of Dave Matthews. Because it was my birthday. And because I would also run off with Dave if he came knocking. Same deal. If Dave and John came knocking together, though, I'm not sure what I'd do. Although I'm pretty sure it would be something that would require me to go to Confession.

Or to Utah.

I had the best surprise birthday lunch ever when Jackie, Mary, Andi, and Pam came to my office and stole me away to PF Changs. I was totally not expecting it. Mary knew. When Jackie asked her if I was in on the surprise, she replied, "No. She's not dressed for lunch. She's wearing fleece."

And I was. Fleece and white socks and dumb shoes. Thank God my friends love me for my witty repartee and my loyal kinship – and not for my fashion sense.

Here's what my pals gifted me with to celebrate my 38th year on this earth:

1. A "Life is Good" purse, a memoir, and a book on writing
2. Merlot
3. A coffee mug (complete with a liquor reference) and a funny book replete with overweight, middle-aged women jokes
4. Personalized stationery
5. A book on friendship and a fun CD compilation (a la the classic 80s "mix" tape)

Oh, could they know me any better?

When I returned to the office, my boss informed me that the team had bought me a massage, that I was to leave work early to get there, and I was then to go straight home afterwards.

Life is good, indeed.

"Wife Number Three"

After a Saturday night filled to the brim with youth basketball, a group of us decided to go out for dinner. Because of other commitments, Pam and I ended up going sans husbands, and we met Brent and Jackie with the kids at a local Mexican favorite. We put the eight kids that were with us at one end of the table, and Pam, Jackie, Brent, and I sat at the other end together.

Our waiter came to our table and asked, 'Hey – are you guys from Utah?"

"The Real Reason"

One of our favorite days began with a winter storm warning and six inches of snow, and the kids couldn't wait to get outside. They built snow forts and played "polar bear hibernation." George told me he even built a snow elephant. (Really, I don't know what that means.) They drank hot chocolate when they came inside, cold and red-cheeked, and they reveled in their chocolate mustaches. I stayed inside and cooked all day. Cooked a meal for new neighbors and another to share with good friends. Cooked in my "Naughty or Nice" apron that Pam gave me – my first real, grown-up apron – my favorite gift this season. It was a good day, a day to remind us what life is all about.

Wrapped in the warmth and coziness of our home, I nearly canceled our dinner plans because the laundry was mounting, the presents were yet unwrapped, and the Christmas cards still unsent. But a mere 30 seconds after calling our friends, Scott and Mary, to reschedule dinner, I had a realization. Today wasn't about dirty clothes, it was about spending time with the people we love. It wasn't about all the details of Christmas, it was about sharing a meal and a glass of wine (or two…or three). It was about watching a three-year-old running around without his pants simply because "it felt good." It was about talking to friends about writing and how essential it is to our lives. It was about being together.

And simply being.

I stood with Sam as Scott played the piano, and I realized how much my 11-year-old had grown. I draped my arm around his broadening shoulders, and I remembered (wasn't it just yesterday?) when I rocked him to sleep in the drafty farmhouse with Paddington Bear painted on the wall. My ten-pound baby is a young man on the verge of becoming a teenager, and with every passing day, we all grow a bit older. I'm no longer the 26-year-old I was when I gave birth to this beautiful boy and sang to him with every breath I had. I am his older mother; he is my growing son. I held him a little tighter as we stood together at the piano. Soon he won't want to be held. I will not waste another opportunity.

In the mad rush of the holidays and the stress of too many presents and too few zeros in the bank account balance, we were reminded today of what really matters.

"Peppermint Prohibition"

Andi called me from the CVS parking lot in a bit of a quandary. Truman had the Final Ear Infection Before Tubes and she was waiting for his antibiotic. We talked a bit about ENTs because Mary Claire had already been through the 3 sets of tubes, tonsillectomy and adenoidectomy rigamarole. I recommended Dr. Adams to her, who incidentally, is the identical twin sister of my OB/GYN, Dr. Adams. They are frighteningly similar. They talk exactly alike. Their mannerisms are exactly the same. When I took Mary Claire to her pre-op appointment, I looked for the stirrups for my feet. That's how much they look alike.

Anyway, Truman was screaming inconsolably because his eardrums felt like they were being poked with a sharp, fiery cattle prod, but Andi and I had a much more pressing concern.

"Dude," she said solemnly, "all the local Starbucks are out of peppermint syrup."

"What?!" I yelled. "How can that be? It's not even December yet!"

How in God's name am I supposed to add to my waistline while soothing my need for caffeine with a steaming hot Peppermint Mocha when there's no peppermint syrup in the entire district?

Hey, Starbucks! This happened last year. Remember?

Could we stock up? I mean, really, it shouldn't be as challenging to find a Peppermint Mocha as it is to find the ever elusive Wii. Isn't there enough stress during the holidays without having to settle for a white chocolate mocha?

Andi described her recent discussion with a barista at the brand spanking new Starbucks in town.

Andi said, "I've heard there are no bottles of peppermint syrup in the district. Is it true?"

And the barista replied, "It is true. But because we're new, I have a secret stash. All the local managers have been trying to get me to give it up, but I'm hoarding it."

Andi whispered to me in her Secret Agent voice, "It's like Peppermint Prohibition around here. But now you know where to go."

And that is what best friends are for.

"Holiday Mystery"

There is a holiday mystery in our small, quiet town. One that requires a little background.

Last weekend, Brent received permission to hunt the geese in between a church and one of our local schools. Yes, you heard me right. In between a church and a school. On a very basic level, that just seems – oh, I don't know – wrong. Not to mention dangerous.

I'm not sure how that conversation might have begun, either.

"Hey, preacher, I noticed you've got a lot of geese hanging out by your pond. Mind if I gear up and shoot some of 'em? Maybe after the service so I don't scare any of the kids during Sunday School?"

It just doesn't seem natural.

Brent and his buddy, however, had the blessings of the pastor, the land owner, the local town officials. And so they donned their camo and went to shoot some fish in a barrel. I mean... they went on a goose hunt. A very challenging one.

While hunting, Brent was texting my hubby messages to the tune of, "Shhhhh. Be wawwy, wawwy, quiet..." Because they're wawwy grown up that way.

Apparently, Brent came home with a few geese. I didn't ask Jackie for the details. I didn't want to know. And I won't be eating any fancy new dips at their house anytime soon.

Later, Jackie and I were frantically searching for last-minute teacher gifts, bus driver gifts, school gift exchange gifts, etc., etc. She was leaving Target and I was in Home Goods when the following phone conversation occurred:

JACKIE: I'm going to kick his ass.

ME: Whose ass?

JACKIE: My husband's.

ME: What is it this time?

JACKIE: There's blood in the back of my SUV. Either he killed and decapitated his mistress and is hiding the body somewhere, or those damn geese bled all over the back of my car.

ME: Is there a lot of blood?

JACKIE: Well, there's more than I'D LIKE THERE TO BE!

ME: (No response.)

JACKIE: Do you think it's the mistress or the geese?

ME: I think either one is pretty feasible.

JACKIE: I'm going to kick his ass.

So, readers, what's your verdict? Which mystery ending do you choose?

Dirty mistress or Christmas goose?

"The Letting Go"

Because I committed to a healthy life this New Year and beyond, I need to mention one more thing.

Letting go.

I've never really been good at letting go and moving on – I'm a grudge-holder by nature. And I come by it quite honestly. It must have some hereditary base.

I've had a situation in my life that has unraveled in the past year. A trusted friendship that turned out to be nothing more than smoke and mirrors. A litany of lies, destructive words, and damaging accusations.

Never before in my life have I experienced such a raw and emotional breakdown of a friendship. Not even in high school. Sure, there was the occasional bit of drama way back when, but nothing compares to this. This betrayal.

Chris and I saw the movie "Doubt" last week. And although he hated the ambiguity and snored through the dialogue, the premise of it had me holding my breath in anticipation throughout. This idea of gossip, of slander, of planting a seed – be it true or untrue – that grows into something so much bigger, takes on a life of its own.

I ached while listening to the priest's homily about gossip being akin to cutting open a feather pillow on top of a building and then trying to collect every single feather that fell to earth or was carried away on a breeze. The impossibility of it. Oh!

Because that, my friends, is exactly what it feels like. When I walk through my neighborhood, when I go to the grocery store, when I pick my kids up from school, I constantly wonder, "What has he heard? What does she believe? What lies has he been fed?"

What feather fell on her doorstep?

Chris tells me on a daily basis to let it go – that those who know us, know our family, know our kids – will be able to separate the fact from the fiction. And in my head I believe this. But in my heart? My heart recoils at the memory of the horrible things that were said about me, about my husband, about my friends, about our family.

The truth of the matter is that I can never allow this person into my life again. This person who twists the truth, who reinvents history, who fills the silences with untruths. This person I used to call "friend." This person who single-handedly tried to destroy my family.

I have built an impenetrable wall around us. A fortress to protect my family, my kids, our reputation. But sometimes it gets lonely inside.

And it would be so much easier to move on if our lives didn't intersect daily, if we didn't live in such close proximity.

But alas. It is what it is.

So, this year, I'm moving on. Forgive and forget? No, I'm not there yet. The wounds are still too raw, the stakes too high. The memory of what I thought we meant to each other still burns a hole in my heart. I miss the illusion. But I know that nothing substantial ever really existed.

I'm moving on this year.

But forgiveness may have to wait until 2020. Or 2099. Baby steps. Baby steps.

"Reunited"

"Would you rather fart on a shark? Or fart on a porcupine?"

Such was the conundrum posed by Mia, five-year-old daughter of our beloved Molly and Jeff.

Molly and her girls (sans Jeff who was sitting through a long overdue class) and Chris, the kids, and I (sans George who was busy building jungles at Luke's) all met up for a Ball State basketball game and a lot of catching up.

We hadn't seen our friends for over five years, have never met their youngest daughter. It's a sad statement on our lives these days – too busy for the things that really matter, too overcommitted to find a weekend that works for all involved.

But, oh, was it worth the wait. Molly and I talked through the entire game. (What? Did Ball State play?) The pre-teens danced tentatively around each other at first and then laughed and carried on over pizza by the end of the day. Elise and Mary Claire hit it off instantly, bound by their shared love of art and the Jonas Brothers.

And Mia? Well, she had a little thing for Chris. Followed him all day, sat on his lap, held his hand. She was sad that George didn't come, but probably would have been sadder if he had come. Inevitably, he would have ignored her because she's a girl. Been dicky to her because she's a girl. Stayed far away from her because she's a girl. And ultimately, she probably would have punched him. Which would have been fine with me.

Five years is far too long to stay away from those who make our lives complete. We promise to not make "next time" such a long time.

"Traversing the Landscape of Childhood"

How do they survive childhood, these children of ours? How did we survive the catty cliques, the gossip, the fickle friendships of our youth?

My Mary Claire is such a tender-hearted girl. She desperately wants her good friends to be her good friends... consistently, devotedly, without conditions.

Instead, she gets, "I can't play with you today. I can only play with one friend today, and it's not you. Maybe tomorrow." Or "I'll call you today..." and so she waits by the phone. Faithfully. Willing it to ring. And it never does.

What makes her so desperate for devotion that she creates a contract that reads, "We promise to always be best friends. Forever and ever."? And still, it sits in her room, unsigned.

I'm not claiming that she's never said a mean word in her life, that she's never done something to hurt another friend. But I know that at her core, she's a kind soul. Her feelings run deep. She's conflicted about seeing "Marley and Me" because she doesn't know if she can handle the end. She doesn't want to watch "Man Vs. Wild" with her brothers because "they just kill animals for NO reason." She writes stories in her journal about friends who are there for each other, who giggle during sleepovers, who share their secrets.

And yet, I watched her shoulders slump in defeat as she stood alone at the bus stop this morning. I saw little pieces of her heart left behind as she climbed on by herself. And she won't want to talk about it when she gets home. She'll just go to her room, turn on "The Rose," and sink into herself.

I was talking to a friend yesterday about the struggles her daughter is having at school. About the bullying she receives. About the lunch table drama. I heard about her backpack being thrown across the bus and being told to "Go fetch it, Dog."

What makes kids so mean? So callous? Is it Darwinian? Are we all really just fighting for our own survival? I can't – in my heart of hearts – believe that's true.

So, I will hang out with my girl tonight. And I will take her to the movies tomorrow, just the two of us. But I won't fill that empty space in her heart.

I'm not the one she wants.

"Tits Magee"

When my kids were twelve, ten, eight, and six, and our lives were overloaded with baseball, softball, lacrosse, school, and acting, I decided to embark with my friends on a girls' weekend. With Southwest drink tickets in hand, we boarded our flight and began a four-day Phoenix adventure – in all its drunken debauchery – for the record books.

One never knows what to expect when seven women decide to take a break from their husbands and 19 children. I must report, however, that the catfights were non-existent and the laughter, abundant.

We stayed at the Phoenix Biltmore and spent a great deal of time drinking poolside margaritas. Rumor has it that Kid Rock and Bruce Springsteen were also staying there during our visit, but they never pulled up a lounge chair beside us. Perhaps it was our raucous behavior on the water slide that kept them away. Maybe they overheard Jackie saying to the unsuspecting teenage water slide monitor, "Why don't you ride me down and see how my friends react?" Perhaps.

We coined many new phrases over the weekend, including "intestinal disturbance," "high vag," and "juterus." The most memorable night, however, was the evening we all dressed up and went downtown to par-tay. As we wandered the streets of Phoenix looking for the best place to hang, Jackie decided to ask the advice of some of the locals. Her first choice happened to be a scantily clad 20-something with boobs literally exploding out of her Saran-wrap-tight tank top. She was so visibly drunk – or high – that she couldn't stand up straight and had difficulty forming complete sentences. She was jittery – possibly from cocaine? No one could tell for certain, although Katy had her suspicions.

Katy and I were walking in the back of the group when Jackie decided to engage this young street corner girl in conversation. Katy leaned over to me and whispered, "Hello, Tits Magee. We're looking for a fun place to hang out. You look like one of us. What would you suggest?"

I then had to stop walking and cross my legs because the 39-year-old bladder, she just ain't what she used to be.

When we were done getting Tits' advice, we all re-grouped to discuss our options.

"She was nice," Andi said innocently. "What did she say?"

"She didn't say anything!" Katy answered. "She was too busy wiping the cocaine off her upper lip!"

We decided to forego Tits' suggestions (whatever they happened to be) and venture out on our own. We randomly chose an open-air lounge that was getting ready to host an 80s cover band. That's right. You heard me correctly. An 80s cover band. Pam and I placed ourselves center stage, front row and waited for Billy Idol and Pat Benetar to make an appearance. The band was good – really good – and the beer was cheap. We partied like groupies through the first set.

During their break, Jackie made her acquaintance with all the band members. "This band loves me," she proclaimed. "And the lead singer? When you get to know her, she's really nice." When you get to know her? After three minutes?

After the second set, Pam and I met a cute young drunkard who spilled her foo-foo drink all over my feet. She was a real estate agent and promised us that whenever we needed to purchase some Phoenix property, she was definitely our gal. "You're so cute," she slurred at me, "I wish you were MY mother!" Then she proceeded to introduce us to the strapping young buck she'd met an hour earlier, and Pam and I – in all our drunken wisdom – lectured her on the questionable safety of taking strange men home with her. We then spoke to her friend, Adam, about his employment status, his good intentions, and whether or not he was sober enough to drive Kelly safely home. We left our new friend, Kelly, with this sage advice (that you must shout in a drunken, loud voice to get the full effect), "Kelly! Don't let him take your money!"

On the ride home, our Jamaican cab driver played "Name That Tune" with us. He'd hum a few bars of a popular 80s tune, and we'd guess it every time. The mood was light, we were having fun, and then he began to sing this song, "I came to America to live the American dream. And now I live in public housing and drive this cab and struggle to feed my family every daaaaay..."

None of us knew that one.

All in all, it was a trip for the record books. Good times with good friends in the oppressive Arizona heat. We indulged in $20 glasses of wine, found out that Andi can start a bar brawl with the best of them, determined that Beth can pull off the dancing-with-Disney-Store-bags-hanging-from-her-arms look, discovered that Katy doesn't really suffer from pica, and confirmed that Angie can pull out the dancing pistols like nobody's business.

Next time, I think we're going to invite Tits Magee.

"Fearless from Row Five"

I recently had the great pleasure of taking Mary Claire to see Taylor Swift in concert along with our BFFs, Jackie and Allie.

Ahem. In the Fifth Row.

It was an amazing experience to watch these two sweet little girls with their jaws on the floor as they listened to their idol croon onstage.

From the Fifth Row.

Allie and Mary have been friends forever. By proxy, of course. Jackie and I have been soul mates since college. Since the days of the flowered bag and meeting "Janet." Our stories are deep and wide and treasured. The girls, too, have forged a lasting relationship. Shaky and tumultuous at times? Yes. But important enough to overcome obstacles and to persevere.

What a special memory, then, to take them to see Taylor, who sang of friendship and love and growing up.

While we sat in the Fifth Row.

She's a class act, that Taylor Swift. And one heck of a performer. Her show wasn't just a concert, it was a production. Perfect for all the little girls who watched her with adoring eyes.

And my favorite part? She chose to leave the word "damn" out of her live performance, even though it's recorded in one of her songs. I have to think it was a very purposeful move. Otherwise, the audience would have erupted into little girl giggles and gasps. But that pretty young thing took the high road. I mean, I'm no prude. And Mary Claire has heard the word "damn" before. Directly from her mother's lips. But I appreciated Taylor's thoughtfulness.

And my second favorite part? Did I mention we were in the Fifth Row?

I didn't know much about Taylor Swift before the concert. I'm not much of a country music fan. I did, however, purchase some sassy cowboy boots to commemorate the occasion.

But now that I've seen that cutie-patootie in concert? I've become her number one middle-aged fan. I've played her music, watched her videos, listened to her interviews. And I have to admit, I'm impressed.

Mary Claire loves that I've taken such an interest. Many of our conversations now revolve around Taylor and go something like this:

MC: I think Taylor must think kissing in the rain is very romantic.

ME: You mean because she sings about it so much?

MC: Duh.

And this:

MC: How do you think they did that "rain thing" at the end of the concert?

ME: I don't know, but it was pretty cool, wasn't it?

MC: Duh.

And this:

ME: Did you know that Taylor Swift used to date Joe Jonas?

MC: Duh.

ME: Did you know that he broke up with her over the phone? Tack-y.

MC: Really? He did?

ME: Duh.

(She then proceeds to "X" his face out on all of her bedroom posters.
You go, girl! Stand up for your sistahs!)

And this:

MC: Why do you think Taylor is so thin?

ME: Well, she performs a lot which probably keeps her in good shape.
And she's a grown woman, honey. She's already gone through puberty.
You know what that is, don't you?

MC: We're not *really* going to have this conversation right now, are we?

And although she's a bit flippant and irreverent (I don't know where she gets that), I can see the little wheels turning in her head when she listens to Taylor's lyrics (and sings them at the top of her lungs).

When I found out that our seats were going for approximately $400 each on the night of the show, I had a brief urge to take the money and run. I mean, we could have bought a lot of books and shoes with $800. Luckily, though, I didn't. Because it was a life-altering memory for my young girl.

And it's a good thing Brian waited until after the concert was over to tell me that John Mayer unexpectedly performed onstage with Taylor at one of her previous concerts. Because if I'd have known that going in, I would have missed the entire show while looking for him in the wings.

And if he had come onstage? Well, I *was* in the Fifth Row. And I could have taken the wimpy security guard down. I know I could have. And Jackie would have bailed me out of jail.

I showed MC the YouTube video of John and Taylor singing together. Our conversation went like this:

ME: Look, Mary Claire, it's our two favorite people performing onstage together.

MC: I thought Dave Matthews was your favorite.

ME: Well, Dave and John both are. They're tied for first.

MC: Why does he make such weird faces when he's playing his guitar?

I don't know, Mary Claire, but if Chris scrunches his face up like Johnny-Baby's and sings, "Come Back to Bed" tonight, he's sure to get lucky. And if he follows it with a breathy rendition of "Crush," well, I can't even say what might happen.

Thanks, sweet Taylor, for being such a fabulous role model for young girls everywhere.

And I especially like this poignant line:

"I didn't know who I was supposed to be. At fifteen."

Amen, Taylor. Take it from someone who hasn't seen fifteen in nearly twenty-five years... there's so much more living to do.

"Urban Legend"

Molly is what we like to call "gullible." She has a kind and trusting heart. And she married the most sarcastic and dry-humored man in the bunch. Jeff can get her – and many of the rest of us – to fall for his antics time and time again. He's a master, really. And he never ceases to take advantage of her trusting nature. But our favorite story of all?

The Hall Bush.

When the boys roomed together in college (in a dirty, sticky, germ-infested, and mold-riddled apartment), they had a coat tree that met an early demise. During some late night party – or possibly just a regular overloading of winter coats – the coat tree snapped in half. So, they propped it up in the corner and affectionately called it "The Hall Bush." After all, it was no longer a true tree. But they were still able to throw their coats at it, so it served a purpose, and was therefore allowed to stay.

Throughout their tenure at Ball State University, the Hall Bush was often called by name. And when Molly and Jeff began dating, she'd never heard it called anything different.

Fast forward about seven years. Molly and Jeff are married, they have a few beautiful daughters in tow, and they're out furniture shopping for their new home. Molly approaches a kind saleswoman to help them with their purchases. Jeff and the girls are standing on the outskirts of the conversation, allowing Molly to discuss what she needs.

"What I'd really like to find is a Hall Bush," Molly explains.

Jeff instantly snaps to attention. As if in slow motion, he mouths the words, "No, Molly…" But it's too late.

"A what?" the confused saleswoman inquires.

"A Hall Bush. You know, to hang coats on."

Jeff is now laughing silently and disengaging from the conversation. He walks away, knowing that he's going to have a good, old-fashioned ass kicking waiting for him.

"Do you mean a coat tree?" the saleswoman asks gently.

"No, I think it's called a Hall Bush. That's what my husband and his friends always called it."

And then in dawned on her. The truth was illuminated with great clarity, and Molly understood that she'd been duped. By her husband and his friends. For multiple years. And that she'd now made an ass of herself in public.

Molly excused herself from the situation and found Jeff in the parking lot rolling with laughter.

"Molly, did you really think it was called a Hall Bush? All these years?"

And suffice it to say that Molly confirmed that she did, indeed, think it was called a Hall Bush. And in no uncertain terms – peppered with phrases such as "son of a bitch," and "bastard," and "asshole" – Molly let Jeff know that she didn't necessarily appreciate his humor.

"No Pain, No Gain"

Jackie, my friend whose athletic abilities don't run much deeper than cheerleading lunges and hurkeys, decided one spring to take up running. Because Jackie had suffered a spontaneous pneumothorax in college (and we therefore liked to call her "One Lung"), I thought that perhaps running might not be her strongest choice.

I was wrong.

Jackie had running stamina that far surpassed my own shuffling abilities. We would meet up in the wee hours of the morning to train, and she was continually dragging my sorry ass behind her.

"No stopping!" she'd yell in her bossy and authoritative way. "Suck it up!"

And so I would.

One morning before the sun had risen, we were jogging on a county road behind the local Catholic Church. I hit an uneven patch of road and felt my ankle snap. My running pants were ripped, my knees bloody, and my ankle, not right.

"Come on," Jackie insisted, "get up. Walk it off. We've still got a couple more miles to finish."

I stood, but was unable to put any weight on my right foot.

"Jackie, something's wrong."

She kept jogging in place.

"Rub some dirt on it. Let's go," she insisted.

"No, I'm serious. This isn't a dirt-rubbing issue. Something's wrong."

Now, let me explain that I have ankle issues. For some reason, my ankles weren't designed to withstand the rigors of my athletic choices. Throughout my entire high school career, I was taped (thanks, Kari), splinted, Air-Casted, braced. My high school softball coach said I was the only person he'd ever known who could sprain her ankle walking across a gym.

But this was different.

"I can't walk on it," I insisted. "You're going to have to go get my car."

With an exasperated sigh, she jogged off into the darkness and left me sitting on the curb at St. Alphonsus Church. People came and went in her absence. Some waved. Most ignored me. I was fairly surprised that no one seemed a bit concerned about a woman with bloody knees sitting alone at church watching the sunrise.

Jackie finally tore around the corner at top speed and threw my Suburban into park. She drove me home and had Chris take her back to her house. My ankle was now as big as my knee.

A couple of x-rays later, it was determined that there was a hairline fracture.

Jackie and I continue to be best friends. We continue to share our deepest thoughts, fears, and desires. We shop together, we take care of each other's kids, we vacation together, we laugh, we cry, we love.

But we haven't jogged together since.

Gross Anatomy

"Eeeewww! That's gross!"

Man consists of two parts, his mind and his body, only the body has more fun. ~

Woody Allen

"The Performer"

Penises are valuable commodities at our house. They far outnumber the resident vaginas (dogs not included), and the word itself is generally much more fun to say. And they tend to give us endless opportunities for inappropriate laughter. Take for instance, the year the five of us (sans George) were holed up in our three-bedroom apartment that we liked to call our own little private circle of hell.

Because the apartment consisted of about 50 square feet, there was no privacy, no interaction that went unnoticed.

Chris and I were sitting with Mary Claire in the family room when we heard three-year-old Sam yell, "Ta-da!" And immediately following, Gus broke into his bubbly peals of laughter – the ones that came straight from his toes. Again, we heard Sam yell, "Ta-da!" And again, Gus's baritone giggles. This went on a few more times before we decided to investigate.

After traversing the three steps it took to move to the back of the apartment, we spotted the boys in the bathroom. Sam was sitting on the toilet with his pants around his ankles. Gus was sitting on the floor in front of him like a rock concert groupie. Sam proceeded to push his penis into his belly and wait for it pop back out. At the precise moment it reappeared, he hollered, "Ta-da!"

He's destined for showbiz, that one.

"Anatomy Lesson"

When Dr. Andrews brought Mary Claire from the nursery, her umbilical cord was still very long.

Sam exclaimed, "Wow, Dr. Andrews! Look at her penis!"

The doctor explained the situation, and later Sam said to me, "Mom, Mary McClaire doesn't have a penis because she's a girl. Girls don't have penises, they have belly buttons."

"Unarguable Logic"

Sam has always been a bit unmotivated. He's a smart kid, a clever kid. But I would never call him a hard-working kid. His lackadaisical attitude toward life reared its ugly head early in Sam's life.

Right about the time we started potty training.

As first time parents, we weren't quite sure what we were doing. (And just for the record, we still don't know the fourth time around.) I relied a lot on books, Chris relied on his instinct. Perhaps we waited a bit too long to begin potty training, but the thought of cleaning up all the accidents and running to every dirty bathroom across town didn't hold much appeal.

Thus, when Sam turned three, he still wasn't trained. Our young son could identify parallelograms and rhombuses, he could read at a 2nd grade level, he could carry on an intelligent conversation, but he still preferred to shit in his pants.

He preferred it so much that he'd often hide behind our frightfully ugly, but oh-so-comfortable Lazy Boy recliner to take care of his business.

When we'd happen upon him, he'd look up at us with his bright, blue eyes and his cherry red cheeks and grunt, "Leave me alone" in a gruff baritone that belied his age.

Chris and I vacillated between frustration and anger. That damn kid could sing a song that included every one of the 50 states and all of their capitals, but he couldn't walk down the hall to willingly use the restroom. And let me just reiterate that Sam wasn't a small boy. Changing his three-year-old diapers almost felt somewhat… dirty.

We started with rewards. That quickly led nowhere. Then we began punishments. We spanked him when he deliberately pooped in his pants. (I know, I know. That's years of therapy just waiting to happen.) Then we began taking away his favorites. His favorite toys, his beloved stuffed animals, his Blue's Clues sheets. The more we took away, the more belligerent he became.

It was a battle of wills. And that boy's will was strong.

One evening, we put Sam to bed on his white sheets in his empty room that was void of anything remotely entertaining. We tucked him in, kissed him goodnight, and wished him sweet dreams.

He looked me squarely in the eye and said, "You can take all my toys away. But I'll always have my penis."

And that, my friends, is when we admitted defeat.

"A Question for the Ages"

"How old does a boy have to be before he stops being obsessed with his penis?" I asked my husband in exasperation.

But then I realized the absurdity of my question.

I most definitely needed to ask someone older than him.

"Abracadabra"

"Mom?" George inquired as I was bathing him one night when he was three.

"Yes, Honey?" I replied, scrubbing shampoo into his silky blonde locks.

"Why are boys different than girls?"

I paused for a moment as I tried to gather my wits. Those who know me well know that I tend to over-explain things to my children at a vastly inappropriate level. Perhaps Sam only wanted to know what a kiss was, but after innocently asking, he was sure to know all the details about sexual intercourse, teenage pregnancy, and the resultant poverty.

"Well, George," I started, "girls and boys have different parts. Boys have penises and girls have vaginas."

280

"I know that," he said. "I've seen Mary's. But there's something much more different about girls and boys."

"What is it?" I asked.

"Girls have hair bows and boys have magic wands."

"Not Quite Netflix"

At age six, we overheard George introducing his pet mouse to a neighborhood friend who happened to be female. Chris and I chuckled as we heard him ask, "Want to pet my rat?"

We probably won't chuckle quite as hard when we overhear it again at age 16.

Gus brought home The Letter this week. You know, the one the school sends home with you to have your parents sign so you can watch The Movie. I mean, he's going to be a middle schooler next year – he needs to learn The Facts.

Sam snickered knowingly when Gus handed it over for my signature.

"You're going to LOVE that movie," Sam laughed. "And wait until Dad gives you The Talk. You're going to love that even more!"

Gus punched him in reply.

"No, seriously, dude, it's like the best movie ever!" Then Sam laughed and walked away. This from the boy who, after viewing The Movie in the fourth grade, promptly went to his room after school to "re-group" in silent reflection. When I assured Sam that he should always feel comfortable coming to me or to his Dad if he had any questions, he responded, "I don't feel comfortable talking to ANYONE about THAT."

Naturally, we joked with Gus a bit more while his face turned about 14 different shades of purple.

After dinner that night – and long after the original conversation had taken place – Mary Claire very randomly asked, "When is that movie?"

I thought perhaps she was talking about the Jonas Brother's 3D movie, or maybe Nancy Drew (which we'd just received from Netflix).

Clearly not on her wavelength, I asked, "What movie are you talking about, Mary Claire?"

She looked at me like I had four heads, rolled her eyes, and replied, "You know! Gus's SEX movie!"

"The Facts of Life"

Because The Middle School Movie was looming, it was time to schedule The Talk. The understanding in our house is that the parent with the matching parts conducts The Talk when the time is nigh.

Chris gave me the signal (the one consisting of an exaggerated pointing to Gus's bedroom door and the mouthing of the words, "I'm going to do THE TALK tonight") and Gus changed into his PJs, completely unaware of the blindsiding he was about to receive.

Chris is experienced with The Talk, having ushered Sam into the well-informed middle school years just 24 short months ago. When he finished his first Talk, Chris asked Sam is he had anything to say. Sam's succinct and immediate reply? "Eeew."

So, I stood outside with my ear pressed against the door as a sort of training session for next year (with the assumed substitution of Part P for Part V, of course).

Chris was very direct, far too loud (no big shock), and intensely matter-of-fact. As I listened to him describe hormones and hygiene, I felt Gus's childhood begin to dry up and blow out the window, leaving the Hot Wheels and Legos behind and eventually settling on the condom aisle at CVS.

I heard the two "Littles" snoring in their own beds and marveled at how swiftly time marched across their baby faces.

Then I heard Chris say, "boobs."

And Gus giggled.

"You know what makes boys and girls different?" Chris asked.

"Well..." Gus started in his deep monotone, "I've been noticing lately that boys often have bigger..."

I caught my breath...

"...Adam's Apples."

My chest heaved with silent, uncontrollable laughter and I prayed my shameless eavesdropping would not be revealed.

And then.

Before I could wave a melancholy farewell to my blue-eyed boy's innocence, it was all on the table. The Mommy Parts. The Daddy Parts. The Meeting Betwixt the Two.

After a brief, uncomfortable pause, Chris said, "So, Gus, what do you think?"

Another pause.

"Well... I think it's a little weird. And a little gross."

Then Chris and I both breathed an audible sigh of relief. Because, really, who wants to think about their ten-year-old sporting a woody while looking at the SI swimsuit issue?

The next day in the car, Gus casually mentioned to me that his Dad had given him The Talk.

"What did you think?" I asked nonchalantly, trying not to pry, but dying to get his take.

"Well...," he admitted with great conviction, "I don't really like what the boys have to do."

And I bit my tongue so I wouldn't tell him that in five years, he'd feel a whole lot differently. It's his fate, after all. I mean, he has a penis. And you know what they say about the Apple and the Tree.

Gifted and Talented

My Kids Are Smarter Than Yours

If there were no schools to take the children away from home part of the time, the insane asylums would be filled with mothers. ~ Edgar W. Howe

"School Rules"

One of the very first, nearly deal-breaking arguments that kept rearing its ugly head during our early dating years was public school versus private school. I was the product of eight years of Catholic school – a luxury my single mom certainly couldn't afford, but insisted upon anyway – and I wasn't willing to consider any alternative for my own children. Every day for eight years, I awoke to the sound of my alarm clock, ironed my white blouse, donned my plaid jumper, and walked three blocks to the safe haven of St. Michael's elementary school. There I learned that the biggest threats weren't on the playground, they were the threats made to my very soul, the core of my being. The Mortal Sins. And let me assure you that the notion of permanent black stains on your soul is enough to keep even the most discipline-challenged on the straight and narrow.

Although my mom and my sister would both disagree, I would vehemently argue that I grew up in "White Harlem" on the wrong side of the tracks. In an apartment complex replete with single parents, unsupervised kids, and young college drop-outs, I cut my teeth on Bob Seger and Marlboro Lights. It was my middle school friends who perfected my enunciation of "motherfucker," and their high school buddies who taught me about blowjobs and Trojans. Thank God I had Sister Helen Therese, Sister Rose Celine, and Sister Veronica Anne to balance my early childhood lessons. I was well-versed in the ways of the world by the time I hit double-digits, but I could also spout the Ten Commandments backwards and forwards. I said my Rosary every night before bed, and I cleansed my soul weekly with a trip to the Confessional and three Hail Marys.

Chris, on the other hand, was a product of the public school system. He, too, ran with a rough crowd of "Eastsiders," but excelled in school and in music. He was proud of his public school education, passionate about teaching kids, and vehemently opposed to cocooning our kids in a private school setting. Ultimately, the source of his paycheck won out over my holier-than-thou arguments, and we agreed on sending our kids to public schools.

And when that decision was sealed, I crossed myself, bowed my head, and whispered, "Forgive me, Father, for I have sinned."

"The Natural"

Like many firstborns, Sam was ahead of his time. When he read a billboard at age three, Chris and I looked at each other in astonishment. Convinced it was a fluke, we'd throw sentences in front of him. "Read this," we'd command. "Read this." And we shook our heads when he deciphered everything we showed him. Friends would ask what we did to help him learn to read. We'd shrug our shoulders. "Lots of TV?" We didn't work with him, he just learned. A journey of self-discovery. It has become the mantra of his young life.

When Sam was little, I took him everywhere, wanted everyone to see him. Needed verification from strangers who saw me and nodded, yes, indeed, you are his mother. I enjoyed strangers ogling his cherubic face, beamed with pride when he'd smile at them. And again, later, when he'd perform for them. "Parallelogram," he'd say when I pointed to the shape. "Rhombus." Rhombus! From the lips of a two-year-old. To say that I was a proud young mother is an understatement. To say that I'm a proud, experienced mother is an honor.

Sweet Sam has grand ambitions and little drive. He's a lot like his father that way. Frighteningly smart, intuitive, socially skilled (a favorite among the grandmotherly type), and eager to please. Eager, that is, until he's required to put forth a modicum of effort. If he's not instantly good at something, he gives it up without a fight. Sam could have been a stellar musician, but building the calluses required to rock some serious guitar rifts proved to be a bit too much for him. So, instead he settled on being able to adequately play a few of his favorites. Although he can play the baritone better than anyone in his seventh grade band, he consistently gets C's in class because he doesn't turn in any practice logs. Doesn't turn them in, that is, because he doesn't practice.

Chris was the same way. A brilliant mind content to skate through life on his innate ability to understand and interpret and make connections – without a great deal of effort on his part. It's worked well for Chris. I assume it will behoove Sam as well.

This oldest boy was a mystery to me when he was born. Different parts, different hormones, different chromosomes. Growing up in a matriarchal family with only a sister left me ill equipped to raise a son. And yet Sam continues to teach me. With his quick wit, his eager smile, and his undying affection, we're traversing through this life together.

"Why don't you spank the other kids as much as you spanked me when I was little?" he recently inquired. And my answer? Because that was what we knew best. It was what worked on Sam, what worked for us. And he's a fine young man who understands boundaries, who respects his elders, who can carry on a conversation with the wall. We've done many things wrong in this parenting experience, but what we've done right is Sam.

"In-School Detention"

In first grade, Sam had a little buddy named Nick with a voice deeper than any grown man's. Nick and Sam were inseparable. They played football together, shot baskets on our driveway, stayed up far too late playing video games, had sleepovers, rode their bikes like wild banshees.

Because they were thick as thieves, they also had their not-so-stellar moments. But as boys, they'd fight, work it out, and never look back.

Then I got the call from Chris.

"Honey," he giggled, "I just got off the phone with Sam's principal."

"What?!" I demanded. "What happened? Why are you laughing?"

"Sam's in in-school detention for a day."

"What?!" I repeated. "What's going on?"

"Well, apparently, Sam and Nick got into a fight on the playground."

"A fight-fight?" I asked.

"Yes. They were punching each other in the privates."

"Excuse me? Punching each other?"

"In the privates."

Chris laughed again. "Sam's principal had him in the office with her. I could tell she was trying to hold it together in front of him while she talked to me, but she called back after Sam left and lost it. She said it was one of the funniest things she'd ever seen."

I was still trying to process the thought of Sam and Nick punching each other's penises.

"We'll talk to Sam about it when he gets home."

And so we did.

We put a movie on for the other three and gathered with Sam at the kitchen table.

"So, what happened with you and Nick at school today?" Chris asked.

"We got into a fight."

"About what?" I asked, always wanting all the details.

"Football."

"Why did you decide it was a good idea to hit each other?" I inquired.

"Well, I took the ball from Nick. And then he said it."

"Said what?" Chris asked.

"He said, 'I guess it's time to punch you in the nuts.'"

I quite nearly fell out of my chair. When did my six-year-old begin referencing his testicles as "nuts"?

Chris stifled a laugh.

"And so we did," Sam explained.

Case dismissed.

But it's still one of our favorite phrases. When Chris acts like a jerk, my first warning is always, "Well, I guess it's time to punch you in the nuts."

"Diversity"

When Gus was four, we enrolled him in preschool at our local Lutheran church. It was a beautiful building, a traditional church painted a bright and cleansing white on the outside. We weren't practicing Lutherans, but we weren't necessarily on the fast track to hell, either. And the hours worked well for my schedule. (Perhaps you might argue that's not a valid reason for choosing a particular preschool. But I assure you that when you have four children under the age of six, convenient scheduling becomes of the utmost importance.)

Gus loved his preschool. Well, he loved preschool as much as he loved anything. Not one to ever click his heels in exuberance over anything, we were happy when Gus smiled periodically about a bright spot in his preschool day. That, to us, was a victory.

While running some late afternoon errands, we ran into Chris's Assistant Superintendent who was very interested in talking to all the kids.

"Sam," she inquired, "how do you like first grade?"

"It's fantastic!" he bubbled. "I love my teacher, and I love eating in the cafeteria!"

"And how about you, Gus?" she continued. "Are you in school?"

"Yes," he replied in his Eeyore-like monotone. "Preschool."

"Do you like preschool?"

"Yes."

This was definitely a victory for us. The year before, Gus had proclaimed that he never wanted to go to school. When questioned why, he replied, "Because there's too many kids and it scares me when the bus goes 'pssshhh.'"

Tough points to argue.

"Where do you go to preschool?" Chris's boss continued.

"I go to the all-white school," Gus replied in reference to the paint color.

Chris choked on his afternoon Starbucks.

"Well," she laughed, "that pretty much describes every school in Zionsville, doesn't it?"

We might have all been thinking it, but I was grateful that she said it first.

"Sad Boy"

Quiet Gus has never been a carefree, happy-go-lucky kind of guy. When he shows the most emotion, it's usually in anger or frustration. We've always called him "quirky," always talked about him as the kid who marches to the beat of his own drummer. But now we have another name to call him.

Sad.

His third grade teachers recommended a psychiatric consultation for him. They're concerned that he's unable to socialize, uninterested in school, disorganized, weepy, lonely, and "very, very sad."

Thinking about his sadness makes my heart break in two. He doesn't seem quite so unhappy at home, but home is definitely his safe place to land. Nonetheless, he really doesn't have any friends. He hasn't been invited to any classmates' birthday parties this year. That fact alone makes my soul ache for him.

I know he has trouble with socialization. He's inappropriate in social situations at best. He doesn't know how to interact, doesn't have any defense mechanisms developed for when he's hurt or angry. And he seems hurt most of the time. Hurt that no one calls him, hurt that no one answers his calls, hurt that he's not his big brother, hurt that he can't seem to find his place in this world.

When your child is in pain, the worst feeling in the world is the inability to kiss it and make it all go away. I can't fix him, I can only love him. And love him, I do. I adore his deep-thinking mind, his guarded hugs, his soulful eyes. I just want his peers to see him like I do. I want him to love himself for who he is.

He teachers have also mentioned adolescent depression. Maybe he's a lot like his Mama that way. Perhaps he does need help sorting his feelings out, help that we've been unable to provide him.

But still, I just want to wrap him in my arms so he knows he's safe and loved. And yet, that may not be enough for Gus. I do know one thing, though. This mother will do whatever she can to help him see the light and happiness in his life. That's the most I can do for any of my children.

I love my sweet, smart, quirky, thoughtful kid. Now I just need to help him learn to love himself.

"What's My Motivation?"

Chris had an early morning doctor's appointment, so I had to take Sam to school today. Though he's only in seventh grade, his first class is at the high school. He's chosen Mandarin Chinese as his language of choice, and spends first period with a gaggle of high school students.

It was fun to spend a few minutes in the car with him in the early morning darkness. We don't often have that opportunity.

"Are you enjoying your Chinese class?" I asked.

"Yeah," he replied. "It's easy. I'm getting an A."

"That's fantastic," I encouraged. "Are you not finding it challenging at all?"

"No," he grunted. "Why else do you think I'd be getting a A?"

"Well," I ventured, "maybe you'd earn an A because you actually put forth some effort."

He chuckled to himself as if to say, well, *as if.*

Then he tossed that stringy, overgrown hair out of his eyes and corrected me.

"Mom, the only A's I get are in my easy classes. I get B's in my hard classes."

"Do you think you could get A's in your hard classes?" I asked.

"Well, probably, but I'd have to work."

And therein lies the problem.

Work? *Work?* What the hell kind of world are we living in when our kids are expected to work? That boy.

He's so damn smart, so damn funny, so damn lazy. Even if I lit a fire under his ass, I'm not sure he'd move.

He's completely uninterested in hygiene and matching clothes. He came down dressed for school in a pair of Gus's jeans last week, thus earning himself the nickname, EMO. (Yes, I had to wikipedia it after Chris said it.)

Green shorts with a red shirt? Why not? It's festive.

We've been talking to him about Malcolm Gladwell's "10,000 hours" theory. We're not sure there's anything that interests him enough to commit 10,000 hours to except, perhaps, Xbox and sleeping.

Maybe dramatic sighing and hair growing, too.

"Fourth Grade Misfit"

Check "A" for "Almost Always" and "N" for "Never." There were two options in between, and those were all the ones I chose. It's difficult for me to say "Never." I'm more of a gray girl than a black and white one. And "Always" seems just as extreme. So, I stayed right in the middle as I checked off questions on Gus's behavioral assessment profile such us, "Does your child hear voices?" and "Does your child say inappropriate things?" It was heart-wrenching to put him into that kind of box. To say that he was not like the other fourth grade kids because he didn't always respond the way he was expected to. He was my little loner, my writer, my dreamer, my odd duck. And I loved him that way. I knew in my heart of hearts that someday, he would be appreciated for his quirkiness and his unique way of looking at life. But not in fourth grade. In fourth grade, he was just different. And kids are brutal.

"Try, Try Again"

We've all been a bit on edge here for the past three days.

Why?

Seventh grade basketball try-outs.

For the first time in his life (and our parenting career), Sam is going through the process of trying out for a school team.

And the competition is fierce.

Most things come pretty easily to Sam. He gets good grades without putting forth much effort and has always been satisfied being a team member, even if it doesn't mean much playing time.

He likes to belong.

But this time, he decided he wanted something and actually started working for it. He practiced ball-handling drills at home, shot free throws, played pick-up games, attended open gym.

This is not the lazy, unmotivated Sam that we normally know and love.

He wanted this.

He came out of try-outs last night – the first night of cuts – trying to look sad. But a smile was curling at the corners of his lips and I knew he'd made it through the first round.

Today was the final day of try-outs. The final cuts.

And he was the first one out of the gym.

As soon as I saw his face, I knew. And the scars that had formed over all the "big" disappointments of my youth felt ripped open at the seams again. Because I could feel his pain.

And your child's pain is worse than any pain you could possibly feel on your own.

We cried together in the car. I told him I was proud of him. Told him it wasn't the end of his basketball career. Told him we would support whatever he chose to do – whether it was lacrosse, another basketball league, or managing the seventh grade team. And I told him that God has a bigger plan. We may not see it now, but I was 100% sure that something better was waiting out there for him.

Oh, that sweet boy. He's such a good kid, such a soft-hearted, kind soul. Yes, he can be dicky at times. Yes, he can be sullen and moody and sassy. But at the core, he's golden.

And it broke my heart to see his heart so broken.

I know that if Sam had come out smiling, another boy would have come out crying. And the whole thing makes me a little sick to my stomach. Because in this world, there are those who win... and those who don't. Those who make the team... and those who have to watch. Those who realize their dreams... and those who have to figure out a Plan B.

But my 39 years have taught me that life's disappointments make us stronger, make us better, change us in ways we could never even imagine.

But when you're 12?

It just sucks.

Hang tight, sweet Sam. Your day is coming.

"Spelling Doesn't Count"

A reprint (unedited) of Gus's answer to "Why Do You Want Spring to Come?" as delivered via his school backpack...

"I'd want spring to come because I just can't take the cold any more even though my B-day is in four day. I want to go a shooting range with my dad, play baseball, have squirt gun fights, go to Penslvaina in a cotadige one hour and 30 minutes from Hershy park plus staying at the small cotidge is free because it belongs to are friend and photographer Brian. That's all folks. See you in my next story."

"The Queen of Bullshit"

Yesterday, I was driving Mary Claire to her before-school Artist's Colony Club meeting, and she informed me that she had an oral book presentation she was scheduled to give that day.

(Procrastination is an inherited Willis trait.)

She handed me a presentation checklist as I was driving and proceeded to give me her two-minute spiel. The purpose? Recommending a book from her classroom library to her classmates.

And in her always-excited, bubbly way, her speech went like this:

"Today, I'm going to recommend a book about oceans by Magnificent E. See Same!"

(That would actually be Millicent E. Selsam, but she said it with such enthusiastic assurance that I could hardly argue the botched pronunciation.)

She then held up the open book to illustrate her next point.

"You will LOVE this book because the pictures are soooo beautiful. There are pictures of squids and octopusses and lots and lots of fish. In fact, the pictures are SO GOOD, you don't even have to read the book to enjoy it!"

And thus ended her compelling recommendation.

Now, I hate to be A Ruiner, but I did gently suggest that perhaps she should alter her semantics to state that the beautiful illustrations would inspire her friends to want to read every word of the book.

"But Mom, I didn't read it!" she explained. "And I really, really liked the book, anyway!"

Apparently, the pictures weren't that inspiring.

The book incident came right on the heels of my sweet girl bringing home a social studies worksheet that posed the following question:

"If you wanted to describe how far west California is, would you use longitude or latitude?"

Mary Claire's answer?

"Yes."

My daughter is going to successfully bullshit her way through any obstacle in life with a big smile and an irresistibly cute speech impediment.

"Back to School"

It's that time of year. Our lazy summer days are dwindling. Soon, it will be early to bed and early to rise. Goodbye to camping trips with friends, swimming pools, and late night firefly chases. Bring on the backpacks, bus stops, and stress-inducing homework.

The beginning of school is a bittersweet time for me. I always loved school as a kid. Back-to-school magazine issues always gave me a little thrill. I loved the thought of walking to school and shuffling through falling leaves. And the smell of those musty, hand-me-down books? Second to none.

But I have adored these summer days with my kids. Bedhead till noon? Bring it on. Picnic by the pool? Check. Breakfast at 10:00 and lunch at 2:00? Yeah, baby.

We've been prepping for school this week. Yesterday, we visited the kids' schools (two in elementary and two in middle – egads!) and found out who their teachers are. We bought spirit wear, filled lunch accounts, paid for school pictures and yearbooks. My checkbook is begging for mercy.

Since when did public school book rental for four kids amount to $1,000? Seriously? And we can't forget supplies, backpacks, clothes, and haircuts. August has become more expensive than December at our house. This Christmas, we're going to ask Santa to stuff school supplies in our stockings.

I'm frantic about Gus entering middle school. He's such an emotional kid, so easily brought to tears. He got frustrated with his locker yesterday and welled up instantly.

You get beaten up for much less than that in middle school.

I talked to him last night about controlling his emotions. I explained how much I loved his kindness and sensitivity, but encouraged him to save 90% of his emotion for home, his safe place. I just want him to find a place to belong. I don't care where it is – as long as it's not with the hard-core fifth grade drug users and prostitutes – but I want him to have a sanctuary at school.

Mary Claire has 31 kids in her class this year. I fear she'll slip through the cracks if we don't stay ahead of the game. And we've never been known for staying on top when it comes to our kids' education. Their education = their job. But damned if that kid still can't say her S's or spell "friend" correctly. She might be a fourth grade social ambassador, but multiplication? Not so much.

Sam is taking Mandarin Chinese at the high school. He either has to ride to school with his Dad in the morning or journey on the high school bus. And I'm sure if he steps on that bus full of older kids, he'll be beaten up, sexually assaulted, called horrific names, and introduced to the concepts of oral sex and bestiality. Because those are the things I worry about. He's anxious about the intensity of his classes. Why? Because he might actually have to put forth a little effort this year.

And then there's George. Devil at home, angel at school. Let's just hope that trend continues. Because the minute School George is tainted by Home George, he'll be on every watch list in the school system. And once he's tagged a troublemaker, I'm sure he'll be destined for academic failure and full-time, lifelong employment at the nearest gas station. And that kid is too damn smart to be doling out lottery tickets and caffeine pills. He should be building a life-size replica of the Eiffel Tower out of Legos, for heaven's sake.

Monday morning, I'll kiss them all goodbye and watch them saunter down the sidewalk with their new backpacks and Target bags full of supplies. And as soon as they get to school, they better start writing with the 120 pre-sharpened pencils that I had to buy for the four of them. Because they have a lot of lead to use.

They'll hop on the bus, and I'll have a blessed six hours of solitude. I'll work. I'll write. I may even end world hunger and help usher in a new era of global peace.

The possibilities are endless.

But I'll still miss them.

Animal Kingdom

Pets We Have Loved and Lost

You enter into a certain amount of madness when you marry a person with pets. ~
Nora Ephron

"Fly Away"

There's nothing better than watching your kids romp happily
with their friends on a hot summer afternoon. Nothing better, unless
you're watching them play with a cold cocktail in your hand. And that's
precisely how we prefer to spend our summer afternoons. With ten kids
under the age of ten, we had three households that spent many late
afternoons drinking, laughing, and haphazardly supervising the antics of
our offspring.

"Mary Claire! Mary Claire!" her fellow four-year-old friends
chanted excitedly. "Come see the robin's eggs!" In a corner of our
neighbor's playset, a robin had built a cozy nest and filled it with three
sparkling blue eggs. The kids were mesmerized, enchanted, intrigued.
They took turns traipsing up and down the ladder to look at the eggs, to
check their health and well-being, to see if they'd hatched yet.

One afternoon, shortly before we all broke rank to bathe our dirty children and send them to their slumbers, we heard the girls screaming.

"Mary Claire killed the babies! Mary Claire killed the baby birds!"

I ran to the backyard to see what was happening and found three broken eggshells on the grass.

"Mary Claire! What did you do?" I demanded.

"I'm sorry, Mama!" she sobbed. "I didn't mean to hurt them!"

Her face was stained with dirty tear tracks and she sobbed inconsolably in my arms.

"Did you drop them?" I asked.

She nodded and wiped the snot from her face with the back of her grimy hand.

"Mary Claire," I snapped, "why in the world would you do that?"

"I was afraid they couldn't get out," she explained. "I wanted to help them crack their shells."

I looked at the mangled pile of eggshells and underdeveloped baby birds and thought to myself that she'd certainly succeeded in helping them crack their shells.

We held a memorial service for the baby birds and buried them in the garden. Mary Claire had nightmares about them for many nights after. She asked numerous questions about heaven and God and the place baby birds go when they die. She wanted to know all about their Moms and Dads and how they were coping with the loss of their babies. She cried into my arms night after night after night.

"I thought maybe they would fly!" she sobbed.

Those babies weighed heavily on Mary Claire's mind for months after the eggshell cracking incident. The weight of her grief was made heavier still by her brothers' torment. Every once in a while, when they thought I was out of earshot, they'd breeze by her and whisper "Bird Killer" in her ear.

"Gas Leak"

"Walter the Farting Dog" is one of my favorite books. Probably because the word "fart" is funny no matter how you look at it. Farts are funny. If you haven't read the book, it centers on an adopted dog named Walter who is loved by his child-owners, but who undeniably has a flatulence problem. The parents want to figure out what's causing Walter's "issue," but the kids don't care. They love Walter no matter what.

Apparently, we've adopted Walter the Farting Dog. Only we call her Lucy. She had such horrible gas one night shortly after we adopted her that it was nearly an evacuation situation. The kids came running up from the basement screaming and holding their noses, and for once, it wasn't a gross exaggeration. The fumes even made their way through Mary Claire's virus-induced stuffiness.

Poor Lucy followed the screaming kids with her innocent look of wonderment. Screaming? Running? Must be play time. The more she gave chase, the faster they ran. The kids all locked themselves into their rooms to get ready for bed, and poor Lucy was left out in the hallway.

When I went to kiss Mary Claire goodnight, Lucy jumped up on her bed like she does every night. Normally, she's a welcome guest. This night, however, she let one rip and it seriously made my eyes water.

"Get her out!" Mary Claire cried. "Mommy, she's KILLING me!" She was actually crying real tears and begging me to drag that pooch off her bed. I escorted Lucy out, calmed Mary Claire down, kissed her goodnight, and went to tuck the boys in.

As I was reading to Sam, we heard a blood-curdling, "NOOOO!" Lucy had wormed her way back into Mary Claire's room. With loud demands of "Get out, get out, get out," Lucy made her way into Sam's room. She promptly whined a bit, put her front paws up on Sam's bed, released some noxious fumes, and walked away.

I couldn't even continue reading because I was crying so hard. Perhaps it was the fumes. Perhaps the laughter. As I said before, farts are funny.

"Swift Justice"

Maggie is rebelling. I think she's over Lucy and the havoc that has been wreaked on her life. While we were at work, Maggie decided to completely demolish a large part of the carpet right by the front entryway. I'm convinced it's her way of saying, "Bring that fucking puppy into the house, and I'll show you a thing or two!" She's never been destructive. She's afraid of being destructive. She's afraid of paper bags and wood laminate flooring, for heaven's sake.

Anyway, her chewing exposed the tack strip and George promptly stepped on it (right after I told the kids to step over it until we had the carpet replaced). He received a tack to the toe and screamed like a banshee.

I told Chris I wanted to catch Maggie in the act so I could beat her black lab ass, and George shouted in a teary, snot-filled wail, "Just beat her ass NOW!"

"A Little Ditty"

Because I had hamsters as pets growing up, I'm a sucker for rodents. Hamsters, gerbils, mice, guinea pigs – you name it, we've had it. Everything except rats. I just can't do rats. At one point, we had two hamsters named Jack and Diane. (Yes, it was at the height of Sam's Mellencamp phase.) Mary Claire and George loved those hamsters with every ounce of being.

And then.

One day, the cage was left open, and Jack made his great escape. He was gone for over a week when Mary Claire asked if we could put some water out for him. I explained to her (because I'm not very good at making stories up on the fly) that our quest to find Jack had probably already become a Search and Recovery versus a Search and Rescue.

She cried inconsolably for an hour or so while I kicked myself for being so literal. And so dumb. I put a bowl of water out, grabbed a couple pieces of poop from Diane's cage, and set them beside the water bowl.

"Mary Claire!" I called excitedly. "You were right! Look! Jack is still alive!"

She wrapped her grateful arms around me and replied, "I knew it, Mama! I knew he was still alive!"

And so we still leave bits and pieces of food around for Jack. Every once in a while, the little ones are sure they hear him scurrying around in their rooms at night. Fueled by thoughts of "The Borrowers," we're convinced that Jack is living a pretty sweet – and amazingly long – life.

"Mercy Killing"

Caroline and Hermione were #2 and #3 in our guinea pig family. Our first guinea pig, Kat, unfortunately met her demise two short days after we brought her home. Although many tears were shed over her untimely passing, we determined that she must have been sick when we adopted her. After all, we've been able to keep these four kids alive for numerous years, and they're a lot more challenging than rodents.

We spent a great deal of time picking Caroline and Hermione out, making sure they were our favorites, buying all the necessary supplies. Caroline was to live in Sam's room, Hermione in Gus's. It was a perfect plan.

And then.

One fine morning, I went to wake Gus up for school and was fairly certain I'd entered a remake filming of "The Amityville Horror." There were flies completely covering his slanted wall above Hermione's cage. (I should point out that because the kids were afraid the guinea pigs were lonely without each other, they'd been cohabitating for the past couple of nights.) And when I say the ceiling was covered "completely," I mean every fly in the state of Indiana had descended upon Gus's room. And they'd brought their Ohio cousins.

"Gus!" I shrieked, as he reluctantly opened his sleepy eyes to the sound of my panicked voice. "Have you noticed all these flies?!"

"Well," he replied nonchalantly, as if a blanket of flies on his wall was a common sighting, "I noticed there were a few yesterday."

"Ewwwww!" I heard Mary Claire shriek from the hallway. She was echoed with a chorus of "Oh, cool!" from Sam and George. "Are those flies?"

I was so completely grossed out that I was rendered incapable of doing anything to help ameliorate the situation. So, I closed the door, shuttled the kids off to school, and called Chris, who is always a voice of reason in my times of high anxiety.

"Well, Honey," he said distractedly, "why don't you just kill them?"

"You don't understand the magnitude of this situation, Chris," I assured him. "There are a thousand flies. At least a thousand. Probably five thousand."

"I guess you'd need a bigger flyswatter then."

Done with his nonchalance, I stated my demands. "I need you to come home right now."

"Katrina, be reasonable," he said. "I'm at work. I have a meeting in ten minutes. You're a big girl. You can handle this. They're only flies."

And with that coldhearted dismissal, I was on my own.

I opened the door a crack and peeked into Gus's room, hoping beyond hope that my earlier sighting was just some crazy, sleep-induced hallucination.

Not so.

They were still there. Buzzing and flying and buzzing some more.

And then I realized that the source of the infestation was the guinea pig cage. And upon closer inspection, I realized there was a writhing, wriggling mass in the bedding.

Maggots.

(I must admit I can hardly write the word because the memory of it brings me such intense horror.)

I closed the door again and called my veterinarian friend, Kerri.

"Kerri, something is horribly wrong with my kids' guinea pigs. Their cage is full of maggots. Help me, please. NOW."

"Have they been outside?" Kerri asked.

"Many times. The kids love to let them run around in the yard."

"I know this sounds gross, but you need to check their rectums to see if you see maggots there."

Excuse me? I'm supposed to examine my rodents' butts?

"And what happens if they have maggots in their rectums?" I asked, fearful of the answer.

"Well, I'm guessing they have blowfly infestation. If they do, they're probably not going to survive. In fact, the most humane thing to do would be to put them down. They're basically going to be eaten from the inside out by the maggots. It's not a good way to die."

And then the retching began.

"If you want me to," Kerri offered, "I can put them down for you. Truly, it's much more humane than making them suffer through this."

After further examination of Caroline and Hermione's nether regions, it was determined that they did, indeed, have blowfly infestation.

We moved their cage to the garage, conducted a fly eradication, and discussed our options.

"I'm not going to pay a vet to euthanize these rodents," Chris proclaimed.

"Well, Kerri said she'd do it."

"And I'm not going to make Kerri drive all the way over here with her new baby to deal with our rodents, either."

"Honey, they're suffering," I argued.

"I'll take care of it."

"What's that supposed to mean?"

"I'll make sure they don't suffer."

"Chris, what are you saying? Are you going to kill them?"

"I'm going to euthanize them. Inexpensively."

"You are not going to take them to a corn field and let them get eaten by coyotes," I argued. "You will not hit them over the head with a hammer. You will not do anything brutal, disgusting, or unsettling." I was crying now.

"Katrina, you have to trust me," Chris said. "I will take care of this."

That night, we gathered the kids together to break their hearts.

"Kids," I began, "I have some bad news for you. Remember all the flies we saw in Gus's room?"

They nodded solemnly.

"Those flies were there because Caroline and Hermione are sick. Very, very sick. I called Dr. Kerri today, and she says that they won't live much longer."

Four sets of bright blue eyes filled with tears simultaneously.

"What's wrong with them?" Mary Claire wailed. "Why are they going to die? Are they sick like Kat was?"

I held my girl and smoothed her unruly hair while I tried my best to explain that bad things sometimes happen, things that make us sad. But that her pets were very sick and it would be better for them to make their way to guinea pig heaven to be with Kat.

"Can we hold them?" George sniffled.

Visions of maggots filled my thoughts.

"No, Honey," I explained. "They're very, very sick. Holding them will only make them sicker. But you can go out the garage and talk to them. Tell them that you love them and that it's okay for them to go to a better place."

And so, one by one, my kids said their goodbyes to their terminally ill pets and cried themselves to sleep.

A little after 11:00 PM, Chris joined me in bed.

"It's done," he said solemnly.

"What?" I asked, putting my book down quickly. "What do you mean?"

"They're gone," he explained.

"I didn't get to say goodbye!" I cried. "What do you mean 'they're gone'?"

"Katrina, be reasonable. They were sick. You didn't want them to suffer any longer. I took care of it. We'll tell the kids I buried them in the garden with Kat."

I was afraid to ask, but couldn't help myself.

"What did you do?"

"I asphyxiated them."

"You what?"

"I asphyxiated them. I put them in a plastic bag and I put the bag on the tailpipe of the car."

I couldn't breathe.

Horrifying. But brilliant in a twisted, gruesome way.

"Did they suffer?" I asked meekly.

"I don't think so. They only squirmed around when I first put them in. Then it was all over very quickly."

I swallowed the bile and blinked back the inevitable tears at the sheer horror of the situation.

"The kids can never, never know," I whispered.

"At least not until they read it in your book," he replied.

"Goodbye, Bob"

"Mom, I've got some bad news."

Gus greeted me in the driveway after work with an apparent sense of urgency.

"Bob's dead."

Now you must understand that we have lots of "Bobs" in our lives. My heartbeat quickened as I ran through the possibilities.

"He had bedding in his mouth. I'm pretty sure he choked."

Then the tears appeared in the big, blue saucer eyes.

Bob, the guinea pig. We'd just returned home from vacation two days earlier. Amber tended the livestock while we were gone, reporting that all was well with the Willis pets.

Not so much for Bob. Maybe he was just too overwhelmed with our return and the prospect of a clean cage.

As I was consoling Gus, Chris came out with Bob's remains in a burial bag.

"We just reclaimed 30 square feet of room in the basement," he said, grinning ear to ear.

I gave him the "Shut Your Insensitive Fucker Mouth" look while he chuckled to himself.

Then I heard Mary Claire from inside the house.

"BOB'S DEAD! BOB'S DEAD! BOB'S DEAD!" She just kept screaming it over and over and over in her near-hysterical, hyper-dramatic way.

I don't know where she gets that inclination.

Then George came out. He was all business. Albeit, sad business.

"Dad and I are going to bury Bob in the garden," he announced. And they did.

The next day, the forecast called for rain. George stood by the window looking anxious as I prepared to leave for work.

"I'm worried about our garden," he admitted. "I'm worried that the seeds that haven't grown yet will drown in the rain."

"Oh, Honey," I said as I hurriedly loaded all my essential crap into my giant satchel, "rain is good for your plants. They need water to grow just like you do."

He looked at me with tears in his eyes.

"What I'm really worried about is Bob," he said. "What if the rain gets in his mouth? He can't close his mouth anymore. What if it fills with rain?"

Oh, my sweet, sensitive boy. He can be such as ass sometimes. But mostly, he's just a smart, kind, soft-hearted, six-year-old who continually melts my heart on a daily basis.

I sat down and held him and explained in my all-knowing Catholic education way that Bob's soul was safe in guinea pig heaven and that his body would become a part of our garden and we'd know when we saw our flowers that he was happily running through fields of Timothy Hay forever. With Kat and Hermione.

That discussion prompted his next question. "What do you think comes first in the sky? Heaven or space?"

Damn. We didn't cover that in Sister Veronica Ann's seventh grade class.

Rest in peace, Bob. We'll miss you.

Well, everyone but Chris.

"House Guest"

While Amber spent her summer with us, she decided to add a new canine companion to the mix. And so we were introduced to Gavin. (Yes, after Gavin DeGraw. Amber's a bit of a fan.) Gavin looked a lot like Lucy, but was unrelated. She descends straight from a line of Dumb and Gavin was a smart and sweet little dude.

He was a good puppy – which is a blessing because his puppy teeth were incredibly sharp and his bladder was like a living, breathing creature. But, oh! That puppy breath...

As always, Maggie wasn't so sure about Gavin. So unsure, in fact, that she reverted back to barking and growling at Lucy as if to say, "You're the one who started this whole puppy thing, you bitch! Now both of you need to get the hell away from my Iams."

Lucy, on the other hand, adored Gavin so much that the two of them spent 99% of their time chewing on each other. Like chicken legs. Her maternal instinct kicked in (despite the fact that all her Mommy parts had been surgically removed long before Gavin arrived), and she'd stand guard over him like a sentinel. When she wasn't biting him.

Amber adored her new little buddy, and I was convinced that when he weighed more than a quarter pounder with cheese, he'd be a great guard dog and companion. And I was sure she'd be able to keep him alive and healthy.

Unlike poor Bob who died on Amber's watch.

Now, I'm not insinuating that Amber was the cause of Bob's death, only that she was the one who was there when the kids discovered him. In fact, Amber probably was the spring in Bob's step during the last few weeks of his existence on this earth. She fed and watered and loved him like he was her own. In fact, if Amber had anything to do with Bob's death, it could have only been that she drove him to a blissful state of ecstasy during which his tiny little rodent heart exploded into a billion pieces of love and gratitude.

Either that, or he choked on his litter. Because Gus was fairly convinced upon his post-mortem diagnosis, that litter choking was the way Bob met his fate.

"Canine Distress"

In was spring time when Lucy declared biological warfare on us.

Perhaps if we'd paid a little more attention to her the night before when she was whining and crying at our bedside in the wee hours of the morning. Perhaps if I hadn't hissed, "Hush! Now you be quiet and lay down before you wake up the kids!" Perhaps if I'd been just a bit concerned. But hindsight is so much clearer.

So, the following morning we awoke to the overwhelming stench of dog vomit and diarrhea all over our bedroom floor. And the upstairs hallway. And in Sam's room. And in the living room. And in the family room. All over the family room. And in her crate. And all over Maggie's favorite Orvis pillow.

There is an unparalleled rankness to illness-induced canine bodily functions. And because our Lucy is a goat cleverly disguised as a Bad Dog, God only knows what she consumed that caused her such intestinal distress. Was it the Nerf football she ate in the yard the day before? Maybe. Or was it the Frisbee that she chewed to pieces? Perhaps. Or, it could have been the jagged remains of the plastic watering can that she carried happily in her mouth when she greeted me after work. (George wailed, "Bad dog, Lucy! Now all my plants are going to DIE because they don't have any water!") Oh, wait! I know – maybe it was the bright pink marker that she chewed to shreds on our living room carpet last week. The one that left her paws stained pink for a good week. It could have even been an arsenic-laced hotdog from my puppy-kicking neighbor. Not that I'm accusing, just speculating. Lucy does tend to bark a lot.

Chris gave the steam cleaner a good workout before he left for the office. Sam ate a bowl of cereal with a candle burning right next to his head. He was willing to risk the singed eyebrows for a modicum of olfactory relief. There's only so much a Yankee candle – or five, or twenty – can do.

We opened every window in the house and the Three Littles shivered through breakfast. "Sorry, kids," I offered. "You'll just have to suck it up. I'm not closing the windows." When we arrived home after work, it still smelled like – excuse my bluntness – a dirty dog ass. So, out came the steam cleaner for Round Two.

Poor Maggie wandered around the house all night looking lost without her favorite pillow. (It, unfortunately, couldn't be salvaged.) She looked at the spot under the grandfather clock where it used to be, then looked at us, then – I swear to my God above – she sighed and walked away. If she could have, she would have said, "You sons of bitches have ruined my life."

And we wouldn't have argued.

Family Outings

"We're Going to Have Fun, Damn It!"

The most wasted of all days is one without laughter. ~ *e.e. cummings*

"The Most Wonderful Time of the Year"

Our annual Picking-Out-the-Christmas-Tree-Outing began in a very normal Willis/Norman Rockwell picturesque kind of way with George flinging himself to the floor in tears because I told him his hat from last year (which was perched precariously on his head like a beanie leaving his ears completely exposed to the elements) was too small.

Once we got into the car, the chorus of "He's touching me!" and "She's kicking my seat!" and "Why do we have to listen to 80s music?" began in earnest. Chris quickly became increasingly annoyed – by the children and the 80s music – and we found that Led Zeppelin was the only thing that would calm him down.

The Christmas tree farm was crowded beyond reasonable capacity, and instead of driving through the scenic displays of evergreens with idyllic smiles on our faces, Chris was grumbling, "This is why I hate this place."

"Let's just go to Marsh and buy our tree then," I snapped. "That will be memorable for the kids." I then went on with my little memory soliloquy, "Oh, Mom and Dad, remember that year we got to go to Marsh and pick out our tree? And then we bought some butter and toilet paper, too? That was my favorite Christmas ever!"

Picking out the tree actually turned out to be pretty fun and relatively painless. Then we went to see the reindeer that smelled like a dirty guinea pig cage times one gazillion. He tried to eat Mary Claire's hat, and she screamed like a banshee, upsetting all the little children around her who thought she, herself, was being eaten by Prancer.

After we talked her off the ledge and took her into the train store, she cried inconsolably because I wouldn't buy her a unicorn for her fairy castle.

When we arrived home, Chris set up the tree and hung the lights. After all the kids completed their arguments about which ornament belonged to whom, and I threatened to call Santa and tattle on their sorry asses multiple times during the tree decorating process, we all decided to watch "The Polar Express" together. And to complete our day of Christmas memories, I promptly fell asleep after the snappy "Hot

Chocolate" number and snored loudly throughout the remainder of the movie. (Which I also vehemently denied.)

We're all about making memories.

"Christmas Crazy Magnet"

Two weeks before Christmas, we were all set to see Santa Claus at the Indiana State Museum. Mary Claire had a Girl Scout Sing event, and we were going to make a memory, damn it. However, when we arrived at the Museum, Mary Claire became ill. I personally believe it was a reaction to the sight of the first floor crawling with little girls with brown and green sashes and their overbearing troop leaders.

It was enough to make me a little nauseous, too.

To make a long story short – and to bear you the actual details of Mary Claire's illness – suffice it to say that our day was cut short, our outing postponed, and our trip back to the car punctuated with the sobs of a young, sick girl and a small, angry boy – who just got gypped out of seeing Santa.

We rescheduled our Santa trip for the following Monday. Because, we rationalized, the museum would surely be less crowded on a Monday than over the weekend.

Of course, we didn't realize that December 22nd was FREE DAY at the Indiana State Museum.

What does that mean? Apparently, it means all the crazy Indianapolis residents come out of hiding and make the lines to see Santa painfully long. And while you're standing in line for over an hour, you are a captive audience for their rambling, inappropriate life stories. But I'm getting ahead of myself...

Sam, our fearless eldest, has always had a visceral reaction to heights. Because I share his fear – although to a much lesser degree – I have always sympathized with him. One of his great fears is crossing the "bridges" that span the upper floors of the Indiana State Museum. He hates using the stairs, hates the openness of the design. To assuage his fears, we agreed to wait for 1,000 years to take the elevator. From the second floor to the third.

Once we arrived on the third floor, we all merrily proceeded toward Santa's house, the one that was just a short bridge crossing and a mere hour and half worth of waiting away. Sam, however, plastered his back against the wall and refused to take a step. He began to cry, and Chris began to lose his shit. Even I thought Sam's reaction to be a bit extreme and a bit... oh, what's the word? Asinine?

I tried to reason with him, tried to convince him to just close his eyes while I led him into Santa's Promised Land, but he became more belligerent. And I became less patient. Much less patient. Chris, having already exhausted all his patience on finding a parking place 30 miles away because the parking garage was full, grabbed him by the arm and forcefully led him to Santa's Magical Wonder Land.

Once there, the other kids spotted a picture-taking sleigh and asked if they could take a turn. I made Sam get in the picture as well. The result? Well, you'll just have to imagine Sam's, "I hate you mudda effers" look. Uh huh. Merry Christmas.

Next, we hunkered down in Santa's line and prepared for a long winter's nap.

For a while, I enjoyed looking at the mass of people congregating in my personal space. Oh, the humanity! Then they began interacting. A plump woman behind me began talking, and it was about 20 seconds into her soliloquy that I realized she was talking to me.

"Do you think anyone would mind if I jumped out of line to take my kids' picture?" she asked. (Her kids were in the "Train Ride" line, which was directly next to the "Santa" line, but moving much more quickly.)

"I'm sure no one will mind," I assured her. "Unless you try to jump on Santa's lap in front of some three-year-olds."

Note to self: Never try to be witty with strangers who might mistake your offhanded comment as an invitation to tell you their life story.

And thus, the rambling began.

"Well, they've got a few more minutes," she explained, "So I'm going to wait a bit longer. My 12-year-old daughter didn't want to come today. She doesn't believe in Santa Claus anymore, and she told me she didn't want to waste her time..."

At this juncture, I attempted to steer my little ones' ears away from the conversation by pointing to the roaming Raggedy Ann. Because, really, what says Christmas more than a life-sized Raggedy Ann?

"But I told her..." (No pause for a breath) "...that she had a five-year-old brother and she was going to suck it up and have her picture taken with Santa Claus for the next 20 years whether she believed in him or not! My husband told her the same thing. He was supposed to come with us today. We'd planned to come on Free Day for over a month, but wouldn't you know it? The doctor scheduled his colonoscopy for today! Of all days! So, he was at the doc's this morning, and he's resting this afternoon. I decided to bring the kids anyway. I mean, it was just a colonoscopy, right?"

Dear readers, how does one appropriately react to a complete stranger talking about her husband's colonoscopy while standing in line to visit Santa and his Head Elf? Really? REALLY?

By some Divine Intervention, she decided that moment was the right time to jump the line to capture forever the wonderment on her 12-year-old daughter's unbelieving face as she supervised her five-year-old brother's magical train ride.

I took that opportunity to use every member of my family to create as much distance between me and Madame Colonscopy as humanly possible.

It was then that I spotted Him. And I'm not talking about Santa.

After rearranging myself in line, I saw my next human anomaly. And he was wearing a shirt – I kid you not – that had these words plastered across the back:

NASHVILLE PUSSY (In Lust We Trust).

Because what says, "Unto You a Child Is Born" more than female genitalia?

I leaned over to Chris and whispered, "Honey, why didn't you wear your 'Pussy' shirt for Christmas? You always look so handsome in it!"

After a mere 39 hours (okay, it just seemed that long), we got to see The Man Himself. Yes, Santa. When he asked Mary Claire what she wanted, it was a total "Christmas Story" moment. Just like Ralphie, her eyes got wide, her tongue thickened, and she froze. But Santa had no time to waste! He had a line of 189 FREE ADMISSION kids waiting to sit on his lap! So, he quickly promised her lots of surprises and moved on to George. When George pulled his wadded-up, three-page list of requests out of his pocket, I think I actually saw Santa reach for a flask.

We went through a few items, and then Santa replied, "Son, why don't you just leave your list in my basket, and I'll make sure you get lots of things that you're wishing for."

George reluctantly climbed off his lap and relinquished his treasured list. I shooed the kids along to Chris, ran back, and dug George's list out of the basket. Because I couldn't bear to be without those dog-eared papers that requested "Powlrod Camra" (Polaroid Camera), "Pozl Bal," (Puzzle ball), and "Pirut sip wif rel gis" (Pirate ship with real guys). It's safely tucked away in my treasure box, the one salvageable remnant from this God-forsaken day.

After Santa, we ventured on to the gift shop because all the kids had received money from Nana and Bob yesterday, and they'd gone nearly 24 hours without spending any of it. Chris and I watched as they milled around aimlessly for another 46 hours, picking up one thing and setting it down, then returning to it at least five more times before making a decision. When the boys were all rung up and Chris approached our weary group with Mary Claire in tow, I very innocently asked what she'd decided on.

"A bag of rocks, a shark's tooth, and an arrowhead."

Moving toward the exit, I heard a voice saying, "I have Crazy Horse in my basement! I really do!"

And I'll be damned if that white-haired, shifty-eyed woman wasn't talking to me! Apparently, the common thread of a fake arrowhead was enough for her to think we shared some kind of Native American bond.

"When my kids were little, we went out West where they were carving that statue of Crazy Horse out of the mountain, and a rock this big (measuring with her arms) fell right in front of us! Well, my kids took that rock home, and it's been in our dining room ever since. I tried to move it to the basement, but when my kids bring the grandkids over, they always ask, 'Where's Crazy Horse?' And so, back to the dining room it goes!"

Are you kidding me? Are you really telling me this? I smiled and nodded and raced down the stairs and out of the building leaving small children in my wake.

Walking to the car, Chris commented, "You were like a Crazy Magnet today." And indeed I was.

To round out the evening, we visited the Circle of Lights, had dinner at the Hard Rock Cafe, and did a little shopping at Circle Center Mall. During that brief time, Mary Claire lost her purse, cried inconsolably about her purse, miraculously found her purse, and then proceeded to accidently drop a ten dollar bill into the Simon Youth Fund coin collector while she was rummaging for a penny to spin. Chris explained to her that she just made a nice donation to some needy kids, but I think all she really wanted to do was stick her little, eczema-ridden hand down into that black hole and fish her ten bucks back out.

"I Want to Ride My Bicycle"

For weeks, my three Littles had been asking me to let them ride their bikes to school. While I was working full-time, it just wasn't an option. I'm one of those crazy parents who believes that a stranger is lurking on the Rail Trail just waiting for three little screaming, arguing kids to cross his path so he can snatch them up, pay for their college tuitions, and listen to them bicker nonstop for the next 18 years. So, I wanted to accompany them on their inaugural bike ride to school to ensure their (and any unsuspecting childnapper's) safety.

And so arrived the day of the Bike Ride to School.

It was a chilly morning, a good, crisp October day. I instructed the kids to wear hats and gloves. Gus and Mary Claire obliged. George did not.

"My hands will slip off my handlebars," he whined as he threw his six-year-old self into the classic Willis slump.

"Fine," I huffed in my mature 38-year-old way. "But I don't want to hear ONE WORD when your hands are frozen."

And off we went.

Let me take a moment to explain that the kids' school is right next to our neighborhood entrance. We are approximately ½ mile back from the entrance, and the kids have ridden this route at least a thousand times. At least.

After about three turns of the pedal, Mary Claire stopped to "rest." Gus began yelling at her (in his ultra-loud Gus way) to HURRY UP BECAUSE SHE WAS GOING TO MAKE HIM LATE, and I almost ran her over from behind, only releasing my feet from my pedal straps by some random miracle of God.

"Mary Claire," I warned, "we don't have all day. You've got to keep moving, or you're going to be late for school."

"But I'm tiiiiiirrreed," she whined.

"I don't care," I snapped. "Get your feet on your pedals and move. We don't have time to sit around and whine. You wanted to ride, now RIDE!"

About this time, George began to complain about his cold hands.

"Zip it," I warned, more than a little short and exasperated. "I told you I don't want to hear it."

"But Mooooooommmmm…"

"Zip it!"

By this time, Gus was so far ahead of us, I couldn't see him anymore.

We ventured slowly past another two light posts, and Mary Claire slowed down to a wobbly crawl.

"Mary, I'm not amused with you this morning. Get moving NOW."

"But it's soooooo haaarrrdd," she whined.

That's when I noticed that both of her tires were flat. Shit.

"Honey, your tires need a little air," I informed her as I softened a tad. "That's what's making it hard to pedal. But we're halfway to school now. It will take us just as long to turn around and go home, and then you'll be late. Keep heading toward school. When you're there today, I'll come pump up your tires so it will be easier to ride home."

About this time, George slowed down, lost his balance, and tipped over. He didn't really "fall" off his bike, he just toppled sideways into the grass. But from his high-pitched screams, you would have thought he'd severed a limb.

"Oh, for heaven's sake, George, stop that wailing!" I said with a teensy hint of irritation as I dusted him off and picked him back up. Multiple bikers sped by us as we tried to re-group on the side of the road.

George's "accident" gave Mary Claire time to catch up, and she proceeded to start complaining all over again.

"I can't DO IT!" she cried. Big, fat tears rolled down her cheeks. "It's TOO HARD!"

"Mary," I explained, "life is hard. Sometimes you have to work at things." I refrained from telling her that if she'd stop mouth-breathing in front of the TV all the time and get outside to exercise, this wouldn't be such a chore. "Now suck it up, get on that bike, and GET TO SCHOOL."

When all was said and done, it took us 40 minutes to arrive – late. It took me seven minutes to ride back home.

It took me less than ten seconds to pour a strong shot of Kahlua into my morning coffee.

"The Last Hurrah"

On the last day of the summer, we lounged lazily by the pool with some of our best friends. Ric Ocasek was in my head as I hummed to myself, "Summer, it turns me upside down. Summer, summer, summer. It's like a merry-go-round." (Really, Paulina Porizkova? You must know something about him that the rest of us don't. Cause he is one rock start that just does not do it for me.)

But the music of The Cars was in my head as we gathered at a different summer pool for one last summer fling. We'd never been there before, and we all cringed at the Posted Rules stating that any child under the age of eight had to wear a wristband and be within arm's length of a responsible adult at all times. Are you kidding me? First of all, there were at least 1,748 lifeguards on duty that day, and they all had their rescue skills down to a science. Trust me, we saw them in action. Second, I'm NEVER within arm's reach of my kids at the pool. In arm's reach of a cold beverage, perhaps, but not in reach of my kids. They can all swim better than I can. And how am I supposed to enjoy a giant Diet Coke loaded with ice if I have to be in the pool the entire day? We promptly chewed the yellow wristbands off with our teeth as soon as we were through the entry doors.

The kids had a pretty good time. Except, of course, when all my boys were hemming and hawing about the water slides. Two of them made the attempt, began the ascent, and then came back down the stairs crying. One of them pouted around for a good half hour because he couldn't bring himself to take the plunge. Lots of fun, indeed.

The girl, on the other hand – you know, the one deathly afraid of her pink, frilly bedroom at night? – she went down every slide about a thousand times. Apparently, all her fears are focused on a scary pink bedroom replete with various and sundry stuffed pigs situated exactly 2.3 steps from her parents' bedroom.

All in all, it was a good day. Backpacks are loaded, first day outfits are out and ready to be donned, fresh breakfast bananas are waiting patiently on the counter. Tomorrow, I'll wave goodbye to a sixth grader, a fourth grader, a third grader, and a first grader. This is The Golden Year. The one where they're ALL in school ALL DAY LONG. And after I throw the discarded banana peels in the trash, I'll mix up the first celebratory mimosa.

"Humans and Animals and Cheese... Oh, My!"

It was time for our annual pilgrimage to the Indiana State Fair. I should begin with a preface stating that I am a huge fan of the State Fair. I love the atmosphere, the animals, the people-watching, the food. Every last glorious friend or meat-on-a-stick inspired concoction.

Our current adventure began in the parking lot. Historically, that's a bit earlier than usual. Typically, we're at least somewhere near the midway when the real fun begins. But as we were pulling into the unorganized, accident-waiting-to-happen debacle known as infield parking, we saw the Grandmammy of All Outfits.

Now I'm the first to admit that I'm not a small woman. I've got some meat on my bones (thanks, Oreos), and I'm fully aware that certain articles of clothing are not longer options for me. Like, say for instance, a black tank top stretched so tightly around rolls of belly fat that the color on the shoulder straps was distinctly darker than the screaming-for-mercy midriff fibers. Yes, they were screaming. I heard them. Chris and I both saw the fashionista at the same time. We knew we were in sync with our lines of vision when the collective gasp of horror escaped from our lips simultaneously.

Two syllables of advice: Muumuu.

It became quickly apparent that I was suffering not only from seasonal allergies, but from those brought on by farm animals, hay, straw, dust, dirt, wood shavings, deep fryers, and tattoo ink. I spent the entire day sinking deeper and deeper into a snot-induced haze. While standing at the Lemon Shake-Up cart (located conspicuously between the Giant Turkey Leg vendor and the Deep Fried Twinkie booth), I sneezed eight times consecutively. And loudly.

"Mom, you're so embarrassing sometimes," Mary Claire scoffed in her pre-pubescent, the-whole-world-is-looking-at-me way as a woman in four-inch stilettos and Daisy Dukes sauntered by.

The part I love most about the State Fair is the animals. Oh, those glorious beasts! The spitting alpacas, the World's Largest Boar, the fuzzy piglets, and the stately horses. But for my suburban kids, farm animals are sometimes mysterious creatures who invoke innocent questions. Like Mary Claire asking, "Why is that pig's butt so big?" when she wasn't actually looking at the boar's rear-end. The World's Largest

Boar also invariably has the World's Largest and Most Obscene Testicles for the entire state of Indiana to view. And like when George said (in his loud, George way), "Look how big that horse's tail is!" I probably don't have to point out that the horse's actual tail was braided and decorated and confusingly close to the "tail" George was referencing. I mean, they're not called "studs" for nothing.

At the close of our fair adventures, we always…reluctantly…take the kids to the dreaded midway. This is most definitely not my favorite part of the State Fair. Why? Let me outline a few reasons…

1. I lose a little piece of my soul every time I pay $8 for four kids to ride down the Super Slide. Once. First of all, they can slide at West Park to their hearts' content. For free. Second, there's nothing Super about the Super Slide at the State Fair except, perhaps, for the SuperBug that is lingering on every square inch and is undoubtedly antibiotic-resistant (thereby rendering my ever-present bottle of Purell ineffective).

2. The Carnies. Don't get me wrong, I like Carnies. I am, in fact, fascinated by them. (Someday you'll probably be privy to a novel written by Yours Truly with a Carnie as the main character.) But I

like my Carnies to have a little more local flavor, a little more County Fair than State Fair. It's just a hang-up of mine.

3. I admit that I have strong safety concerns about rides that look like they're held together with paper clips and Band-Aids. I'm a huge fan of amusement parks. That's because I like rides that have permanent homes. I don't so much go for rides that are moved every other day from Indianapolis to Des Moines to Bryson City by aforementioned Carnies.

4. Although I like people-watching at the State Fair, I don't necessarily enjoy close-contact mingling with some of them. It seems like the midway is more tattoo than skin and that at least half of the young children have urine-stained shorts that were just perched on the seat my kids are climbing into next. Yuck. That's all I have to say.

This particular midway adventure was so loud, so crowded, so overwhelming that I felt I'd been molested by the time we ran at full sprint to the antibacterial soap stands.

And last but not least, I'd like to talk about State Fair art. Here's the question I'm ruminating on…

How does one come to the conscious decision that his or her chosen artistic medium is going to be cheese?

Yes, cheese. Because tonight, we saw a 1,500 pound cheese sculpture. It was more than impressive. It was downright inspirational. People were snapping pictures of the cheese; people were contemplating the cheese; people were filming the cheese; people were wondering whether or not the cheese was still edible. It was more than a conversation piece. It was a first-class piece of pasteurized art.

Here's my thing – there's a story behind that cheese. There's a woman – an artist, no doubt – who one day sat down and thought, "I'm going to create my masterpiece. What shall be my medium? I've got it! Gouda!" Or maybe she was inspired when she bit into a niblet of Brie. So, this cheese artist thought about it, she planned it, and then she sat down and created a 1,500 pound replica of the State Fairgrounds covered bridge. Out. Of. Cheese.

I'm awestruck.

"Pure Perfection"

These only come along every once in awhile, but I think today can be counted as a Perfect Day. It began with a hot Starbucks coffee at the Farmer's Market with my favorite husband and my favorite daughter.

My favorite boys slept peacefully at home while we picked ripe plums, peaches, fresh green beans, and homemade whole wheat bread.

Shortly thereafter, we drove Sam to the high school so he could line up with his baritone to march in his first Fall Festival parade. The night before, he'd shown me how he was instructed to roll his feet while he marched so his instrument wouldn't shake too much.

Can you say "deja vu?" Because if he was not the reincarnation of his father at that precise moment, I don't know who he was. I wholeheartedly remembered my 18-year-old, aware-of-every-appearance-snafu self (except, perhaps, for the female mullet I sported throughout much of my high school career) proclaiming to my 17-year-old boyfriend that rolling his feet was *only* for band performances and Speedos were *only* for swim competitions.

And I've been bossing him around ever since.

After we dropped Sam off, we all saddled up on our bikes and rode the Rail Trail to our parade watching spot where the kids collected more candy than they do on Halloween.

We screamed and yelled and whooped at Sam and his friends and shamelessly embarrassed every one of those self-conscious pre-teens. But damn, they sounded good! And a seventh grade band that plays Journey's "Any Way You Want It?" Count me in as a groupie.

After the parade, we lunched at home and saddled back up to ride to the Fall Festival. The kids rode a few rides, Chris and I walked around holding hands and greeting friends, and we didn't bring home any cheap, stupid blow-up guitars or flimsy dart guns. A victory, indeed.

I bought a cute, kicky aluminum water bottle that reads, "She packed up her potential and all that she had learned, grabbed a cute pair of shoes, and headed out to change a few things." How fun is that? Mary Claire didn't get it, even after many long-winded explanations. But that's okay. Someday when she can think about "all she had learned," she'll understand.

Chris also bought me an artsty-fartsy necklace with a "K" pendant made out of an antique typewriter key. How cool is that? How perfect pour moi? It's my new wear-everywhere inspiration that screams, "Write, damn it! Write!"

And best of all? No goldfish. Not one. Two years ago, we brought home six. And they all died the following weeks... one by one by one. We had a series of toilet-flushing funerals, enough tears to last until the next Fall Festival, and a cupboard that's now loaded down with unused fish bowls and fish food. Thank God for the small miracle of not having to live that tedious nightmare over again.

A stop at Dairy Queen on our ride home resulted in happy kids and chocolate-stained shirts. Then Chris and I ordered pizza for the kids, put them in sleeping bags in the basement under Sam's watch, threw "Karate Kid" into the DVD player (because Mary Claire and George are currently becoming Karate masters), and headed to Noah Grants for a rare and overdue evening out.

We sat in the alleyway that felt a bit like Tuscany. Or at least what I imagine Tuscany – having never been there – might feel like. We indulged in sushi and filet and split a bottle of Woop Woop Shiraz. So what if our $31 bottle of wine had a screw top? Who cares if Chris's after dinner Scotch rang in at a whopping $16? We had a fabulous time reconnecting, talking about the future, visiting with some friends sitting nearby, and flirting with each other like teenagers.

Because, really, we're not that far away from the teenagers we once were, are we?

Okay, okay. So, we're old and fat and happy. (And not so fat anymore now that we've both lost 20 pounds.)

And I wouldn't have it any other way.

Finding God

Religion or Something Like It

True religion is real living; living with all one's soul, with all one's goodness and righteousness. ~ *Albert Einstein*

"God and Thank You Notes"

I feel as if I'm failing my children in two significant areas of life. First and foremost, I feel they are missing out on the gift of a religious upbringing – something that both Chris and I were blessed with. It's not that I don't have a strong belief in God myself, it's just that Chris and I can't seem to find a place where we both feel comfortable. And we can't seem to drag our asses out of bed on a Sunday morning, either. The combination is proving morally lethal for our kids.

When George first began preschool at the local Methodist church, his teacher asked each of the children what they would give Jesus as a birthday present. The other religiously well-fed children gave thoughtful, appropriate answers like, "a lamb, a warm blanket, a winter coat." George, however, gave the question a bit of thought and then promptly informed his teacher that the perfect gift for Jesus would be a

"Bowling for Soup" CD. I mean, who wouldn't want to listen to "Trucker Hat?" We sing it all the time. Hell, we even went on a family outing to the "Bowling for Soup" concert at the Myrtle Beach House of Blues. Apparently, George didn't want Jesus to miss out on some serious rocking.

So, my first concern is that my kids don't really know much about God, Jesus, the Bible, and the Catholicism that molded and shaped every minute of my youth, every synapse in my brain. We're good people at heart – we live (as much as possible) by the Golden Rule, but my kids couldn't tell you what the Golden Rule is. I am a firm believer in the Ten Commandments, but my kids think that the Ten Commandments begin with, "Thou Shalt Brush Thy Teeth Twice Every Day." And they still don't obey.

One of the greatest gifts my mom gave me as a child was a Catholic school education. Growing up without a father wasn't easy, but growing up without God would have been much harder. I talk to my kids about God, but I know they don't quite "get it." He's right there with Santa Claus and the Easter Bunny. Maybe a few steps ahead of the St. Patrick's Day leprechaun who also doubles as the Lucky Charms mascot. I definitely need to step up to the plate. Father, forgive me, for I have sinned. It's been over a year since I took my kids to church on a Sunday that wasn't Easter or Christmas. We need more than four Hail Marys to save our souls.

My other misgiving is my inability to teach my kids the proper thank you note writing etiquette. When I was growing up, not writing a timely and thoughtful thank you note was akin to committing a mortal sin. (See previous paragraph for the Catholic school reference.) I used to love writing thank you notes. I could schmooze with the best of them, and I adored describing in full, mind-numbing detail how perfect my Easy Bake Oven really was, and how wonderfully soft the resulting chocolate chip cookies were. Once I had four kids in five years, I couldn't even remember how to spell "thank you." I was so sleep deprived and reeking constantly of spit-up that a trip to the Hallmark store for a box of note cards was as elusive as an all-expense paid trip to Hawaii.

I gradually stopped being grateful on paper (but never in my heart), and my kids have never learned the art of proper thank you note writing. Now that they're older and can bathe and wipe themselves (well, at least most of them can most of the time), I've realized with horror that this essential life skill is an unknown entity to my kids. I'm sure my mom is ashamed. I know my aunts and uncles are appalled. No one is as embarrassed as I am, though.

We're going to sit down as a family tomorrow and pray to God to help us learn to write a proper thank you note.

"The Great Unknown"

Perhaps one of our most disturbing lack-of-God stories came from overhearing a conversation between 3-year-old George and his best friend, Luke.

And the conversation went like this:

LUKE: I don't like Jesus.

GEORGE: Who's Jesus?

It's tough to argue which stance is more disturbing. To know and recognize Jesus and then to decide that you just don't like Him? Or to not even know who He is? Yeah, that's bad on multiple levels.

"Hallelujah"

Our past Easter was an affair to remember. It started out a bit shaky, though, when we opened our Paas Tattoo Egg Kit (specifically chosen for the tattoos) to discover that the tattoos had been carelessly omitted from this particular box. In the spirit of the holiday, however, we decided not to send a scathing letter to Paas quality control, rose above it, and dyed some spectacular eggs despite.

And you know what else we did?

We went to church.

For some, this isn't a monumental feat. It is, in fact, a weekly occurrence akin to going to the grocery store or mowing the lawn. People get up on Sunday, get their kids dressed in their finest duds, and drive to their chosen house of worship on a regular basis.

Not so much for the Willis Tribe.

It's truly a Festivus Miracle when were able to make the decision to go, get all the kids up, get everyone dressed and fed, and actually arrive at the church – all on the same day. And somewhere near the beginning of the service.

But we did it. We planned, we executed, we sang the Hallelujah Chorus. Chris and I even sang the soprano and bass parts from memory, just like we used to in Chamber Choir. It was a sight to behold.

And after we came home, and I did the laundry, and put away the dishes, and paid the bills (okay, I opened the bills), I succumbed to the lure of the couch. With Lucy.

After I arose from my glorious Easter nap, we played Life Twists and Turns and Eye Spy Snap. The kids watched Easter movies, and we all ate too much chocolate.

A fine Easter, indeed.

"Scary Jesus"

There's been a lot of Jesus talk in our house lately. No, we haven't started going back to church on a regular basis. That would definitely interfere with our Sunday morning coffee-drinking laziness.

But with the kids in "The Greatest Christmas Pageant Ever," with the Christmas season in full gear, and with us using the Lord's name in vain far too frequently, Jesus is getting a lot of face time in our house these days.

Which reminds me of my favorite Jesus and Mary Claire story.

Remember not too long ago when Mary Claire had trouble sleeping in her own bed? Remember when we'd trip over her in the morning because she'd set up a campsite on our bedroom floor? Remember when my eyes were glazed over for days on end because she'd regularly tap me on the head at 3:00 AM and ask to get in bed with me? Remember when Chris would yell at her to go back to bed and she'd cry loudly enough to wake up the boys, the dogs, the mice, AND the fish?

Remember those days? Me, too.

During Mary Claire's Sleepless Phase, we had many discussions about her safety and security. We assured her that we'd wake up if we heard anything funny in the house, that the dogs would bark if there was an intruder, that we would never let anything happen to her, that Bloody Mary was just a story, that Jesus was always with her and that she, therefore, didn't need to be afraid.

Well, apparently, the Jesus-Always-Being-With-Her story? It stuck.

The next night, she came into my room in the wee hours of the morning, and her little heart was beating out of her chest.

"I'm afraid, Mommy," she said. "Jesus is in my room somewhere, and I can't see him. I don't want him in my room if I can't see him. What if he jumps out and scares me? What if he tries to talk to me? What if I hear him in my closet? Please get him out of my room!"

Can you say, "backfire?"

A friend was recently relaying a story about her eight and six-year-old daughters. They were fighting with each other, rolling around on the floor, and generally causing mayhem with one another.

My friend said to her girls, "Remember that Jesus said 'Do unto others as you would have them do unto you.'"

Her six-year-old emphatically replied, "No, Mommy, that's NOT what Jesus said. He said, 'Do to others whatever they do to you first!'"

We have Scary Jesus and my friend's kids have Vengeful Jesus.

I don't know about them, but perhaps it's time for us to kick up the home-churching a notch or two.

"A God for All"

We joke about "home churching" our kids when friends ask us about our religious beliefs. "Home churching is a lot like home schooling," we explain. "Except that diagramming sentences takes a back seat to God."

But a quick conversation with my BFF this morning made me

think a great deal about why this truly has become our modus operandi.

I was born with Catholicism coursing through my veins. I attended Catholic school for eight years. I wore the plaid, pleated skirt (with my athletic shorts underneath for those high-intensity kickball and dodge ball games), genuflected when appropriate, confessed (most of) my sins to my beloved priest, learned the Ten Commandments under the watchful eye of Sister Helen Therese. I am Catholic. I will always be Catholic. It is part of who I am, just as much as my blue eyes come from my wayward father and my sense of humor comes from my witty and sarcastic mother.

For all eternity, I will be grateful for my Catholic upbringing. I cling to the traditions and teachings of my youth more than I willingly admit. Do I believe everything the Catholic church teaches? Not by a long shot. But I believe in the beauty, the wonder, the tradition, the mystique of Catholicism. Always have. Always will.

Chris was raised in the Methodist church. He won't admit to it now, but as a teenager, he did the Methodist church tour as part of a singing duo known as "Christian and Quick." (And he'll be less than pleased with me for revealing that.) I share that particular detail, however, to illuminate the fact that he was not just a Sunday morning Methodist. He was a METHODIST. His belief system was as integral a part of his youth as mine was.

And therein lies the rub.

When we first began talking about marriage, religion continued to rear its ugly head. As a good Catholic girl, I swore I would never raise my kids anywhere but in the arms of those who had received all the same sacraments I had. As a staunch Methodist boy, he was unwilling to comply.

And that, my friends, was nearly the beginning of the end.

So, what did I do? I prayed. I said the Rosary. I communed with the Holy Spirit, I drank a lot. I asked God for guidance.

And His answer surprised me.

Because I found myself releasing my vise grip on the beliefs taught to me via my beloved organized religion. I didn't release my grip on my own beliefs, just on some of the teachings that never really settled well with me to begin with.

And that was the beginning of a long journey of religious reflection.

In college, I studied Catholicism, Judaism, Buddhism, Lutheranism. If it was organized and had a name, I couldn't get enough of it. I read the Bible, both as an instrument of faith and as a work of literature.

My own religion, in turn, became more internalized, more private, more reverent.

But my God never changed.

I went to Methodist churches, Lutheran churches, Episcopalian churches.

And my God never changed.

My realization wasn't earth-shattering, but it was a personal awakening. I believe in God. Not the Catholic God. Not Buddha. Not Jehovah. But God. My God. In all His many forms.

Do I believe that my God is the only God? Well, I believe that there is just one God. But who am I to say that He doesn't manifest himself in different ways to different people across the earth? Perhaps the Native Americans saw Him as the wind and the rain. And perhaps that windy, rainy God was the same God that I rely on every day of my life.

My big personal awakening was that I don't believe in a religion. I believe in God. I believe in a moral compass that guides my life and the lives of my children. (Well, all my children except for George. We'll still working on that one.) God, for me, does not equal religion. God is goodness, kindness, acceptance, love. He is the Golden Rule.

My belief system may not be right. But I did not come by it lightly. I will never take it for granted, and I would never force it onto someone else.

I would much rather live my life, my faith, my beliefs by my actions than by my words. Will I fuck it up? Most certainly. That's part of being human. (So is my inclination toward profanity.)

The funny thing about me is that I love to go to church. A traditional Mass thrills me to no end. I love to see how other people celebrate their own individual beliefs. I must admit I'm not a big fan of the big screen TV churches. I prefer the quaint quiet of a musty chapel and an intricately carved crucifix. But I would never begrudge anyone the joy of worshipping where they are most comforted, where they are most secure.

It's just that for me, that some place tends to be with my kids and my husband and the other people I hold most dear. Sometimes it's in our home, sometimes it's riding our bikes, sometimes it's camping in the woods, sometimes it's playing Scrabble in Brown County. My sanctuary – and where I feel closest to my God – is when the "religion" part of my religion is not first and foremost.

I understand that writing about God is like opening a Pandora's Box. I might as well say that my political beliefs lean toward socialism and that I have sex with goats. (That got you thinking, didn't it? You're wondering which – if either – of those statements is true, aren't you?)

So, I feel I must state that I don't believe my beliefs are the right way, the only way, the chosen way. I love good, honest, sincere people – black, white, green, Asian, Jewish, bipolar, fat, skinny. It just doesn't matter.

What matters is a kind, caring, generous heart. What matters is that we're all taking this journey together. We're each carving our own path, but those paths – when you look closely at them – really aren't so different after all.

I'll never force you to take my path, but you're always welcome to join me. And if you need me to walk with you for a while, I'm happy to meander your way.

That, to me, is what God is all about.

Adding Insult to Injury

We've Got the ER on Speed Dial

It is better to take many injuries than to give one. ~ *Benjamin Franklin*

"A Ban on Power Tools"

My kids may be accident prone, but they come by it honestly. Chris and I have the scars to prove it. I've got the remains of ten stitches to the forehead that I received while chasing my cousin, Sherri, around the family room and subsequently sliding into the wall. I've got a matching six-stitch scar on my chin from bowling in my saddle shoes and falling on the actual bowling ball – while it was still in my hand.

Chris, however, likes to do injuries Big. And for that reason, he's no longer allowed to use power tools without at least two other people present – one to drive him to the ER, and one to clean up the blood.

When he and I were dating, he spent a lot of time working at the farm (the one we'd eventually live in as newlyweds). He spent many summer days pulling fence posts, trimming tree limbs, mowing acres of overgrown land. During one particular day of labor, he managed to slice through a tree branch with a chainsaw – and then continue on to his own leg. He then drove himself to the hospital to receive ten stitches to the thigh.

During a camping trip a few summers ago, he hit himself with an axe while splitting wood. Not once, my friends, but twice. The first hit left a permanent scar, but didn't require further medical attention. The second hit, however, wasn't quite as simple. By the time we tore down camp the next day, his finger was swollen, hot, throbbing, and generally disgusting. Two rounds of Keflex later, the infection finally healed.

And we can't forget about his broken rib – the one he received when he leaned over the bed of his truck to load up a half-full keg after the Cook-Out/Shoot-Out. Lesson learned? Always empty the keg first.

But my favorite story of all has to be what we now refer to as the Power Saw Incident.

Before we moved into the Willis farmhouse, we did a lot of preparatory work. Chris and his friends tore out a false ceiling, moved a wall, cut and installed new baseboards and moldings, and my mom and I spent many hours cleaning, painting, and decorating.

Our bedroom was fashioned in a French country style. (Not ducks, I liked to explain, but provincial.) We painted the floor with a faux-brick pattern, bought a beautiful patchwork quilt from Pottery Barn, and

Chris was building a closet for me – complete with sliding doors designed to look like antique barn doors.

He was working on these doors in the detached garage one beautiful Sunday afternoon when I heard him call me with some urgency. I left Mom with the paintbrushes and went out to see what he needed.

What I saw, instead, was a scene straight out of a horror movie.

Chris's hand was wrapped in blood-soaked towels, and blood had sprayed over the expanse of the garage and all of its contents.

"I need to go to the hospital," he explained calmly. "I checked the floor, and none of my fingers are there, but I don't want to unwrap my hand because I'm losing a lot of blood."

Oh, God, I prayed. Don't let me faint. Don't let me faint. Don't let me vomit. Don't let me faint.

My mom stepped out onto the porch for her beloved cigarette and called over to us.

"Is everything okay?"

"No, Mom," I explained. "Chris cut his hand on the table saw. I need to take him to the hospital. Will you be okay without me?"

"Honey, why don't you let me drive?" she asked, sensing the shakiness in my voice.

"Oh, Jesus," Chris whispered under his breath. "I'll bleed to death before I get there if your mom drives. I need you to drive me," he insisted. "But I need you to drive me safely. Please don't freak out on the way."

And so the three of us loaded up into his truck and I barreled down the gravel road toward the hospital, shifting with all the skill of a 15-year-old driver's education student.

He ended up only needing five stitches, but the amount of blood that he left behind in the garage suggested a massacre of greater proportion. And he contends still that numbing shots to the digits were far more painful than any accident he's ever incurred.

Two days later, Chris interviewed for his first high school mathematics teaching position. He looked dapper in his suit and tie. And his heavily bandaged hand.

When he sat down with the Principal, he broke the ice with this classic line, "It's probably a good thing I'm not interviewing for an industrial tech position, right?"

"Bunk Brothers"

Because the apartment in Muncie was so small and because we believed our boys were old enough – despite manufacturer warnings to the contrary – we purchased bunk beds for them when they were four and two.

I'm sure it will come as no surprise when I tell you that we were jolted from our TV watching reverie one evening with a loud crash and Sam's howls of pain.

Not only had he wriggled past the wooden guard rail and fallen out of the bunk, he'd managed to land on an end table, thus truly capitalizing on his accident experience.

We carried him gingerly to the bathroom, checked for broken bones, and watched in horror as welts and bruises began forming all over his battered little body.

I picked up the phone and called Dr. Andrews.

"We don't see any signs of broken bones," I explained, "but he's bruising quite a bit. I'm afraid there's something we might not be seeing."

"You need to take him to the ER," Dr. Andrews instructed calmly. "They need to make sure he doesn't have any internal injuries. But Honey, be prepared for them to ask you some pointed questions about how this happened. A badly bruised four-year-old is bound to raise some red flags."

Abuse? Were the hospital employees going to consider us potential abusers? The thought of it made me nauseous as I plucked Mary Claire out of her crib and zipped up Gus's jacket. Chris carried Sam tentatively in his arms, and we made our way to Ball Memorial Hospital.

By the time the doctor came in to examine Sam, he had calmed down and was back to his charming self. He giggled during the examination and willingly showed the doctor all the spots that hurt the most.

"Now, Sam," the good doctor began, "I want to ask you some questions. And I want you to answer them, not Mom and Dad." He glanced at us to make sure we understood. "Is that okay with you?"

"Okay," Sam agreed as Mary Claire babbled to herself.

"How did you get hurt, Sam?"

"I fell out of my bunk bed."

"Did you fall onto anything?"

"My table. And I broke my lamp, too."

"Were your parents in your room?"

"No, they were watching TV."

"Is there anything else you'd like to tell me?"

Sam thought for a minute.

"Well," he began in his old-man way, "I've decided I'm never going to do that again."

"Do what again?" the doctor asked kindly.

"Try to spit on my brother from the top bunk."

My face burned with embarrassment and surprise.

"Is that what you were doing?"

"Yeah. I leaned over to try to spit on him, but I slid out of the bed instead."

Oh, dear God.

"Yes, Sam," the doctor agreed, "I think it would be best if you didn't try that again."

"Fragile Fingers"

In his defense, George wasn't really running with scissors. He was making paper snowflakes. Nevertheless, he ran some ultra-sharp scissors into the base of his left index finger right before we called the kiddos up for bed.

Apparently, he hit a major artery (do you have one of those in your index finger?) because there was so much blood. I'm not kidding – it was geyser-like. The kids were all screaming in the basement, "George cut himself! He's bleeding! He's bleeding!" I was hoping to get a two-for-one deal at the hospital because I was quite sure Mary Claire was going to have to be treated for hysteria. (Her emotions tend to get a little raw and uncontrolled, just like her mama's.) But God love that girl, she was into the band-aids immediately like a good little nurse. Only we didn't need band-aids, we needed highly absorbent towels.

After numerous x-rays, the good doc at the ER determined that George did not damage anything internally. It's just a deep puncture wound – no stitches necessary – and we need to keep our eyes peeled for signs of infection.

The interesting twist to this story is that George's best buddy, Luke, was at the hospital just last week with a thumb injury. He walked out with six stitches and multiple highly painful digit shots.

Now sit down and grab a cup of joe, because this story is a good one.

Luke had just returned from the grocery store with his family where he was treated to a new toothbrush and a new tube of toothpaste.

He promptly told his mother that he was going to "oweganizth hith thtuff."

What exactly does that mean? According to Jackie, that means he wipes his bathroom counter down with Lysol and neatly lines up all his "products."

Yes, he has product. He's the only six-year-old metrosexual that we know.

He has deodorant, hair gel, various and sundry lotions and creams, and of course, his new toothpaste. Apparently, all that product is working. One look at his beautiful face proves that something is most definitely working.

So, the story goes that he was trying to open his new toothpaste to no avail when he decided to grab his trusty pocketknife for assistance.

The knife made both an entry wound and an exit wound. He stuck that baby clear through the meat of his thumb, just barely missing his tendon.

Oh, those boys.

And to add to the irony, right before George's Scissor Incident, he was delivering Cub Scout popcorn with his dad. And what did George choose as his popcorn sales incentive prize?

A pocketknife.

"Oh, Snap"

Snap.

That's the sound Sam's clavicle made at 11:30 PM after a Colts home game. Thanks to our kind friend and former youth football coach, we had first row seats at the game – right in front of the cheerleaders (much to my boys' delight). And we were granted the opportunity for the kids to run on the field afterwards. The running quickly became a pick-up football game, which resulted in the first official Willis broken bone. The six of us hung out at the St. Vincent's Peyton Manning Children's Hospital until 3:00 AM just to solidify the complete Colts experience.

Alas, our friend, Peyton, did not make a post-game appearance.

After his accident, Sam had spent some time reconciling with the early end of his first travel basketball season. But his sadness was assuaged with the knowledge that he can still bowl on the Wii.

Thank heaven for small miracles.

Parent of the Year Awards

There's Always Next Year...

If you must hold yourself up to your children as an object lesson, hold yourself up as a warning and not as an example. ~ *George Bernard Shaw*

"All Spanked Out"

There are two very distinct phases of my parenting life. Jackie likes to refer to the early years as the "Farm Trina" era. Farm Trina was a parenting badass. She didn't stand for any sass, didn't put a kid to bed any later than 8:00 PM, and was always ready with a quick finger flick when her precious brood got out of line.

Fast-forward to now. Farm Trina has gone soft. After four babies, endless amounts of diapers, potty-training debacles, and preschool tantrums, Farm Trina has lost her edge. Now she's simply Me.

Case in point:

During one of George's inappropriate dinnertime soliloquies in which he was most likely discussing:

A. Poop

B. Farts

C. Butts

D. All of the Above,

Sam pointed out that in my prime, I would have spanked him (Sam) faster than the speed of sound for the same behavior and then ushered him promptly to bed – without dinner.

Those were the days.

Farm Trina would have definitely given George a swift smack to the rear and sent him to bed hungry. The current, much milder me is the one we like to refer to as "new and improved thanks to the magic of pharmaceuticals."

The simple truth is that I'm too damn tired to discipline like I used to. Let's face it – after I've worked out at 5:00 AM, gotten four kids dressed and on the bus, made two grocery store runs (because I forgot something the first time around), paid a couple of late bills online, drunk two McDonald's Diet Cokes (requiring two separate jaunts to Mickey D's), signed five different permission slips, written a couple of data sheets, cleaned up dog vomit, booked a summer vacation for a family of six, fed the mice, done three loads of laundry, written a chapter of the Great American Novel, made dinner, scrapbooked a couple of pages, wasted way too much voyeuristic time on Facebook, worked through some third grade story problems, administered spelling quizzes, unloaded and reloaded the dishwasher, and eaten a sleeve of Oreos, I'm TIRED.

My legs are tired, my brain is tired, my eyes are tired. Hell, even my uterus is tired.

So that, dear Sam, is why you drew the short disciplinary straw. It is why you are polite, well-mannered, amiable, smart, and charming. It is why your baby brother is loud, obnoxious, rude, sullen, and inappropriate.

You learned all those positive life lessons in the heart of home. George will have to learn them in reform school.

"Speech Therapy"

Mary Claire has the Mother of All Speech Impediments. She can't say her "S's." When she tries, it results in something resembling a "Th" with a bit of spit dangling off the end. As a little side note, she has some trouble with her "R's," too. Think Wabbit.

And to add insult to injury, she had the following litany of teachers before she even reached first grade:

1. Mrs. Hoops, preschool

2. Mrs. Corich, preschool

3. Mrs. Herbst, kindergarten

When she would come home from kindergarten, Chris and I would ask about her day.

"What did Mitthuth Hubtht teach you today?"

"We leawned about dinothauws. They make me vewy newvouth."

And being the stellar parents that we are, we'd giggle.

Every day, it was the same. We'd ask about Mary Claire's day, and she'd expound with her broken "S's" and "R's."

Finally, one day she became irritated.

"I have a quethon fow you guyth," she spat – literally. Her baby blues were wide and her chubby hands placed dramatically on her hips for emphasis.

"Why you call Mitthuth Hubtht 'Mitthuth Hubtht' when hew *name* ith Mitthuth Hubtht?!"

And, dear readers, if you can answer that particular question with a straight face, I'll hand over my Mother of the Year Award to you.

"Rock Stars and Double Digits"

When Sam turned 11, we engaged in this scintillating conversation:

ME: Aren't you excited about being double-digits?

SAM: I was double-digits last year.

ME (in a lame attempt to think on my feet): Yes, but now you're same double-digits.

SAM (walking away while shaking his head sadly): Mom, sometimes I worry about you.

Me, too, Sam. Me, too.

For Sam's 11th birthday, we took him to see his rock idol, John Mellencamp, at Conseco fieldhouse. I actually joined the Cherry Bomb Club to get pre-sale tickets. With my official Cherry Bomb Club membership, I was also eligible to enter a contest to win band "Meet and Greet" passes. And believe it or not, I won.

Sam and I were sitting in the stands waiting for the Meet and Greet to start while Amber and Chris sipped lattes in the nearest Starbucks and waited for us. These rocker gals walked up to us and offered us backstage passes (apparently because Sam was so darn cute and I mentioned that it was his birthday).

Before I continue this story, I should note in the spirit of full disclosure that I'm madly in love with John Mellencamp and his bad boy self. He's on My List. You know, the same List that John Mayer and Dave Matthews share the number one spot on. The List of men I would leave my husband for if they came knocking. Because it could happen.

With impressive, all-access passes around our necks, we sprinted to the backstage party room. (Well, I did the sprinting and Sam was merely dragged along behind me.) When they let us in, we were surrounded by very darkly tanned men with very diamond-clad necklaces and women who had bigger collagen-enhanced lips than my ass. Seriously. We sat down and tried to act cool.

Before I knew it, Elaine Irwin Mellencamp had sidled over beside me. Okay, so she doesn't actually sidle. She glides on air. She is the most beautiful, graceful, stunning, head-turning human being I've ever laid eyes on.

And her ass is as big as my big toe. No, it's as big as my middle toe.

I pointed her out to Sam (discreetly, of course) and told him to drink her in. Assured him that he'd never again have an opportunity to sit beside a woman this stunningly beautiful unless he learned to play the guitar like Jimi Hendrix.

Then we saw John.

He stood outside the party room door and I was afraid to breathe because I didn't want to scare him away.

But he never came in. He came close — within 20 feet. And if I'd had a few drinks, I might have thrown myself at him and willed the security guards to do their worst. But instead, I just stared. At him. And his wife.

And I'm pretty sure she's on My List now, too.

"Good Mother"

Not so very long ago, I asked my friend, Mary, if she enjoyed Sue Miller's book, "The Good Mother." And Mary quite vehemently replied,

"I didn't like it. She had sex in the same bed her daughter was sleeping in. I don't think she was a very good mother."

Okay, so I've never had sex in the same room with my kids. (Except, of course, when each of them was conceived. And whether they were actually "in" the room with me at that moment is a question for the pro-choicers and the pro-lifers to duke out. Okay, and I might have had marital relations in a shared vacation hotel room with the tide crashing in the background after one too many glasses of red dinner wine. But I digress.)

Regardless, I'm pretty sure I'm not a very good mother.

And here's why.

I lambasted my kids this afternoon. Umm. Lambasted might be an understatement. After one too many piles of dirty underwear lying around on the floor in search of the elusive laundry basket that was two inches away... after one too many spills of McDonald's soft drinks in the Suburban because they weren't deposited in the trash cans that were two inches away in the garage... after one too many pairs of shoes that were run over in the garage because they weren't put back into the appropriate shoe drawer that was two inches from the entryway... after one too many stinky, mildewy towels on the floor because they weren't hung on the hook that was two inches away… Well, quite frankly, I lost my shit. I think I even said "ass" (or something like it) while I was screaming.

Okay! Okay! I did say "ass!" I yelled the word "ass!" I yelled it at my kids. Like this:

"I'm sick and tired of working my ass off all day long just so I can come home and be your maid! I'm your mother, not your damn housekeeper! And I'm tired of living in a pigsty! You kids are old enough to be contributing members of this household and to take care of your own shit!"

That's pretty much verbatim.

Unfortunately, it didn't stop there. Poor Amber and Andy were here while the tirade spiraled out of control. They avoided all eye contact as they hastily cleaned up spilled drinks and shepherded the kids to the car. In total silence.

Once in the Suburban, the yelling and picking didn't end. Oh, no. Ask my husband. It goes on… and on… and on. Forever.

I actually said to Sam a couple of times, "Take those damn headphones off! I'm not done yelling at you yet! And what in the hell are you all crying about?!"

In hindsight, I'd probably classify that as a rhetorical question. I'm pretty sure I know what they were crying about.

Once my head stopped spinning around like a wobbly, unstable, unmedicated top, I actually felt a wee bit bad about my three-year-old behavior (if, of course, you know any three-year-olds with a mouth like a sailor). But I didn't apologize. I get that directly from my mother. That unapologetic gene ran straight from her uterus through my umbilical cord and wedged itself right into the blackest little corner of my soul.

They deserved it, I rationalized. Those precious little faces deserved to have their crazy mother curse at them for misplaced underwear, didn't they? So, it could have been worse? Right?

Be careful how you answer. Are you a good mother?

"Pre-Teen"

My firstborn, ten-pound bundle of joy that turned our world upside down and ushered us into the adventure known as parenthood. That smiling bundle of joy draped in spit-up bibs and swaddled in baby blue blankets. Our gift from God, the love of our lives, the beautiful boy who turned heads everywhere we went...

He's 12.

And although I will always love him unconditionally... Although he is permanently etched into my own heart... Although I wouldn't hesitate to lay down my life for him...

I must admit that I don't always like him.

Say, for instance, like today. On the basketball court.

Or this evening at the dinner table.

It's not his long, unruly hair (although tonight I was tempted to grab my scrapbooking scissors and shear him like Samson), it's not even his burgeoning pre-teen acne, or the jeans that are always just a smidge too small.

It's that shit ass attitude.

Sometimes Sam can be the kindest, sweetest, wittiest, most engaging kid on the planet. And other times... Well, other times he's just a dick.

Yes, I just called my son a dick. If it's good enough for his dad, it's good enough for him, too.

This parenting into the teenage years is going to be challenging for me. I'm much better with poopy diapers and ear infections. I'd even go through potty training again to avoid this sullen, disrespectful, woe-is-me, pre-teen angst.

(And those of you who know me well will surely remember that potty training was my own personal circle of Hell.)

When we have four teenagers in the house? And one of them is a GIRL?

Well, then, may God have mercy on us all.

"Slumber Party for Scaredy Cats"

I had a visitor in my room last night. And the night before that. And the one before that. He would roll over and die if he knew I was telling you this story, but it's just so coincidental how the apple never falls far from the tree. I feel it's my duty to share.

Although Sam is nearly a teenager, he's definitely not a lion heart. In so many ways, I love this about him. He's sensitive, he's kind (most of the time), he's aware of other people's feelings. But on the not-so-positive side, he's a scaredy-cat – just like his mama.

Earlier this week, Sam thought it would be a good idea to watch a snippet of "A Haunting." His rationale? It was on The Discovery Channel. Surely anything on The Discovery Channel wouldn't scar him for life, right? Wrong.

Five minutes of "A Haunting" was enough to do him in. He can't sleep, can't turn his lights off, can't get it together when it's time to go to bed. In short, he's a mess.

Last night, he came into my room requesting sanctuary from his imagination. Because I'm pretty sure it's all kinds of inappropriate to let my near-teenager sleep with me in my bed, I told him he could bring his sleeping bag in and camp out on the floor.

Of course, I had a hidden agenda.

As many who know and love me understand, I'm obsessing over the notion of applying for a Creative Writing MFA program. Bennington College – the alma mater of my beloved Donna Tartt – is my number one choice. Bret Easton Ellis also graduated from Bennington, and because I've never read anything he's penned, I thought it would be good to explore some of his work. So at the library yesterday, I picked up "American Psycho."

Not my best idea ever.

In the wee hours of the morning, I was sitting in my bed – sans Chris, who was conferencing in St. Louis – transfixed to the most horrifically disturbing piece of fiction I've ever laid eyes on. And like the train wreck that we can't turn away from, I could not put it down. I was powerless to stop turning the pages, both repulsed by the graphic violence and enmeshed in the satire and brilliance.

The reviews on the book cover proclaimed Mr. Ellis's literary genius. "American Psycho" has been hailed an American classic. Mr. Ellis may be brilliant, his satire spot-on, his dialogue entrancing. And yet, there are incidents in "American Psycho" involving nail guns and live rats that I could have lived a lifetime without envisioning. Those images are now seared into my brain. The work of a genius? Perhaps. But work that I should never have exposed myself to.

Reading this book (or what I could finish before I had to finally put it down – my brain spent, my body shaking) was like watching the movie "Seven." What was so disturbing to me was that someone had to actually create that plot. A work of fiction? Yes. But what happened to the women in "American Psycho" was not anything I could have ever imagined in my wildest, darkest dreams.

And so, when Sam came knocking on my door around midnight, I gladly opened it for him. We were comforted by each other's presence in some twisted, co-dependent way. He had refuge from all ghostly presences, and I was safe from nail gun wielding, psychopathic multi-millionaires.

And neither one of us will be allowed to read or watch anything scarier than "American Idol" (which has it's own brand of creepiness) ever, ever again.

"Welcome to the Jungle"

In third grade, Gus announced that he was going to be Student of the Week.

Excitedly, I asked, "What did you do to earn the Student of the Week title?"

"Nothing," he shrugged. "Everybody gets to do it. It's just my turn."

Kind of like the draft. Or jury duty.

As part of his special week, Gus had to complete a poster about himself. There were pre-fab areas for him to fill in, such as "What's Your Favorite Color," "What Do You Want to Be When You Grow Up," and "Who Is Your Hero?"

I was anxious to see who would be identified as Gus's hero. I was thinking it might be his dad, or one of his grandpas, his favorite author, a Colts player, maybe even his mom.

Silly me.

When I looked at his completed poster, I nearly choked on my coffee.

Gus's hero?

Slash.

Of Gus 'N Roses fame.

Somewhere in the past nine years, we've gone terribly wrong with that kid.

Welcome to the jungle, Baby.

"Spelling Bee Champ"

Mary Claire needed a little help with her homework on the night of our 14th wedding anniversary, and I was a bit frazzled during the "Witching Hour" as we call it around here. I'd fed the kids a quick dinner at Subway (plain turkey sandwiches sans condiments with a side of sand just to make sure they were dry enough), rushed home to supervise homework, was planning to take Sam to his football game, take The Littles to play practice, meet the babysitter at the football game at 8:00 for a kid hand-off, and then sneak away for a late night anniversary dinner with my beloved of 14 years.

We were on a schedule.

Mary Claire sat at the table while I scurried around like the Tasmanian Devil.

"Mom," she asked innocently, "how do you spell sick?"

"S.I.C.K.," I replied quickly as I threw a load of laundry in the washer.

"No," she argued, "not sick! SICK!"

"S.I.C.K.," I repeated, the annoyance in my voice quite evident to everyone in the house who had ears.

"No, Mom," she wailed, "I need you to spell SICK!"

"Mary Claire!" I shouted, "I have spelled it for you twice! What are you trying to ask me?? Are you trying to say 'six'?"

"No, Mom," she said as tears filled her big, blue eyes, "I need to spell siiiiccccckkk."

As if saying it much more slowly would cause me to understand. And maybe even be – oh, what's the word I'm looking for?

Motherly?

Chris, sensing that I was about to lose my cool, quickly intervened.

"Honey, use that word in a sentence for me," he requested. (He's such a damn teacher.)

She was sniffling audibly and wiping her eyes, grateful at long last for an adult who didn't yell at her in her hour of need.

"The storm clouds were dark and sick."

"You mean 'thick,'" he concluded. "Th...th...th...Get your tongue out in front there, Sweetie. Th...th...th."

"It's T.H.I.C.K.," I replied curtly.

I mean, if he's going to take all the credit for being nice and patient, then I'm at least going to pull out my spelling prowess.

Sheesh.

"Den Mother"

Gus has found his new calling. And it's just what Chris and I were hoping would not be his forte. Yup. He's a Cub Scout. And darn proud of it. Because I've coached Sam's basketball team, I thought it best to even the score by offering to be a Cub Scout Den Leader for Gus.

And then I found out I had to wear The Shirt.

Oh, the sacrifices we make for our flesh and blood.

After finishing our first popcorn sale extravaganza, Gus ended up as the second highest seller in our Den. What he might lack in charisma, he more than makes up for in tenacity when door-to-door selling is involved. He wasn't afraid to go for the sale, no matter what the response, and I think he eventually wore most of his customers down with suggestions of a less expensive product, or a Christmas present, or a donation to the soldiers overseas. Whatever his formula, it worked.

I thought for sure that when it came time to pick his sales prize, he would choose the much-coveted Marshmallow Blaster. But, alas, when the final decision was upon him, he opted instead for the Buck Knife.

The long-anticipated knife arrived at the next Tribe Meeting. In his gangly and uncoordinated way, he ripped that baby out of the box and wielded it like a sword. He couldn't have been prouder. I thought it would be a flimsy, dime-store knock-off, but it's sharper than anything in my kitchen.

We had a long talk about when he's able to use the knife (only when Chris and I are with him), where he's able to use the knife (to whittle at home or while we're camping), and that he's NEVER EVER allowed to take it to school.

To which he replied, "I KNOW that, Mom. Jeez. If I take it to school, my teacher might think I want to STAB someone."

Okay, Gus. Something like that.

That treasured knife was his constant companion for the next three days. He couldn't have been prouder if he'd won the Nobel Prize. But we kept the ER on standby just in case.

"Once an Editor, Always an Editor"

I have the sweetest daughter in the world.

Yesterday, she handed me a carefully constructed, scallop-edged, handmade card that read (verbatim):

"Dear Mom. You are soooooo sweat and kind. I love you and I see whats in side you. Your the best mom!"

My eyes welled up, and I hugged that girl close while I showered her sweet-smelling head with kisses. I thanked her a million times and hung the card on the magnetic strip by my kitchen desk. She went back downstairs with a huge smile on her pretty, freckled, little face.

Then I resisted the very strong urge to grab my red pen and fix the misspellings and grammatical errors.

"Dear God, it's Katrina. There's something seriously wrong with me…"

"The Power of Pharmaceuticals"

Every day at 9:00 AM, my Blackberry rings to the tune of Jason Mraz's "I'm Yours" as a reminder to take my happy pill.

It's an interesting – albeit unplanned – statement, I think, that I chose "I'm Yours" as my reminder song. As in, "I'm yours, Little Green Pill. Do with me what you will. Mold me into the happy-go-lucky girl my family and friends love. Keep my blood pressure down and save my kids from an OCD-induced, toilet-scrubbing, banister-sanitizing, out-of-the-wild-blue-yonder cleaning frenzy."

"Mommy," Mary Claire asked during a Saturday morning jaunt to the baseball fields, "why does that song play every day on your phone?"

"It's a reminder for me to take my medicine," I replied.

"Why do you have to take medicine every day?"

"It helps me to not be so anxious."

"What's anxious?"

"Well," I stumbled, "you know how sometimes my voice gets a little loud? And my face gets red? And I yell at you kids even though you don't really deserve it?"

"Yes!" Gus, Mary Claire, and George all responded in unison.

"My medicine helps keep me from overreacting like that. It makes me yell less."

Without missing a beat, Mary Claire replied, "I think DADDY needs to take that medicine, too.

"Yeah," Gus added, "I think he needs to take THREE of those a day."

"Crazy Crocs"

On the morning of Crazy Dress Day at Pleasant View Elementary, George proudly announced, "I'm going to wear my Crocs backward."

Okay. Whatever that means.

"And I'm going to wear the mullet wig and wear my shirt backwards and inside out." That, I could understand.

"Honey," I said calmly, "I'm not sure what 'wearing your Crocs backwards' means, but you need to wear socks because it's cold outside today."

"But I caaaaaaan't wear socks with my Crocs backwards," my six-year-old whined. And because I was busy packing lunches and finger-combing wigs for The Middles, I dropped it.

Then the daily Morning Crunch began. After much breakfast dawdling and bickering over cereal choices and general 8:00 AM grumpiness, we were cutting it close to bus-arrival time, and I was (surprisingly enough) running low on patience.

"Two minutes until the bus comes," I announced and The Middles scrambled to get jackets and backpacks arranged.

And then there was George.

Sitting on the garage floor and trying (need I say unsuccessfully?) to shove his bare foot into his backwards Croc. I can't even accurately describe what he was attempting to do. You're just going to have to go with me on this one.

"George, I told you that isn't going to work," I snapped. "Now run upstairs and get some socks. You can get mismatched socks if you want. But hurry up because you're going to miss the bus."

He threw himself to the ground.

"But I've worn them backwards before!" he wailed. "Why isn't it working nooooooooow?"

"George," I yelled, "we don't have time for this! Now get upstairs and get some socks on!"

And the wretched sobbing commenced.

"If you DO NOT get moving RIGHT NOW, I'm going to give you something to cry about!"

I have become my mother.

And so he stomped upstairs amidst heaving sobs of defeat because his backwards-Crocs plan was thwarted on Crazy Dress Day.

"Now stand with your brother and sister and SMILE!" I shouted as I commemorated the occasion with my new fancy camera. And so we have a picture that will last forever. One with three of my kids standing side-by-side in wigs and hats and mismatched clothes. The two bigger kids smiling wildly and the littlest one with red-rimmed eyes and a look on his face that plainly says, "My mom is a bitch."

The stuff memories are made of.

"Life's Big Questions"

I've never claimed to have all the answers. And yet, my kids continue to ask questions. Incessantly. Now, I know that curiosity is a good thing. And I love that their little wheels are turning. But sometimes, the constant interrogation brings me to my knees. Here's just a sampling of a few I've received in the past few weeks, most completely random and out of context:

1. Why can I taste Afrin in my mouth after you spray it in my nose?

2. How does Dad get the star on top of the Christmas tree?

3. What's for dinner?

4. Why does Lucy shed so much?

5. Can I have a snack?

6. When can we go to the waterslide pool?

7. When can we go back to Disney?

8. When is dinner?

9. Why does the sun always set on the same side?

10. Why does Johnny fart so much?

11. Can I have a snack?

12. Why can't I fall asleep?

13. When are we going to Nana and Bob's?

14. Can I have a glass of water?

15. Why is George so annoying?

16. Why do you listen to sappy love songs all the time?

17. Can I have a snack?

18. Why do I have to eat vegetables?

19. Is macaroni and cheese healthy?

20. Why can dogs poop in the yard when we have to use the bathroom?

21. Why don't we ever fly on a plane?

22. What's a mortgage?

23. Why do you call Daddy an ass?

24. Why do curling irons get hot?

25. Were you alive when George Washington was alive?

26. Why don't you ever stop singing?

27. If you publish a book, are we going to be in it?

28. Why did you pick Daddy to marry?

29. Do guinea pigs go to heaven?

30. How do you know you're clean when you're done wiping?

And that's just a smattering. I realize that I could open up some really good dialogue and embrace some strong teachable moments with a lot of those questions. And sometimes I try. And inevitably, in the middle of explaining the structure of a sinus cavity, the questioner has moved on to question #847. And then I'm left just talking to myself. Which was all fine and good before I started taking the medication, but now...

I often want to just scream, "I don't know all the answers!" But those of you who know me well know that I would never admit to not having all the answers. And I'm reminded of my friend who gave that very answer to her young son. His reply?

"Maybe if you'd asked all the questions when you were little, then you'd know all the answers."

That's tough to argue.

"I Can See Clearly Now"

Two of our kids wear glasses. Four of them probably need them. We'll figure it out someday.

Sam got his glasses in first grade. His teacher first brought it to our attention, thought that perhaps we should have him evaluated. He didn't seem to see very well from a distance, couldn't always read what she'd written on the board.

He was, in fact, more nearsighted than me. And I've worn glasses since college.

When we got him his first pair of glasses, the drive home was a miracle to him.

"Mom, I can read that billboard!" he said.

"Mom, I can see that road sign from here!"

"Mom, the trees actually have leaves, not just little blobs of green!"

You'd have thought we'd learned our lesson. But not yet.

Gus was in second grade when he began complaining about headaches. He'd go to the nurse day after day. And day after day, we'd get a phone call about Gus's latest visit.

"Gus, why are you going to the nurse every day?" I asked. "Is someone bothering you? Are you having trouble with your work? Are you trying to get away from someone?"

"No, Mom," he denied. "I have headaches every day. It feels good to lie down."

"Gus, you need to stop spending so much time in the nurse's office," I instructed. "You're going to fall behind in your school work. You're going to have to suck it up and get back to business."

"Okay," my compliant little boy agreed. Because that's what Gus does. He complies.

And when we took him for his annual eye exam over the summer? He got glasses. And you know what else? He stopped having headaches.

When Mary Claire starts complaining, perhaps we'll listen. Maybe we won't get it until it's George's turn.

Maybe we'll never get it.

"Setting a Good Example"

Gus doesn't speak much, but we've learned that he listens.

To everything.

Intently.

While loading the troops up in the car one day for a fun family outing, Sam crawled to the back seat and asked Gus to close the Suburban door.

Gus grumbled as he unstrapped himself to reach the handle. He slammed the door with authority.

"Damn it," he mumbled, "I have to do everything around here!"

"What did you say, Gus?" I asked.

His face turned red.

"Whaaaat? YOU say it!"

Touche.

"Well, Gus," I explained, trying to hold on to a shred of my parental authority, "even if you've heard me say it, I don't want you saying it. We shouldn't say those kinds of things in this family."

"Yeah!" George piped from the backseat. "Because when Mom says it, she says '*God*damn it!'"

Getting Away From It All

Or At Least Packing It Up and Taking It Somewhere Else

Find what brings you joy and go there. ~ Jan Phillips

"Dreams of Disney"

When the kids were 6, 4, 3, and 1 (and the one-year-old was not yet walking), Chris and I decided it would be a good time to take a summer trip to Disney World.

We've never been known for our smart planning.

But we persevered. We booked adjoining rooms at the All-Star Sports hotel, we bought three-day Park Hopper tickets, we loaded up the Suburban, and we began our journey.

With four kids under the age of six.

To the Happiest Place on Earth.

In our defense, there were some more than magical moments. When Mary Claire saw the parade of princesses, I thought she might pass out from excitement. When George touched a life-sized, furry version of

Tigger at a character breakfast, he squealed with delight. When the boys embarked on the Dumbo ride? Pure, unadulterated bliss.

One day while leaving our hotel rooms, we spotted an armadillo resting under a nearby bush.

"Wow, Sam," I remarked. "I've never seen a live armadillo!"

"Yeah," he agreed, peering closely, "I've never seen a dead one, either."

Of course, we didn't really think about how hot it would be in Orlando in late July. And we didn't really consider the fact that George would be strapped to one of us in his Baby Bjorn the entire time we were there. But the pictures are a good reminder. When we look at our first Disney album now, we're not only shocked by how little the kids are, but by how red all of our faces are. And how sweaty our hair is.

We returned to Disney for a surprise Christmas trip when the kids were 13, 10, 9, and 7. It was an entirely different experience. Instead of spending our time stopping for snacks and waiting in line for Peter Pan's Magical Flight, we Fast-Passed our way through the Rock 'N Roller Coaster, the Tower of Terror, Soarin', Test Track, and Everest. (I can still hear Mary Claire chanting at the top of the hill, "I don't want to see the Yeti. I don't want to see the Yeti. I don't want to see the Yeti.")

Riding the bus back to our Wilderness Cabin, we witnessed a young family fold their strollers up, take their backpacks off, and settle in with their four exhausted, half-asleep children — all under the age of six.

And we marveled at how crazy they were.

At how crazy we are.

"Car Trouble"

We were packed to the gills, locked and loaded, and ready to begin our Myrtle Beach vacation after a short 13-hour drive with our four young children. It all went wrong somewhere in the South Carolina backcountry.

With less than two hours left until we reached Mecca with a beachfront view, the Suburban began to smoke and sputter in the oppressive heat. Surrounded by nothing more than wilted orange cornflowers and a boiling expanse of highway that shimmered in the distance, we pulled over to assess the trouble.

Chris, being the Renaissance man that he is, immediately diagnosed the problem as a coolant hose gone bad. We were losing coolant by the second, and the engine was overheating. Storm clouds were rolling in, the temperature was well into the 90s, and the kids were anxious. We did what any self-respecting family would do. We called AAA.

Problem is that our Triple A membership had expired. So, while Chris was going through the automated renewal process (to the tune of a couple hundred dollars), his cell phone died.

By this time, we were all out of the sweltering car and standing on the deserted roadside. Sweating.

"I'm going to walk back to the last exit and see what I can find," Chris informed us. My head immediately filled with visions of roadside serial killers coming out of the brush to off our entire family.

"No way in hell," I responded. "We're going with you."

So we locked our week's worth of clothes, snacks, and beach paraphernalia into the Suburban and commenced our journey.

After about half a mile of walking and whining, we reached the exit. Mary Claire's blood pressure and general anxiety rose as the storm made its way closer.

As we stood at the exit, a kind, large, loud African American woman pulled up in a very tiny car.

"You babies in trouble??" she shouted.

"We're looking for a gas station or a convenience store," my husband explained. "Do you know where the closest one is?"

"Back that way," she replied, pointing in the direction from which we came. "About four miles."

I tried not to cry as I imagined walking my hot, weary family four miles to the nearest phone.

"I don't usually do this, but because you got the children and all, can I offer you a ride?"

I looked at her car, looked at Chris, looked at my kids, and was instantly rendered unable to make a decision. Would we fit in the car? We didn't have car seats. Would she kidnap, rob, and kill us? Was the four-mile ride to potential safety worth the risk of piling into her micro-machine?

"Yes, thank you," Chris offered. "We would very much appreciate a ride."

Decision made.

I sat in the front with George strapped on my lap. Chris sat in the back with Mary Claire on his lap and Sam and Gus squished in beside him. I'm not sure how many laws we were actually breaking at that given moment, but I suppose desperate times call for desperate measures.

Our savior talked our ears off for the next four miles, and we graciously offered her our last $20 in cash for her troubles. She dropped us at a convenience store – or the closest thing to a convenience store in the South Carolina backcountry – and left us standing bereft and sweaty at the entrance.

We were truly in the middle of nowhere. The only thing we could see for miles was a small, disheveled house next to the store with two elderly black men sitting on a bedraggled golf cart. They eyed us with a mix of curiosity and suspicion as we fell out of the car like circus clowns.

Chris found an outside electrical source for his phone charger and re-connected with Triple A. I took our hot, tired kids into the convenience store and bought them each a frozen treat from a rickety, rusted deep freezer.

Just as we were finishing up our transaction with the cashier who was less than friendly – who, quite frankly, bordered on downright mean – a large bolt of lightning and rumble of thunder knocked the electricity from the small building. The kids cried and spilled ice cream as they tried to crawl onto any available part of my body, and Chris, again, lost his connection with Triple A.

The golf cart duo who had witnessed every second of our convenience store activities offered us a ride on their golf cart. I'm not sure where they were planning to take us, or how they were planning to get us all there, but we politely declined as the kids' cries permeated the silence around us. At this point, you could actually see the line of black clouds slowly making its way toward us. It was menacing, to say the least. And although I tried to tout the wonder of Mother Nature's glory, the kids were not impressed.

"Are we going to diiiiiieeee?" Mary Claire sobbed.

"No, honey, we're not going to die. We're going to see some pretty cool lightning, though."

"Are we going to be hit by liiiiiigghhtniiing?"

"No, honey, that's not going to happen. You have to trust me."

"But we're going to diiiieeeee!"

At that most precious of moments, Chris entered the dark, muggy convenience store to inform us that a taxi was on the way.

Apparently, rental cars were available, but could not be delivered outside a certain radius. And we were definitely outside a certain radius. Hertz may deliver to some, but not to those of us most desperate.

As the storm clouds rolled closer and Mary Claire's sobbing became more edged with hysteria, a long, black sedan circa 1988 pulled into the drive. Our chariot.

Chris loaded me into the taxi with the kids and promised he'd be right behind. Triple A was sending a tow truck, and he'd grab a cab once the car was unloaded. Reluctant as I was to leave him in the middle of that God-forsaken place, I knew I had to get Mary Claire to the condo or risk her long-term mental stability. And by that time, Sam had joined the chorus of fear. The two of them ping-ponged their anxiety back and forth until it had escalated nearly to the point of no return.

Our taxi driver kept us one step ahead of the storm as she told us uncensored stories about her wayward kids and their drug, alcohol, and promiscuity problems. I'm fairly certain my kids learned more about life in that 45-minute trip than they could ever hope to learn in a "Creating Positive Relationships" class in middle school.

With no more cash in hand and a $200 tab on her meter reader, I begged our driver to swing past the ATM machine.

"Please, please, please," I pleaded. "I don't have any cash." I was then torn between leaving my kids as collateral in the car or pulling them out into the eye of the storm while I withdrew a large, unexpected chunk of our vacation fund. While the ATM spit out my twenties, I anxiously glanced at the taxi as I envisioned our driver peeling away from the corner with my precious cargo.

But they were safe. The fare was too much to forfeit.

She dropped us at our destination, and I ushered my tired, anxious kids into the condo lobby. Which was closed. Now, this presented a problem because we were unable to claim the condo key that would grant us our entrance.

"What are we going to dooooo?" the kids wailed.

Fueled by desperation, I catapulted myself over the counter and began to check all the drawers, most of which were locked up tight. With the security camera pointed right at me, I began to fashion my explanation for the police report. And then. A drawer opened. And in the middle of the drawer was a key. With our condo number tagged on it.

Miracle of miracles.

In the midst of our convenience store trauma – in between power outages – we were able to reach the dear friend (whose condo we were staying in) to tell her of our travel woes. She contacted her Myrtle Beach-resident parents, and they met us at the condo with an extra car and a grocery bag full of breakfast food and essentials. Like the three wise men bringing gifts to the Baby Jesus, they could not have been a more welcome sight for sore eyes.

And the donuts? That was the only thing that stopped the flow of Mary Claire's tears as the storm came crashing in around us.

While we were carrying the food to the third floor, Chris arrived in his minivan taxi. I died a little inside as I watched him shell out another $200 in cab fare, and he then began to unload our week's worth of clothes and amenities onto the condo lobby floor.

In the process, an entire bottle of rum crashed and shattered all over the tile. I sopped it up with a beach towel – praying that I wouldn't lacerate myself – and was more than a little tempted to suck the remnants directly out of the towel. Kind of like a teething blanket of sorts – for adults. It seemed a damn shame for all that lovely alcohol to go to waste.

"The Way We Were"

There are very few friends we can travel with for extended periods of time, but we find we work well with the Archers and the Zahns. Perhaps it has something to do with the tumblers of red wine that are consumed. That, inevitably, has to make anyone feel a bit more relaxed and affable.

One of our most memorable vacations was a trip to the North Carolina side of the Smoky Mountains where we rented a beautiful mountain-top cabin and ingested far more alcohol than any liver should be subject to.

We hiked in the Smokies, went river rafting, horseback riding, marshmallow roasting, train riding, and ice cream eating into the wee hours of the morning.

Never mind that I nearly had a nervous breakdown driving to the top of the Smokies or that Jackie and Jody lost their cool when wasps invaded their rooms.

While we were gone, Jody sold her house. First day on the market. We got sentimental, a little weepy, engaged in dirty talk, and laughed until vodka came shooting out of our noses.

When we returned home, we discovered that our separation anxiety-ridden pup, Maggie, had pooped all over Sam's bedroom and the basement. There was a large conglomeration of ants in the laundry room, and a stowaway cockroach in my purse.

After steam cleaning, ant spraying, and thoroughly checking every article of clothing and food product that made the return trip, we finally got unpacked and settled into our routine.

Jody returned to pack her PODS and prep for her move to Chicago. Jackie commenced prepping for a couple of work trips, and I continued planning my conference trip to San Francisco.

Life marches on.

Barbra said it best: "Memories light the corners of my mind. Misty, water-color memories of the way we were." Sappy? Yes.

But true.

"What Happens in Vegas"

In our late-30s, Chris and I lost our Vegas virginity with our best friends in the universe. Jackie and Brent met us there, and we partied like rock stars. Middle-aged rock starts, yes, but rock stars nonetheless. We most definitely stayed up later than we have in a long, long time.

While Chris and I were in the security line at the Indianapolis airport, I realized that my driver's license was not in my purse. Now, you must understand that I'm a nervous flyer, anyway. My head tells me that air travel is safe, but my heart assures me we're heading straight into the side of a mountain. To add the lost license stress to my fear of flying almost sent me straight to the St. Vincent's Stress Center. No passing "Go," no collecting $200.

By the grace of God, I had my Social Security card and my voter registration card in my purse. When I showed these to the security gal, she marked me as an "SSSS" and told me I'd have to go through additional security. What do you think "SSSS" might stand for? I was sure it was something sinister. All I could imagine was a full body cavity search by a burly woman in a hidden concrete bunker. Luckily, that wasn't the case, and after careful and intense examination of my cell phone and my digital camera, I was good to go.

Vegas is one of those places that everyone should visit at least once in a lifetime. I mean, really, where else can you see at least ten billboards chock full of boobs in every city block? From cigarette smoking 70-year-old slot machine junkies to the CFMP-wearing 22-year-olds in Band-Aid attire, there's no better place to people watch (which, incidentally, is one of my favorite pastimes). Jackie and I spent a lot of time shopping, but I spend even more time gawking. Blatantly.

I lost my prescription sunglasses and a decent amount of money, but still managed to have a good time. The incident that put me over the edge occurred when we were denied admittance to a nightclub because I didn't have an ID. I'd been drinking a wee bit before we went (well, the drinks ARE free when you're gambling!), and when the bouncer said "no," I grabbed my boobs and shouted, "Come on! Do these look like the boobs of a 20-year-old?! For God's sake, I'm a 36-year-old housewife with four kids!"

He wasn't impressed. Neither was Chris.

"Rainy Season"

After being buried alive in a work project that nearly did me in, we took off for a week of bliss in St. George Island, Florida.

It was beautiful. Stunning. Breathtaking. Picture perfect.

Short-lived.

Five out of the seven days we were there, my photos captured the buckets upon buckets upon buckets of rain. "The worst bout of rain I've ever seen in my 15 years on the island," proclaimed one native. "Even hurricanes are better than this — at least they do their damage and leave. This just keeps going on and on and on..."

And that, my friends, was our Spring Break.

But I'm not complaining. I'm really not. We had a couple of good days, enough to get sunburned and return home with sand in places that sand should never be found. We have three bags full of beautiful shells, memories of bald eagles flying in our back yard, and pictures of dolphins jumping in the bay right off the edge of our private dock.

And we truly did have a good time. I mean, if we hadn't spent so much family time together, how could I have added these gems to my list of Favorite Family Quotes:

MARY to SAM: Your armpits smell like crap!

GEORGE to the OTHER KIDS: We're playing Nazi tonight! (Yahtzee)

ALLIE to ME: Please don't buy another bottle of wine, Aunt Trina. I'm afraid you're going to get The Drunk.

And my favorite conversation of all? The one that took place between my sweet, well-behaved, socially appropriate six-year-old and me in the parking lot of a McDonalds in Alabama...

ME: If you kids don't get in the car RIGHT NOW, I'm leaving you in Alabama!

GUS (nervously): Would you really leave us, Mom?

ME: Of course, I wouldn't leave you, Gus. But I need you guys to bust a move.

GEORGE (yelling, as usual): If you leave me in Alabama, then I'll have to punch you in the nuts!

ME: I don't have nuts, George. Now get in the car.

GEORGE: Then I'll punch you in the penis.

ME: I don't have a penis, either.

GEORGE: Then I'll punch you in the vagina!

I think any reasonable person would agree that it's a miracle George made it out of the parking lot in Alabama to his warm, cozy bed in Indiana.

"History Lesson"

On one of our favorite family summer vacations, we traveled for seven days through the annals of American history, briefly visiting Antietam and Mt. Vernon. We touched historic landmarks, including the

Washington Monument, the Lincoln Memorial, the Jefferson Memorial, and the FDR Memorial. We talked about our nation's battles as we viewed the monuments dedicated to WWII, Korea, and Vietnam. We trekked through the Museum of Natural History, the Museum of American History, the National Archives, the Bureau of Printing and Engraving, the National Zoo, the Air and Space Museum. We honored our fallen heroes at Arlington National Cemetery, we watched the changing of the guard at the Tomb of the Unknown Soldier, we toured the nation's Capitol Building, and we gazed with wonder at all my literary heroes at the Library of Congress.

And the following is what my sweet daughter chose to highlight in her vaction-recap email correspondence with her friend, Elise:

"I miss you to. And I didn't get to see you at dc! That was sad. Gess what? On our last day a storm came and as we where going to bed THE FIRE ALARM WENT OFF!!!!!!! We all ran out of our room! But mom just had to get dressed. Dad said just throuh on a bra. The kids are cring and seaming. Sam said don't put up your hair right now we have to go outside. George and I runing down the stairs as fast as we coued. When we got outside I was so happy because it was a false alarm. So how was your vacshon? Good? So was mine. Soory I have to go. Bye!"

Yes, my bra is mentioned. My bra. Not climbing all the steps to the Lincoln Memorial to see her historical hero. Not bowing our heads at the graves of JFK and Jackie O. Not spending $28,498 for an in-depth week of American history. (Okay, that's a slight monetary exaggeration, but just a slight one.)

Next summer, we're just going to wash our skivvies, set off our fire alarm, and call it swell.

"Summer Camp"

The day after my kids completed their stint in a summer production of "Charlotte's Web," I dropped Mary Claire off at camp. She's the first of my kiddos to express an interest in sleep-away camp — with her best buddy, Allie. I was so excited for them both. We explored together — checking out the lake, the cabin, meeting her counselor. But she looked so little in that cabin full of girls. A young third grader in a sea of 10 and 11-year olds.

It rained last night. Mary Claire doesn't like rainy nights. I kept expecting her to tap me on the head and crawl in bed next to me. But she's two hours away. It's a strange feeling, this rite of passage. I want her to have a wonderful time – I hope she's making memories that last forever – but I miss her already.

She's tough. It's true. She nearly had a throw-down with her brother on stage Saturday night. Perhaps they shouldn't have been cast as husband and wife. "Homer Zuckerman and his bitch." That's how Jackie described them. I'm not sure the Zuckermans were ever supposed to be a bickering, old, crotchety couple, but that's how Gus and Mary Claire portrayed them. I kept expecting Gus to yell, "Jesus, Edith! Stop nagging me, woman!"

And yet, she's a tender heart, too. I hope the girls are nice to her. I hope the thunder holds off, that the spiders stay away. I pray they're watching her with eagle eyes while she's swimming in the lake.

And I'm fairly certain that Friday can't get here soon enough.

"Do You Canoe?"

We're a family of campers. I never thought I'd be a camper, was never interested in a tent. I have an irrational fear of spiders and an even more irrational fear of the Friday the 13th movies. But as a Father's Day surprise for Chris and Brent, Jackie and I planned our first multi-family camping outing, and we were all hooked.

Since that first trip, we've invested in all the gear. Between the Archers, Brian, and us, we have enough camping supplies to sustain a small village. It's always the same set-up: one tent for the kids, one tent for Brian, one tent for the other adults, two dining tents, one food preparation area, and a giant circle of chairs around the campfire.

On the last trip, we even added a white sheet strung between two trees and a movie projector for an after-hours movie screening of "Big Man on Campus." But I'm getting ahead of myself.

Yes, we've had insect and arachnid run-ins. In fact, we once found a tick in a place no tick should be found. On Gus. But if he knew I was mentioning the infamous Dick Tick, he would be mortified. So don't tell him.

During the tick-infested trip, Luke had to have one removed with tweezers. We had deer so close to our campsite that we could see their tick-filled ears. There were ticks in the shower, ticks on our chairs, ticks everywhere. When we arrived home, nothing went inside the house without first being run through the washing machine sanitary cycle. Including the kids.

We've seen spiders the size of baseballs.

We've had run-ins with snakes.

We've been visited by raccoons who had the dexterity to unscrew the lid from our jar of peanuts.

We've had multiple pocket knife injuries.

We've fought over barbeque chips.

And yet, we still love the great outdoors.

On our most recent camping trip, we were anxious to introduce the Fabers to our favorite summer adventure. We told them to bring a tent and a food supply and to plan one night's dinner. The rest was up to us.

Because the Fabers added three girls to the mix, we split the young ones into boys' and girls' tents and added Molly and Jeff to the adult tent. Brian still brought his own. And we always strategically placed him next to the kids' tents. He is, after all, the only one who hears Mary Claire wander aimlessly in the dark in search of me after we've all passed out from red wine and vodka drinks around the fire.

On our first full day of Faber camping, we decided to rent canoes. Molly assured us she'd been canoeing before. She felt confident in her abilities. And because Jeff had never been, she thought it would be best if she and Jeff and Mia went together. After all, Mia was the youngest and needed the reassurance of her parents.

I was in a canoe with Allie and Maddie, Brian had Mary Claire and Elise, Jackie had Luke and George, Chris had Gus and Johnny, and Brent and Sam were partnered up.

Brian was the first to capsize.

The girls did relatively well through the trauma. They only whimpered a bit. Elise lost her shoe, but I caught it downstream.

Then Molly, Jeff, and Mia went over.

The rest of us were waiting downstream for them. We could see them in the distance, could tell that they were going to go under, but couldn't do a thing about it. They got back in the canoe. And then capsized again.

Jackie and I could see Molly shaking her arms. We thought it was a victory move. An "I'm going to conquer this thing!" sort of war cry.

But as she walked her canoe closer to us, we could tell that she wasn't war whooping at all. In fact, she was crying hysterically.

"I'm done!" she yelled. "That's it! I'm going back!"

"Molly, Honey," Jackie pointed out gently, "you can't go back. The river only moves one way. You have to keep going."

"I'm not putting Mia back in that canoe!" she yelled. "She's traumatized already! We were catapulted from the canoe the last time! CATAPULTED! I'm not doing it anymore!"

Brent then tried to talk her off the ledge.

"Molly, why don't you and Mia ride with Sam and me? Jeff and Brian can ride together. Chris can pull your canoe behind him."

"No!" Molly cried. "I'm not getting in another canoe! I'll walk back. I'll just leave our canoe here. I'll pay for them to come get it later. But I refuse to get back in a canoe!"

"Oh, shit," Jackie whispered. "I've never seen her like this."

"Me, neither," I agreed. "She's truly freaking out."

Mia was shivering and crying.

"Mommy, please don't make me get back in! Please don't make me get back in!"

The girls were trying to comfort her.

"It's okay, Mia," Mary Claire said. "We tipped over and we're okay. And look – Maddie and Allie haven't tipped at all. If you ride with Brent and Sam, they'll take good care of you."

By now, Molly was losing her shit. I've never seen her so upset.

Somehow, the boys convinced her to go with Brent's plan and they forcibly placed poor Mia between her mother's legs on the floor of the canoe.

There was no further capsizing the rest of the day, but Molly never enjoyed the ride.

Later, Sam explained to me that every time they'd see a bit of white water, Molly would cry and beg, "Please, guys, please don't tip! Please don't tip!"

Sam and Brent would both reassure her and guide the canoe expertly through the moving waters.

Mia fell asleep from terror and exhaustion halfway through the trip and didn't wake up until we were done.

She'll probably never get in a canoe again.

Around the campfire that night, Molly eventually began to relax a little. By the next day, she even giggled a bit about her reaction. And a week later, she was convinced that she needed to redeem herself on our next camping trip by renting canoes again.

"You guys," she explained, "I don't know what happened to me. I truly lost my shit. But I know I can do this. Next time, let's do it again."

Jackie and I aren't as convinced. We might just sit by the beach instead.

Balance

Why Is There an Elephant on My Teeter-Totter?

Life is like riding a bicycle. To keep your balance you must keep moving forward. ~

Albert Einstein

"Spinning Plates"

When you're a mother of four young kids, it's tough not to be an extremist. At least it's tough for me. It seems that we're in a constant state of flux, that we're eternally attempting to strike the perfect balance of self, family, work, play, and sanity. I often imagine the circus performer who expertly balances a multitude of simultaneously spinning plates.

There are reasons I never wanted to join the circus.

My plates seem to be constantly falling to the ground and shattering beyond repair. And then I have to go to the store and buy new plates. And sometimes if I don't have enough cash, I have to charge them. And then I'm paying an exorbitantly high interest rate on plates that I should have never dropped in the first place, so I bury my head in the sand and cry.

Suffice it to say that maintaining a healthy life balance isn't a simple task. It is, in fact, Herculean in its size and intimidation factor.

And yet, every day, with slingshot in hand, this Momma/David goes out to slay the Balance/Goliath with renewed energy and resolve. Until my rock tumbles lamely at his feet and he decides to chew my head off instead.

"Doing it All"

Snow days in our house are a cause for celebration. Gathered around the fire with hot cocoa in hand, singing Kumbaya, and making family memories. Or, perhaps, me in my cloffice, Chris snow-blowing the driveway, Sam with a 102-degree fever, Gus playing Xbox, and The Littles making a grand mess of the basement that I completely reorganized the previous day.

On such a morning, I work to the sounds of the All-American Rejects and my then four-year-old singing "Dirty Little Secret" at the top of his lungs. When Sam was four, he sang Barney songs. Somehow, from the oldest to the youngest, I've lost some of my parenting prowess.

The previous week, I'd had the grand idea to move everyone's toys from their bedrooms to the basement. I was tired of messes in the bedrooms, messes in the family room, and messes in the basement, so I decided to contain the mess on one floor. Underground.

It took me an entire day to move everything from the third floor to the basement. (Can you say, "overindulged?") I mean, really, we could rival a Matchbox factory with the number of toy cars that we own. So, during the move, I organized, purged, and divided things into various and sundry toy bins and Rubbermaid containers. (Ah, Rubbermaid containers, the brilliant inventions that make my life complete.) Jackie reminded me that I do this on an annual basis (at least). She assured me that by the fall of the following year, I'd be moving everything back up into their bedrooms.

It's that bit of OCD in me. I can't help it.

During the reorg, I received an email about an open audition for a production of "Nunsense" at a local dinner theatre. I was up most of the night thinking about how I could make it work. I wanted desperately to audition, but couldn't reconcile being away from my kids every night for a month. And the production ran every weekend in April.

An impossible task.

I believe we products of the 80s were all sold a bill of goods when we were told we could "have it all." Eventually, something has to give. Be it a career, a family, a dream, an ambition, there aren't enough hours in the day to "have it all."

I'm trying to determine at this point in my life how to map out my future years – the ones that are slipping by like water through my fingers – to be able to experience some of the things I've dreamed about doing. The problem is, by the time I'm able to do a dinner theatre show, I won't be able to dance because of arthritis, and my boobs will be hanging down to my knees.

Who wants to cast a geriatric wanna-be as Maria? I won't be very convincing singing "Climb Every Mountain" from my wheelchair.

Don't get me wrong, I wouldn't trade my life for anything in the world, I just want to be able to add a little more to it.

Too many dreams, too little time.

I'd love to write more, but I just heard a little voice from upstairs yelling, "Mom, will you please wipe my butt?"

Broadway, here I come.

"Little House on the Prairie"

WWCID?

What Would Carolyn Ingalls Do? It's my new mantra.

I'm ready to downsize, ready to go back to the basics. I've grown weary of Webkinz and Xbox and pre-packaged fruit drinks with straws attached. Convenient? Sure.

But I've grown weary.

Every time we drive by a rustic, cozy, little cottage in the woods, I want to sell all our worldly possessions and live a simpler life. Do we REALLY need five bedrooms? Do we REALLY need three toilets to clean on a regular basis? (Okay, semi-regular basis. Okay! NOT REGULAR AT ALL!) And the stuffed animals? Don't even get me started.

Watch me get all deep here, but I think we're losing sight of what really matters in life. I mean, we've trained George to give us what he thinks is the right answer. It goes something like this:

ME: George, what is the most important thing in your life?

GEORGE: You, Mom. And my friends. And the rest of my family.

The same conversation with Mary Claire goes like this:

ME: Mary, what matters most in your life?

MARY: Umm. The Jonas Brothers. And pigs. And Pop-Tarts.

And Sam's answer – invariably – is "pie." Why? Because he thinks it's funny. Do you think he's funny? I don't, either. Maybe you have to be eleven to think he's funny.

When I ask Gus, this is the answer he provides:

GUS: Were you talking to me?

But I digress.

Some days I really do want to chuck it all and go back to the beginning. I always wanted a big house, a suburban neighborhood, the right schools, and hardwood floors.

Now I just want to be Carolyn Ingalls.

Mid-life crisis? Who knows. But if Chris pulls out a fiddle and starts singing me a little tune while I nibble on some Johnny-Cakes and sew some bonnets, he might just find himself getting lucky tonight.

"Riding the Coaster"

The roller coaster of life is making me want to vomit lately. I think I had my first true anxiety attack on Mother's Day weekend. Where is my Xanax?

These lives we lead, they're hard, aren't they? Even when nothing is truly wrong, there can still be lots of little things that aren't quite right.

I'm still struggling with work. Still trying to define who I am. Still trying to pay too many bills with too little money. Still chasing my tail.

And I want to feel like I'm important. I want to feel like I belong. I don't feel that way at work. I feel insignificant, over the hill, outside. And it bothers me.

But then I look at them, my children. And I know that I'm significant. They run to me when they hear the door opening in the evening. Doodybug still wraps his sweaty little arms around my neck as he's waking up in the morning. I mean something. I am their mother. What could possibly fill me more?

"Working the Numbers"

If it's darkest before the dawn, then I'm expecting a magnificent sunrise tomorrow – the brightest, most inspired sight I've ever seen.

Because I'm in the depths tonight. The deepest, darkest of depths. And I'm struggling hard to keep my head above water.

I don't know if I can figure this out. I don't know if I can make this work. Do you know how hard it is for someone who wants to be the best at everything to suddenly become no better than mediocre at anything? I stand by the assertion I made in my 20s that women really can't have it all. Something gives. Something bends. Something eventually breaks. You can't give 100% at work and 100% at home. I was an English major, but I do know that $100 + 100 = 200$, and that's 100% more than anyone has to offer. (Except, of course, for those overachievers who always give 101%. That's 99% more than they can give.)

This return to work has become a reinvention of myself. Who am I? What is it that defines me? What is truly important in my life? I can easily say that my husband and my children are #1, but that doesn't mean they can always have 100% of me. Because being the best wife and mother at this point in my life means contributing to our financial stability and future. It means teaching my school-age children that their mother wasn't put on earth solely to serve their needs – that I can, indeed, be a contributing member of society. That I can think, reason, make a difference.

But when George calls from Nana's too sick to go back to school but crying because he wants to come home, and my boss has kindly (but in no uncertain terms) noted that I need to be in the office, that's when my heart is ripped in half. That's when I feel like a dog toy being yanked in both directions by two muscular, determined canines.

Yes, Work, I know that I need to be there because you're running a business and paying me to be a contributing employee. Yes, George, I know that you want to be with me when you're sick because I'm your mom and you're only five. No, Self, I don't know how to be everything everyone needs me to be.

This life that I have known and loved for the past decade is gone. And I'm deeply mourning the loss of it. I won't stand in my PJs and wave goodbye to the kids from the front patio. Instead, I'll sit in the car until they board the bus and wave from my window as I drive to work. I won't load them up and take them to the pool every day this summer. Instead, I'll listen to the babysitter tell me about their swim lessons and their brave cannonballs into the deep end.

I want to move ahead, want to forge a new path, but my heart can only hold so much guilt, and my head can't seem to reconcile my old self with the new one that I have to re-create. I'm sure there are new memories to make, new adventures to seek. I'm sure I'll find new kinds of fulfillment. But I'm not there yet. I'm still slapping at the surface of the water, trying not to go under, fighting for every breath, and hoping beyond hope that my feet touch the bottom soon.

"What Matters"

I studied my sleeping kids – their flushed, peaceful faces – and came to this conclusion:

My job as their mother doesn't help pay the mortgage. But without them, this house is nothing but a lonely mess of bricks and mortar.

"Resolutions"

The first day of our New Year opened with a hot cup of tea and a bowl of fresh orange slices. You might wonder what's so strange about that. Then those of you who know me might realize that oranges are not equivalent to Oreos.

This year is shaping up to be a year of big changes for the Willis Tribe. When all is said and done, we'll have a teenager. We've never had one of those before. We might pursue a life change that takes us out of our beloved Indiana. We've never done that before, either.

And in the midst of our Big Plans, I hereby solemnly swear that by this time next year, I will be 75 pounds lighter than I am today. Now some of you skeptics might be saying, "Yeah, yeah, I've heard that before. Isn't she supposed to be running the Disney Marathon in less than two weeks?" And I'd have to hang my head in shame. Then I'd have to go into the gory details of my hip injury. And who wants to hear that?

Suffice it to say that I've learned I cannot complete a marathon until I lose 75 pounds first.

The event that sealed the deal was a conversation I was having with Gus a week ago. I explained to him that we were all going to start eating healthier – that we were going to stock up on fresh fruits and veggies instead of Hershey bars and ice cream – and that, as a result, we would all be healthier and I would be skinnier. And that wide-eyed boy looked at me with pure, unadulterated curiosity and said, "I wonder what you'll look like when you're skinny."

For 12 years, my life has revolved around those four little munchkins and their father. Those 12 years have been the most memorable, most emotional, most educational, most important years of my life. And while I was enjoying the ride with an ever-present bag of peanut butter M&Ms, I lost sight of the person in the mirror. And then I just stopped looking.

But Gus's comment... oh, that comment opened my eyes. My kids have never known me as anything but fat.

Sure, I remember the Glory Days of size six jeans and a concave stomach. I remember bikinis and mini-skirts and rock-hard thighs. I remember going out for a run and coming back five miles later barely winded. I remember. Chris remembers (and probably cries at the beauty of that memory). But my kids don't remember. They've never had the opportunity to know that person.

I'm not going to be the Fat Mom anymore. I don't want to have a heart attack. I don't want to have diabetes and high blood pressure. I want to be able to run without risking hip dysplasia or whatever the human equivalent is.

Big changes, indeed.

And while I'm re-discovering the wonders of grilled chicken and daily exercise, I'm also committed to finishing my novel. Not the one starring Desiree Delilah. I'm going to be finishing "The Wandering Man" – the story of James, my lost, searching soul who told me his story in a dream. (Corny? Yes. True? Absolutely.) I can't escape from him, can't stop thinking about him. I sit down to write, and the words fall from my fingers. I think, perhaps, this is what true writing must feel like.

So, there you have it. A novel written in the midst of a budding teenage hormonal firestorm and fueled primarily by orange slices.

Should be an interesting year.

"Overwhelmed"

I've done it this time. I've really done it. I'm walking around with The Fray reverberating through my brain.

"Everyone knows I'm in over my head, over my head..."

I've been overcommitted before. But this time. This time I've hit the mother lode. I know it's duller than dull to hear your friends complain about how busy they are. About how their lives are sooooo much harder than yours. But humor me, will you?

Take tonight for example. Chris had an awards ceremony downtown, so I was running solo. Mary Claire had Girl Scouts, Sam had lacrosse practice, George had a baseball game, and all three of The Littles had "Charlotte's Web" rehearsal. You know, the summer children's theatre program I agreed to direct? The one that over 80 kids auditioned for when we were expecting maybe 20? The one we double-cast so more kids would have an opportunity to participate? The only lucky break I caught was not having a softball game to coach. Because I'm the coach of the eight and nine-year-old Novas. Oh – and my colleague at work went into labor a week early, so I have a 20-page whitepaper to finish. By Friday. And just to round things out, I joined another book club today. (And let me just clarify that I haven't attended my current book club for over three months.) Did I mention that I joined a gym, too? And signed up for personal training twice a week? And committed to spinning on Tuesdays and Thursdays at 5:45 AM?

If I stop to think about how much I've agreed to do – and how poorly it will all probably be done – it makes me want to curl up in a ball and cry.

But you know what's really doing me in? The straw that's breaking the camel's back?

Stamps.

The price of postage stamps went up two cents today. And I have an entire unused roll of 42 centers. So now I'm faced with a dilemma. Should I try to squeeze a painful trip to the post office in this week so I can buy a roll of two-cent stamps, or do I just stick an extra 42-cent stamp on my eye doctor's envelope and eat the extra 40 cents? Because I'm sure she'd like to get paid for the frames that are sitting on my nose right now. Logically, it's an easy answer. But on principle, I just can't throw that 40 cents away. And so the bill sits on my desk, unpaid. I have a sinking feeling that the eye doctor is going to ban me from her office, and my eyesight will continue to deteriorate at a rapid pace. Eventually, I'll go blind. And I'm guessing it's damn hard to drive your four kids to all their activities – let alone write a 20-page whitepaper – when you're blind.

Lesson learned. This is what happens when you say, "yes" one too many times.

"A Recap"

"How I Spent One Day During the Summer I Agreed to Direct Our Local Children's Theatre Production"

1. Wrangling 80 excited kids who strayed within inches of falling three feet from the edge of a stage.

2. Listening to 40 kids forget 80% of their lines four days before their first performance.

3. Telling one child for the 843rd time that her costume was not yet ready.

4. Trying to explain to a multitude of seven and eight-year-olds what to do if someone forgets a line.

5. Painting a fair scene with glow-in-the-dark paint that looks mysteriously like a bodily fluid that shall remain nameless.

6. Telling my own child for the 394th time that if he doesn't stop jacking around, he'll be grounded for the remainder of the summer.

7. Wishing that I had poured just a smidge of vodka into my water bottle.

8. Sucking my husband into the deep, dark depths of yet another project that I couldn't refuse.

9. Granting at least 32 children restroom privileges.

10. Experiencing intestinal distress resulting from too many kids not knowing their lines, their cues, or their blocking.

11. Praying to the Good Lord above that everything will miraculously come together before Saturday morning.

12. Talking a seven-year-old off the ledge when she realized how big the stage was and how little she felt on it.

13. Smiling from ear-to-ear while watching 20 adorable kids sing "Personality" at the top of their lungs – complete with some sweet dance moves.

14. Feeding my children Subway for the 28th time in two weeks.

15. Wishing that Subway still had a frequent customer card.

16. Dreaming of those halcyon days when I was working 60 hours a week.

17. Avoiding the angry stares of the one parent who believes I am the devil incarnate.

18. Explaining to my 12-year-old that I cannot help him with the lights and sound because I know absolutely nothing about lights and sound. And then watching him figure it out on his own.

19. Counting small heads as they return from snack break to ensure everyone has, indeed, returned.

20. Basking in the glow of 80 happy, wondrous faces when they first stepped on the stage of their new venue.

21. Trying to squeeze some billable hours in during some of Charlotte's lengthier soliloquies.

22. And tonight? Eating a giant bowl of ice cream while I rest my weary bones – now that it's after midnight.

Tomorrow's schedule? Back to the theatre at 8:00 AM. Only four more days until we open.

"Simple Delights"

A little less than two weeks in, but this new diet is changing my life. I know that sounds dramatic. I know it's only been two weeks, but I'm awakening to a world of food that I never knew existed.

For the past 39 years, I've eaten like a ten-year-old. Couldn't get enough pasta, starch, carbs, ice cream. The more processed, the better. Mashed potatoes? Yes. With a side of macaroni and cheese, please. And better bring me a chaser of white bread and butter. Fried? Um. Of course.

Who knew that spices could make such a difference? And that fresh veggies on the grill could make my mouth water? And that fresh brown eggs from a local farm could taste like manna from heaven?

Who knew?

In the past 12 days, I've lost 16 pounds. I know that's a crazy amount in such a short time, and my weight loss is beginning to taper off a bit. But damn, do I feel good.

And you know what's even better?

This new life I've discovered.

We're getting up early on Saturday mornings. And instead of stuffing our faces with donuts and bagels, we're going to the Farmer's Market. We're picking out fresh fruits and vegetables, whole grain breads, and the best effing black bean soup I've ever had in my life.

It's a community that I was never a part of. Now I can't wait to go back again and again and again.

It's no secret that this suburban life I once pined for hasn't turned out to be all I dreamt it would be. I've had more neighborhood drama than I could have ever possibly imagined, more heartbreak from what I believed was a true friendship than I care to admit.

When I think about the farm we used to live on – the lace curtains blowing in the breeze, the swing on the side porch, the dogs running in the backyard – it's almost more than I can bear. I hated living on the farm then. I thought there was so much more to life than corn and beans and fresh air.

But now I'd give anything to return to that simplicity. To surround my kids with the true pleasures in life. The simple joys. The sun shining through 100-year-old windows. A sturdy tree in the back yard that's older than all of us combined. The night breeze blowing into each of our rooms.

My life is fabulous. Don't get me wrong. But I've realized how serene a simple life can be. How fulfilling. How spiritual.

We'll go back someday.

We've already begun.

"Naked Fajitas"

I'm embracing this new South Beach lifestyle. We're all about eliminating the White Devil over here (i.e, white flour, sugar, and all the crappy, gut-growing substances I once held near and dear to my heart). But 25 pounds lighter, I'm starting to feel like a teenager again.

And my favorite new discovery?

The Qdoba naked chicken fajita with extra black beans.

There are many reasons why I love this enticing concoction. First and foremost, I love to slink up to the counter and breathlessly order a naked chicken fajita in my best Lauren Bacall voice. There's just something innately sexy about saying "naked" and "fajita" in the same breath. And something bordering on dirty, too.

Top it off with a smidge of all-but-forbidden guacamole, and it's a sinful feast of decadence.

Fajitas – in general – always bring to mind my brother-in-law, Kevin's serving story. Back 163 years ago when we were all young and able-bodied and waiting tables... (sidebar: I personally believe everyone should have to wait tables at some point in their lives. It makes you much more appreciative of the hell that is serving food to the public. Once you've had someone say to you, "Just leave our food and go away. We don't want to see you for the rest of the night," you acquire a whole new perspective on the human race.) Anyway, fajitas were a new and novel item menu back then. (Yes, that's how old we are.) Kevin had a patron who said (in his best NASCAR voice), "I'd like to try some of them new fajitas (rhymes with Ore-Idas)."

Yeah, that sounds doubly dirty.

I discovered yesterday that I don't like cilantro. My tastebuds determine it to have a less-than-subtle essence of soap. And I know what soap tastes like. I had my mouth washed out with it on a regular basis as a kid. Usually right after I yelled, "SHIT!" or called my sister a "Penis-Head." Penis was my favorite word in grade school – not quite bad enough to earn me some time in the confessional, but bad enough to make my sister tattle on me. The satisfaction of the name-calling, however, was well worth the inevitable Dove soap punishment.

I suggest that next time you're in Qdoba, you should saunter to the counter, do a little shimmy, and order something "naked" (and sans cilantro). You might even want to wink at your Qdoba server, or talk dirty to him in Spanish. (That's Jackie's favorite trick.)

Trust me, it will give you a little thrill. And we all could use a few of those once in a while, right?

All Work and No Play

Rejuvenating a Near-Death Career

She never quite leaves her children at home, even when she doesn't take them along. ~
Margaret Culkin Banning

"Jumping Back In"

After much hand-wringing and nail-biting (on my part, not on Chris's), we decided once the kids were all in school that it would be in our best financial interest for me to go back to work full-time. The prospect of four kids in college (along with their perpetual student father) was a bit daunting, to say the least. I agreed to it on one condition – that I could do what I love best, write.

And thus began the resume assault on the town of Indianapolis.

After a couple of weeks, I had two corporate writing/editing job offers – one from a steady-Eddie (but a bit dry) bank in downtown Indy, the other from a young, entrepreneurial tech company. Although my technical knowledge is limited, my banking prowess has also proven to be a bit lacking. Based on company culture alone, I accepted the tech job offer and officially became a Marketing Copywriter.

450

The next week was a crazy exercise in finding before and after school childcare, buying a few outfits that were a bit more presentable than my bathrobe and sweats, and convincing the dogs that I wasn't abandoning them.

After being at home for ten years and dabbling in part-time positions, I was going back to work full-time. The prospect was scary, exciting, and intestinal distress-inducing all at once. I think I felt like Sam must have felt on his first day of middle school. He wasn't worried about the work itself, just about getting his locker open.

I was primarily concerned with driving the right way on all the one-way streets to my downtown parking garage. The writing part seemed easy – it was the elevator that challenged me.

"Say Uncle"

My epiphany came on a cold March morning in Starbucks. As I stood waiting for Chris to bring the extra set of car keys, I had a silent breakdown, tears and snot coursing steadily down my face. I didn't care about the people staring curiously – me, the one who invented self-consciousness. But at that moment in time, all I could think was, this isn't working. That's it. That was the epiphany. My life is not working.

It was 6:30 AM when I stopped for gas upon my return from work. You might wonder why I was coming home from work at 6:30 AM when most people are just leaving for work at that time. Well, we'd just come off of a long night that that involved our seven-year-old, Mary Claire, and a great deal of vomiting. Chris and I drew straws at 4:30 AM to determine was going to stay home from work with her this time. Suffice it to say this was not our first winter illness, not our first day home from work with sick kids. Because he has the Alpha Job, I lost – short straw or not. I begrudgingly loaded my sorry, tired, sweatsuit clad self into my car and drove to my office in downtown Indy to gather resource material for the whitepaper that was due by the end of the day.

When I arrived at the office, I found that someone else had been using my desk and could, therefore, not find the edited hard copy document that I was searching for. Not looking my personal best and clearly battling bedhead, I decided not to stick around long enough to ask anyone for assistance. So, I drove back home to the tune of a beeping low gas light.

As I pulled into the Zionsville Marathon station, I decided that I should buy some lottery tickets as well as gas. After all, our luck couldn't get any worse. I rationalized that we were due for some good fortune. And if good fortune meant an unearned, lucky windfall, then, by God, we'd take it. So, I pulled my billfold out of my purse, turned the car off, locked the doors, and proceeded to swipe my debit card.

Have I mentioned how cold it was on this March morning? Our friend, Ben, would call it a "lion" day. He learned about "lion" and "lamb" days in preschool. Turns out, it was a day I'd have been relieved to have actually been eaten by a lion.

So, my card is approved (thank God for small miracles), I choose the unleaded variety, and the hose is not long enough to reach the gas tank. Damn!

I unlock the car, pull forward a couple of feet, and proceed to lock the keys in the car upon exiting. Really, in retrospect, it's kind of funny. I mean, Lucille Ball would have made it entertaining. But at that moment in time, I wasn't laughing.

Because my cell phone was also locked in the car, I ran into the station to use the pay phone. The attendant pointed to the lonely phone across the frozen tundra of the parking lot. I bought a couple of lottery tickets, zipped those sure-fire winners into my pocket (which, by the way, was very empty because my gloves were also locked in the car), and trudged across the icy parking lot. It was so cold that I'm sure if I'd stuck my tongue to the phone, it would have frozen. I would have also probably died from some third world disease.

I dialed our home number and Chris answered nervously on the second ring. As we're all well aware, nothing good ever comes from 6:30 AM phone calls.

"Honey, I locked my keys in the car."

"Oh, Katrina, you didn't," he sighed.

"I did."

"Where are you?"

"The Marathon station."

"What about OnStar?"

"Well, when Union Federal became Sky and then Sky become Huntington, our auto deduct numbers changed, and I never bothered to update them. We can try it, but I'm not sure it's still active."

"Oh, Katrina."

"I know!" I insisted. "I know. What are we going to do?"

"I'm going to drive the other set of keys over."

"With all the kids?"

"No, I'll just leave them here. They'll be okay for 15 minutes."

"Oh, Chris, are you sure?"

"Honey, what else do you think I should do? Mary Claire is back in bed. Do you want me to wake her up?"

"No, just hurry," I instructed. "But be careful."

Click.

I was so out of sorts that I stood shivering beside the Suburban for a while before I realized that Starbucks was open and I did, indeed, have my billfold. My small miracle of the day. So, I ordered my venti two-pump peppermint mocha and a cup of the day for Chris and stood impatiently by the door, sipping my fattening concoction, but not enjoying that first minty whipped cream sip nearly as much as I should.

Two young men sat beside me talking passionately about their church and their ministry, and I eavesdropped shamelessly. As I listened in on their conversation about God and His plan for their lives and their congregation, I felt the nervous breakdown slowly working its way into my body. My hands began shaking, my breaths became shallow, a lump formed in my throat.

Busy people came in and out of that Starbucks as I clutched my coffee in my hand and cried. And cried. And cried. I didn't make any dramatic, sobbing sounds to give myself away, but the few people who bothered to glance my way knew that I was crying. The snot and the blotchy red patches on my face were dead giveaways.

When Chris's Volvo came into view, I stepped outside to meet him at the Suburban. I handed him his coffee, and he silently handed me the keys.

"Why is God punishing us?" I cried.

"Have a good day, Sweetie," he replied, familiarly ignoring my doomsday question. "I'm going into work. I'll see you later."

His face was pale, his upper lip a bit sweaty. I knew he wouldn't last through the day. By 2:00 PM, he'd succumb to the Willis Plague.

By 8:00 AM, I knew what I had to do. It was time to start writing.

"Out of Shape"

Is it returning to the work force after being home with my kids for ten years that's so difficult, or have I truly lost that many brain cells? I can't seem to wrap my mind around the "big picture" – or any minor details, for that matter. I feel like I can complete tasks – well-defined, effectively communicated tasks. But take initiative? Come up with an original idea? Those concepts aren't even on the horizon.

When I was a part of Corporate America at age 25, I was going to take the world by storm. I was forward-moving and fast-thinking. Now I feel like my brain is in slow motion. Everyone else is running in front of me, and I'm shuffling behind, struggling for every breath. My work life is a scary parallel to my running life.

"You're Gonna Make It After All"

Working downtown has its ups and downs. On my good days — while walking back and forth from the parking garage — I often fancy myself as Mary Tyler Moore.

You remember…

"Who can turn the world on with her smile? Who can take a nothing day and suddenly make it all seem worthwhile? Well, it's you girl, and you should know it…"

It put a little spring in my step.

Granted, Miss Moore and I are pretty different. She was young and perky. I'm middle-aged and over-tired. She was a budding business girl looking for her big break. I was coming out of full-time motherhood retirement for a second shot at gainful employment.

We did, however, share a seventh grade teacher. Of course, that information came straight from Sister Veronica Ann, and she also insisted that Sri Lanka was pronounced "Sire Lanky."

And another major difference between my and my girl, MTM?

I'm fairly convinced that Mary Tyler Moore never slipped on the ice and fell on her giant ass in the middle of downtown Indianapolis. Fairly convinced. So, in that particular way, we're very different.

And the saddest part of the story is that I wasn't even spinning around gracefully whilst throwing my cute, kicky hat into the air. Nope. Just walking.

"On the Other Side"

So, I sat in my "hug" (since I left the work force in 1997, the "cubicle" has morphed into the "hug" – but only in the hippest of offices), and I looked around and thought, this is not me. This is not my life. This is not who I am. Young, frighteningly smart 20-somethings zoomed by me on their way to important meetings, talked over my head, texted amazingly fast and grammatically correct messages on their iPhones, and I stared at the pictures of my bright-eyed kids and wondered why I wasn't home in my sweats cooking them a much-loved dinner of smoked sausage and shells and cheese. The old me wanted to rush to an important meeting so I'd feel respected, intelligent, worthy. But the real me knew that my self-worth was nothing compared to the intense love and adoration that those little blue-eyed imps wrung from my heart each and every day.

Write! I shouted in my own brain. Write! Write something provocative, edgy, new. Write passionately, write intelligently. But all I could do was pine for my kids, for my home, for the dog hair on my flowered arm chair, for the sweats languishing in my dresser drawer. I once deplored toilet scrubbing, but at that point in my life, all I wanted to do was make my toilets sparkle and shine. I wanted to clean my tile with a toothbrush, to reorganize all my kids' closets.

What's that they say about the grass being greener?

"Learning the New Ropes"

Another minor breakdown today. It's hard for me to be 38 and to suddenly have a boss. Pride? Probably. But for the past ten years, I've been the boss. I've been the boss of dirty diapers, of unmade beds, of vats of laundry, of morning sex, toilet cleaning, of hugging and snuggling. I was the part-time boss of a small non-profit, but I had a big time title. Executive Director. Now I'm at the bottom of the Org Chart, and it's definitely not the most reaffirming place to be. Sometimes I want to scream, "Look at me! I'm 38 years old and I've accomplished a lifetime of feats! I had four babies via four c-sections in five years! I run a home with six people, two dogs, a guinea pig, and a fish. I run, I blog, I write, I read, I have dear friends who love and appreciate me. I can shoot a three-pointer better than any kid in the neighborhood, and I can still throw a fastball that will burn your hand right through the glove. I get up at 4:30 AM so I can make it into this office by 9:00 – on a good day! I'm smart! I'm ambitious! I could do any job in this office (except, perhaps, the technical ones). But I made a CHOICE. A choice to stay home and raise my kids and support my husband while he pursued his educational dreams. That doesn't make me less of a person."

That's what I want to yell. But instead, I stay silent. And I watch. And I learn.

"Searching for Answers"

Pondering Life's Greatest Questions

1. When you return to the corporate work force after spending ten years at home raising your children, do you really have to start from scratch? Do you somehow lose all the experience you acquired via blood, sweat, tears, and sacrifice prior to choosing to raise contributing members of society (and I'm not considering Pouting and Booger Eating as valid contributions)? Can you have once performed strongly as a team leader, a manager, a director, and then suddenly forget how that process works? Or is that just

the common consensus among those who haven't taken a workforce sabbatical for something monumentally more important?

2. Do dogs have feelings? Does Lucy feel slighted when I run with Maggie in the morning?

3. Can chocolate stains every really wash completely out of white t-shirts?

Okay, so Question #1 is really the only one I'm struggling with.

"In Over My Head"

You know what annoys me? People who say they're overworked, way too busy, always tired. I mean, who isn't tired? Who doesn't have too many things on his or her plate? Who says such obnoxious things?

Turns out I do.

Because I'm so damn tired, so damn overloaded, so effing busy, I feel like the stitches that are holding me together are slowly but surely unraveling. Every day, I feel a little further behind, I get a little less sleep, I drink a little more coffee. Eventually, it's all going to come to a screeching halt. Perhaps when my completely sleep-deprived brain raises a red flag, detaches itself from my spinal column, and marches off into the sunset. Maybe that's how it will all go down.

Between working full-time, taking on freelance jobs that allow me to segue out of full-time work, sending four kids back to school, playing chauffeur for all their extracurriculars, filling out all their paperwork (are they applying to become international undercover espionage experts?), rehearsing for the lead in a community theatre production, training for my first marathon, finishing my third novel, and trying to squeeze a shower in every now and then, every minute of my day is beyond full.

Grocery store? What's that? Clean laundry? Never heard of it. Bills paid on time? Ha! I've decided that I'm willingly embracing the Red Letter Payment Plan. When the bright, red letter arrives – the one that's threatening to turn off the gas, the cable, the electric, etc. – that's when it gets paid. And only if I remember to open it or dig it out from the bottom of the Mt. Everest-sized pile of unopened mail on my kitchen island.

My life is spiraling out of control. I've read about sleep deprivation as a form of torture. Now I understand it. My mind is no longer fully functional. I'm seriously over-committed and unarguably under-rested.

There. I said it. I just became my own Biggest Pet Peeve.

"Living the Dream"

I've been dreaming a lot about the life of a novelist, and I'm convinced it's the life that I want. Sitting in my cloffice, drinking coffee in the morning and wine after 5:00. (Okay, after 11:30 AM.) Never getting out of my pajamas, acknowledging the kids once in a while as they rot their brains but strengthen their fingers playing Guitar Hero. All while I create new worlds of humor and love and intrigue from daybreak into the wee hours of the morning.

Yes, indeed, that's the life for me. Problem is, when I spend so much time dreaming about it, I'm not actually making it happen. It's hard to write when you're thinking really hard about your novel and you don't want to interrupt your brilliant thoughts by actually picking up the laptop and using it.

I think maybe I'm afraid of the failure. Of the inevitable rejection. I'm feeling somewhat like a nervous middle schooler. Will my editors like me? Will people want to read what I write? Do I have anything worthwhile to say?

For God's sake, Publishing Word, will you go with me?

(Check "yes" or "no.")

"Bifurcated"

Those who know and love me well know that I am, indeed, insane. My career path instability definitely drives that point home.

When I returned to work full-time, I had breakdown after breakdown. Was I jilting my kids? Was I gone too much? Was I doing the right thing for my family by earning an extra income? I felt like I was gone far too much, and yet I still wasn't putting enough hours in at the office. And then.

Then the pendulum swung all the way to the other side. Because I became convinced that if I had to work, I wanted something more high-powered. I missed being the boss. I missed having influence. I missed the whole ego trip that went along with it. I intentionally chose to re-enter the workforce full-time as a copywriter because I didn't want the stress of a high-powered career. But then I decided I wanted my Executive Director title back.

Crazy? Yes.

But at this point in my life, this minute, this second, things were better at work. Perhaps it was my attitude that improved, but nevertheless, I was enjoying my work more and more. Watching the wheels turn inside my office had been enlightening. Did we need better internal communications? Indeed. Were we utilizing our human talent as effectively as we could be? Probably not. Were we losing a portion of our vibrant, entrepreneurial spirit as we grew into a mid-size business? Most assuredly, yes.

My answer to this? Corporate Communications. A department that would bring us all back together, that put us all back on the same page. Our home base, if you will. I always tell my kids that no matter what happens outside our doors – and challenges and disappointments will inevitably happened – that this home is their Safe Place. I want them to always feel loved, cherished, respected here. I don't think our professional lives should be much different. If my children feel like they can take risks and push themselves and sometimes fail – but still return to their Safe Place – couldn't my co-workers feel the same way?

And so the Household CEO becomes Corporate Mom. Wouldn't my fellow employees feel supported in their risks, their ideas, their adventures if they had a Safe Place to land? Shouldn't they feel well-informed, part of the team, worthy? Won't they ultimately be more successful if they come from a solid base? And perhaps we could even provide some blankies when the going really got tough.

My poor friend, Nicole, who had to sit with me in Au Bon Pain multiple times while I cried my eyes out and let the battling demons inside me take over, would most definitely roll her eyes at this change of heart –

the one that was probably directly related to my dear Jody's new, glamorous, high-powered position in Chicago.

I wanted to go to New York! I wanted to be wined and dined and pampered by my corporate executives! Hell, at that point in my life, I wanted to BE a corporate executive!

I'm so shallow sometimes.

Within a month, Jody and I were both crying on the phone about how hard it is to be a good wife, a good mother, and a good employee. Within two months, we had both left our corporate lives behind, donned our slippers, and grabbed our Swiffers.

Perhaps you could just refer to us both as Home Executives.

"Becoming the Master of My Domain"

It took me a while to realize it, to admit, to confess it publicly, but I can't do it all.

And here's the thing.

That's okay.

My return to Corporate America taught me that I don't want to return to Corporate America after all. Once I got through my soul-searching, sanity-crushing year of full-time work, I realized something. I'm not a full-time worker. Full-time wife? Yes. Full-time mother? Yes. Full-time writer? Yes. Full-time office worker? Not so much. It took me nearly four decades to realize it, but I'm not happiest at a conference table — even if I'm running the show. I thought being in charge would make me happy, but I was sadly mistaken.

So, I've once again officially become the Master of My Domain, Queen of the Cloffice, Mistress of Laundry. The full-time money doesn't seem to matter as much when I'm trading it in for my soul. I'd rather sell my house and live in a shack than constantly run on this endless, thankless, aimless hamster wheel called full-time employment in Corporate America.

I've found the perfect balance of using my brain, exercising my writing muscle, and contributing the family bottom line by becoming a freelance writer. Documenting the ins and outs of customer relationship management and digital marketing may not light my fire, but doing it from the calm obscurity of my cloffice definitely brings a smile to my face. Avoiding the commute, the mind-numbing meetings, the team building exercises, frees up my time to hug my kids, share a glass of wine with my husband, and document our family trials and tribulations.

And when the paycheck arrives in the mail? Well, that's just an added bonus. I may not be a fast learner when it comes to self-actualization, but once I get it, I've got it for good. And this, my friends, is where I'm supposed to be.

"Checklist"

When I stopped working full-time in Corporate America, I developed a short list, titled "What I Plan to Do with My Free Time." And I'd like to share it with you.

1. Finish – and then publish – a book

2. Blog more

3. Volunteer more in my kids' classrooms

4. Drink coffee with my friends on a regular basis

5. Keep a steady supply of clean underwear in my kids' drawers

6. Wash my windows

7. Organize my cupboards and closets

8. Have more sex

9. Read, read, and then read some more

10. Clean the fish bowls weekly

11. Train the mice to do quirky mouse tricks

12. Rub the dogs' bellies

13. Cook dinner

14. Channel the muse in my cloffice

15. Replace my living room carpet

16. Open my mail

17. Snuggle with my kids

18. Bake cookies (and eat cookie dough)

19. Support Chris

20. Actually train for the marathon I committed to

21. Figure out where the strange smell in my kitchen is originating

22. Scrapbook

23. Organize my pictures

24. Buy a fancy new camera to take more pictures

25. Find a fabulous new agent who adores every word I pen (or at least offers me some good, sound advice on what to do with all the crap that flows from my fingertips)

26. Teach a writing seminar

27. Sing

28. Keep my toilets sparkly

29. Visit my mom and sister more often

30. Eat more egg rolls

31. Plan our family sabbatical

32. Talk Chris into one more baby (Just kidding! Maybe...)

33. Continue avoiding yard work at all costs

34. Save lots of money on gas

35. Clip coupons

36. Pay our bills on time

37. Keep the light bulbs changed

38. Learn how to play something other than The Pointer Sisters' "Fire" on the guitar

"Leisure Envy"

At 11:23 PM, I was finishing up some copy on a proprietary call accounting system. Riveting? Umm, not so much. Lucrative? Well, it's definitely helping with the never-ending onslaught of sports registration fees, school lunch money, rapidly disappearing 12-packs of toilet paper, overdue library fines, and mental health-inspired bookstore trips.

But my book?

Well, it's not writing itself.

And that's the conundrum. How does one continue to contribute to the family's bottom line, wash all the dirty underwear, vacuum the mounds of dog hair, shop at the grocery store for overpriced convenience foods, assist with the nightly homework battle, and still find time to pursue a dream?

Oh, sure, I write whenever I can. But at the rate I'm going, I'll be in assisted living before I finish Chapter 5.

I'm not really complaining.

Okay, I am.

I know so many women who don't have to work, so many families who aren't dependent on a second income. And many of my non-working female acquaintances choose to do, well, not much of anything. I'm not begrudging them that choice. I'm begrudging them the luxury of making that choice. Because if I had that free time, by God, I'd be writing the next Great American Novel.

Envy has always been my favorite of the Seven Deadly Sins.

I'm a covetous person by nature. Forgive me, Sister Veronica Ann. I know that it's wrong to feel the way I do. I know there's a special circle in hell for the covetous... (Oh, wait – that's Dante, not Catholicism.)

I don't necessarily envy other people's *things*, but I envy their *leisure*. (And perhaps money doesn't buy happiness, but I would definitely argue that it buys leisure.) If I could just re-claim four to five hours a day, I'd be working on my tenth novel by now. But it's not to be. At least not while my kids are playing lacrosse, the most expensive club sport in the history of the world.

And so I sit bleary-eyed at my beloved Mac in the wee hours of the morning and attempt to string together some engaging, semi-coherent, coffee-inspired prose.

And I get a bit distracted by the Mysterious Enigma known as the publishing world. So I Google agents and publishing houses and book advances, and I find myself getting sucked into the swirling vortex of cyberspace death. (How in the world do I segue from a Google search on book publishing to a riveting account of how to train your pet mice to perform rodent tricks?)

And then all I can think about is that middle school bus that's scheduled to arrive at 7:00 AM. And the middle school boy that I have to drag from his beloved bed at 6:30. And there's not enough coffee in the world to fuel that particular task.

Perhaps it's not time I'm lacking, but focus.

But as the night turns to morning, dear readers, the siren song of my down pillow calls. And so I bid thee au revoir.

After all, I can always write tomorrow.

"Brainstorming"

I had a freelance work meeting this morning with one of my favorite former colleagues ever. She's young, willowy (something I aspire to, but will never be), smart, creative, sarcastic, and a little bit dark at times.

My soulmate.

She could be my daughter. I mean, if I was a promiscuous, sexually active 13-year-old slut, she could most definitely be my daughter. But less willowy. And afflicted with lots more issues.

Anyway, we were gathered at Panera this morning to do some brainstorming. And when we got down to business after updating each other on our lives, she explained, "Well, we need to brainstorm a bit about..."

And I just started giggling.

I was envisioning violent thunderstorms of thought and creativity, and I was immensely tickled.

"My brain," I explained to her, "doesn't really storm. It's more like showers. Scattered showers. Less than a 30% chance."

And the sad truth? That was a pretty accurate forecast.

"Soul Boogers"

I just finished reading a book.

This, in and of itself, is not writing-worthy news. I finish lots of books. Two or three a week, actually. This one, however, was different. Why? Because a former BSU classmate of mine penned it.

And it was...

Breathtaking.

Brilliant.

Beautiful.

If you're a fan of the short story and tend to prefer your writing on the dark side, stop what you're doing, log on to Amazon.com, and buy "We're in Trouble" by Christopher Coake.

Right now. (I'll wait.)

Chris's writing talent makes me feel like every word I write is nothing more than drivel. I don't typically like to be a close-fisted kind of gal. I like to believe that there's enough to go around – that if we all approach the world with open hands, we receive just as much as we give.

But I'm pretty sure I haven't received that kind of talent.

Hey, God? My hands are open. Just wondered if you'd noticed.

I probably shouldn't compare my writing to Chris's. After all, he writes about death and dying and love and the complexities of the human soul.

I write about boogers.

But I *know* boogers.

The complexities of the soul? I'm still working on that.

I'm probably just disenchanted today because I discovered that my favorite low-fat yogurt is chock-full of High Fructose Corn Syrup. And in the eyes of South Beach dieters everywhere, I might as well be stuffing my face with white bread and French fries.

Damn those Yoplait execs for smiting me with HFCS. I mean, I gave up my Homemade brand Cookies and Cream ice cream, didn't I? I stopped the Oreo binges and hid the Peppermint JoJos! I even ate cauliflower disguised as mashed potatoes tonight. And you know what? As pretty as it looked, it still tasted like cauliflower.

I've given up my starches and sugars... and now... now my yogurt?

And how about my writing? Will I ever be talented enough to write about the complexities of the human soul, or will I forever be condemned to describe dog farts and dirty laundry?

The sum of my talent, I'm afraid, may be limited to vivid descriptions of body odor and adolescent angst.

And I'm not sure I can face that fact without a limitless supply of Yoplait by my side.

"Eloquence Escapes Me"

There are many things I do well.

I can fire a softball from centerfield to home with laser precision. I can change a diaper while simultaneously holding an infant and coaxing a preschooler into bed. I can belt out an aria that would make you sit up and take notice.

Listening? I'm a great listener.

My penmanship (when I put forth the effort) is fairly nice.

I can sing any bad 80s lyrics that you can't recall, and I can spell anything if I've seen it in print at least once.

I'm pretty good at conceiving and growing babies. (The parenting part is still questionable.)

After several critical fails, I've learned to become a true and loyal friend.

Chris might add a few others to the list of things I excel at...

But what am I definitely not good at?

Speaking in front of a group.

That group might consist of my family, my closest friends, my book club members, my work colleagues, complete strangers... it doesn't matter.

I learned in Catholic School that where two or more are gathered in His name, God is there. In my own existence, where two or more are gathered, my tongue inevitably fails me.

One on one, I'm great. I can have heartfelt, meaningful, intelligent conversations with my husband and my best friends. I can converse with any stranger in a room.

But put me in front of crowd? Epic fail.

I've never been a good verbal storyteller, have never been able to pull off a witty joke. When I sang in front of crowds, I always had to rely on a beta blocker to soothe my jangled nerves. But even singing was better than speaking. Because singing allowed me to prepare, to rehearse, to learn every note precisely.

Off the cuff, I'm a disaster.

It's not that I don't want to be the center of attention. I do, in fact, enjoy a performance now and then. But I'm a bad verbal performer. I cannot form a coherent sentence if I have an audience consisting of more than two living, breathing human beings.

And not only can I not convey my most scintillating thoughts and feelings, but I actually excel at blurting out stupid, nonsensical shit directly from my gaping maw. Phrases such as, "stuff and stuff..." and "blah, blah, blah..." and "ummm."

And my favorite self faux pas? Incorrectly using a word, a cliche, or an idiom. As in, "Keep your nose to the ground." Ahh, that would actually be, "Keep your ear to the ground." Or perhaps, "Keep your nose to the grindstone." Wrong body part? Wrong destination? You pick.

Those who don't know me well must think I'm a blubbering idiot. Those who do know me well probably think twice about their choice of companions.

I used to think my inability to express myself adequately was attributable to early onset Alzheimer's. Now I'm pretty sure I'm just a dumb ass.

My written words may not always be resplendent, but they sure as hell beat their verbal opponents. Every time.

That's not saying much, though.

I think Lucy and Maggie might express themselves more eloquently.

And they eat their own poop.

"Focus"

It's no secret that I'm working on a novel. Writing a book is hard. Harder than I remember. I wrote one in high school (bad). And one in college (worse). Those didn't seem quite as challenging as this one. (I'm hoping that means my current novel might have a bit of merit.)

I think about my book all the time. Obsess about it, really. I wonder if the topic is engaging, if the characters are true, if the story line is believable. Then I go out on the Internet and research books like mine. And publishers who might be interested in this sort of book. And author blogs. And what the weather is currently like in San Francisco.

Eventually, I sit down to write. And words spill out of me like volcanic lava. Or not. And when the words do come, I examine them at least 50 times, rearrange them, look them up on dictionary.com to make sure I'm using them correctly.

I've got over 10,000 words written (love that Microsoft word counter), but they're not yet cohesive. (I just went to look up "cohesive" and got distracted by Dooce.com and a horrifying story about two young children being shot in Indianapolis.)

Maybe it's not the writing that's so difficult. Maybe it's my adult-onset ADD.

It's the sitting-down-to-write part that gets me every time. Once I'm here, I love to spew out all my thoughts, ideas, and opinions. I just can't seem to get to my desk to do it. With four kids and a thousand different activities, a husband who's working on his doctorate and/or at work all the time, two dogs, four mice, a fish named John, a house, never-ending laundry, an overgrown lawn, and a part-time job with full-time hours, it seems my writing often ends up on the back burner.

Now please excuse me while I start some dinner. And feed the dogs. And run the kids to karate. And work out at the gym. And chase some dust bunnies that are bigger than Lucy. And scrapbook some of our favorite family memories. And check in on my mom. And research the best summer vacation spots. And read the latest novel by Julia Glass.

My novel? It's coming. Possibly by 2053.

Reflections on Motherhood

The Adolescent Years

There is no such thing as an ordinary person, and no human being has ever fully seen or appreciated another. We are too vast. ~ Paul Richards

"Pieces of Me"

George lost a tooth this weekend. Looking at his gap-toothed smile makes me smile in return. I remember when he was born and his eyes were still squinty, his cheeks not yet pink and chubby – when we thought perhaps we'd used up all the good-looking babies and should have stopped while we were ahead – and I look at him now and my heart skips a beat. When he's not being spanked or grounded, I truly could eat him up. Such a love in my heart for that sweet, rotten, handsome boy, the one who rivals his Daddy in volume.

I watched Mary Claire sleep the other night – her blankie pulled up to her cheek, her fingers in her mouth. And I remembered her as an infant in the same pose – her tiny toes sticking through the slats of her crib. That sweet baby smiled all the time. As the third in four years, she knew she had to wait her turn for attention. And she'd sit patiently in her high chair, smiling at the antics of her big brothers, until it was her turn. Now she listens to "The Rose" when she feels sad or betrayed. Her kind and caring heart is a true gift.

Sweet Gus, our sick, sick boy. When I see him on stage, I wonder at the journey he's taken thus far in his ten years. From the brink of leaving this world far too soon to growing into such a fine, deep thinking, young man. He's such an enigma to me, and possibly even to himself. But I can't help but think that he's destined for great things. He's a still water that runs deep, and I'm anxious to see what changes he will bring to this world.

And then there's Sam. Such a short time ago, he was my fat little baby who spit up nonstop. Now he's smart, sullen, and moody like a pre-teen should be. And yet he still hugs me, still cries when he's sad, still wants me to be with him when he's afraid. He's discovering who he is, who he wants to be, who his true friends are. He firmly shakes hands with every adult he meets – he makes his mama proud, that one.

I marvel at this journey we're all taking together. Me – who once dreamt only of becoming a powerful career woman, who had no ambitions of marrying or having kids – here I am with a husband I adore and four kids who define and shape every day of my life.

People often ask if I'm sad to see my kids grow up, if I cry when they boarded the school bus for the first time, if it made me weepy when they no longer wanted to kiss me goodbye in front of their friends. And I tell them the truth. It doesn't make me sad. I can't be sad when they have so much happiness in them, so many discoveries to make every day, so much living to embrace. These tiny pieces of me are becoming individuals before my very eyes. Every day, I learn something new about them. Every day, I am so very grateful for these gifts I have been given.

Unworthy, yes. But so very, very grateful.

"The March of Time"

On the day I turned 38, George came home from school, the Boys and Girls Club, and Chris's office with pockets stuffed full of pictures. He spent a good amount of time digging them out of his pockets and then handed them to me. They were all folded into small, lopsided squares. The corners were bent, and the papers themselves were warm. Carefully drawn on the inside were images of little stick-figured boys holding hands with stick-figured moms.

They were the best birthday presents ever.

Nine short months later, my oldest turned twelve. Just one year away from being a teenager.

Wasn't it yesterday that I breathed in the baby soft smell of his freshly washed newborn hair? It wasn't so long ago that he giggled and cooed and wrapped his chubby arms around my legs, was it? And now...

Now he's a preteen – full of raging hormones and angst and the occasional facial blemish. He stinks when he forgets his deodorant, but he still needs to be reminded to brush his teeth.

I can't bring myself to go near his big, man-size feet. And don't even get me started on his toenails. And still, his beloved Paddington Bear – worn down to the stuffing in so many places – sits by his bedside every night.

He's a joker. His sense of humor, sharp and quick. His brain is always moving, always thinking ahead. But he still crosses the line between funny and obnoxious, he still needs The Look when he's taken his jokes a step too far.

Only three more years before he starts to drive, six more years before he becomes a man. He'll be infinitely smarter than I could ever hope to be. The world is at his feet – if he'd just get off the Xbox long enough to take it by storm.

When he was 11, Sam informed me that he was 50/50 on the whole Santa Claus thing. I think he was afraid if he admitted to no longer believing, he'd no longer be receiving. Now he's closing in on the dreaded teenage years, but still such a child in so many ways.

Sam and Gus slept together in Gus's room that next Christmas Eve. George and Mary were together in George's room. Watching them sleep and remembering the Christmas anticipation I felt as a child made my heart skip a beat.

They are good kids, kind kids, smart kids. The have the entire world at their disposal, and it's my job to teach them to embrace it.

That's a big undertaking.

It's challenging to teach when the teacher is still learning. But, I suppose, that's what life is all about – constantly moving, constantly growing, constantly absorbing. The task of raising them to be productive, relatively happy, well-adjusted members of society is overwhelming. But I wouldn't trade it for the world.

That Christmas, Sam, Gus, Mary Claire, and George found a Wii and Nintendo DSs under the tree, but the greatest gift they will ever receive is the gift of love, stability, and opportunity. Chris and I will continue to give that gift to them.

And my greatest hope is that someday, they will learn to provide it for themselves.

"Ch...ch...ch...changes"

Ralph Waldo Emerson once said, "For everything you have missed, you have gained something else, and for everything you gain, you lose something else."

There is so much happening in our lives right now. So much changing, shifting, morphing. We're passengers on a ship in a tumultuous sea. We're holding on for dear life – trying to enjoy the view while simultaneously trying not to barf over the side.

So many changes. Changes for us, changes for our friends, changes in our friendships. Things we once believed to be forever... well, maybe not so much anymore. Forever is tricky that way.

God is a jokester, isn't He? (Yes, Chris, God just showed up in my prose again.) Just when you think you have it all figured out, He laughs and says, "Psych!"

(Really. He might say "psych." Maybe He says "Fo Shizzle," too. I dare you to prove me wrong.)

But the bottom line is this: He's the one in control. I think we learned that lesson very well when we nearly lost Gus. The relinquishing of our perceived power, the opening up of our tight-fisted hands. The most important lesson of our lives.

Chris likes to call it "our circle of influence." When I get a little controlling (yes, I get that way occasionally), he likes to draw a teeny, tiny, imaginary circle with his finger.

"This," he explains, "is your circle of influence."

Then he uses both of his arms to draw a giant, imaginary circle around his little circle.

"THIS," he continues, "is outside your circle of influence."

And, ultimately, it's true.

I can't force anyone to be a part of my life. But I can embrace those who choose to be. I can't be assured that the jobs, the house, the cars we have today will be the same ones we have tomorrow. But I can continue to work hard and make plans and map out a future – albeit one with a flexible path.

And what can I do every day? Love my husband. Respect him. Laugh with him. Cry with him. Support him. He is my constant. My rock. The one I can always rely upon. My other half. Often, my better half.

And I can embrace my kids. I can hug them, teach them, cuddle with them, look in at their sleeping faces and feel that overwhelming sense of humility rising in my chest. These babies of mine who are really not babies anymore. Part of me, part of Chris, but uniquely individual. Some stinky, some not. Some sweet, some bitter. But always – unequivocally – loved and cherished.

Today is not tomorrow and tomorrow is never guaranteed. So, I will continue to be thankful for what I have today. Right now. This instant.

After all, it is enough.

"A Big Life"

In the halcyon days of my youth, I thought I was important. Defined by my academic success, my athletic endeavors, and my wide, but tight, circle of friends, I existed in a world that revolved around me, around my wants and needs, around my neuroses and angst.

When I was blessed enough to bring another life into this world, my universe expanded. With Sam, with Gus, with Mary Claire, with George – my world became exponentially bigger, my self-absorption, much less significant. My own needs? Largely unimportant. (Although I must admit that Chris and I abide by the oxygen mask rule that is driven home on every flight – you must put your own oxygen mask on before you can assist others. We're no good without oxygen. And so, we breathe, we re-group, we reconnect with each other often and with great purpose and enthusiasm.)

Parenting is a tenuous and fragile gift. The responsibility for the safety and well-being of four other creatures is a daunting task indeed. But when you check on a flush-faced, sleeping toddler boy with his pudgy hand tucked safely and securely into the front of his diaper, and when your little girl picks up your phone call and greets you with high-pitched, babbling, nonsensical excitement, you understand that your life has become Big.

A Big Life is a gift. A treasure. A never-ending ride complete with a cocktail (shaken, not stirred) of laughter, tears, fear, humility, joy, anticipation, excitement – and the occasional shot of Vodka.

Will I still feel that way when my adolescents become teenagers? When their Carters are tossed aside for Abercrombie and Fitch? When their beloved blankies morph into cell phones? And their rosy, baby cheeks are filled with acne?

We're on the cusp of trading diapers and bedtime stories for deodorant and slammed doors. But like every other phase of life that has rolled our way (sometimes like a speeding train), we're embracing our journey. After all, it brings us one small step closer to sending them off to college, downsizing, and drinking our morning coffee in silent solitude.

Or something like that.

"The Next Chapter"

Seventeen years after I graduated, Chris and I had the opportunity to return to Ball State University for an Emens Scholars reunion. Campus has changed so much since we've been there. It feels so familiar and yet vastly different. It's not our school anymore. We've been usurped by an army of young, energetic, ambitious kids who have the world at their feet.

It's amazing to look at their bright, eager baby faces and realize that these college kids are closer to my own kids' ages than they are to mine. I'd like to believe I'm still young and hip. But my kids – and my mirror – keep telling me otherwise.

It's been 17 years since I was a student at Ball State. *Seventeen years.*

When I was 17 years old, I had the world at my feet, too. I had a heart full of teenage angst, washboard abs, and a new boyfriend. (Who, incidentally, in seven years became my husband.)

Chris and I will celebrate 15 years of marriage next month. *Fifteen years.*

When I was 15 years old, I played on a nationally ranked AAU basketball team, I was beginning my high school career, and I was surrounded by a vast circle of friends – many of whom I adore, but none of whom I keep in close contact with anymore.

Sam will turn 13 in November. (Yes, go ahead and say it in italics.) We are going to be parents of a teenager. Soon, he'll be beginning his own high school career, determining which friends to associate himself with, and figuring out how to find comfort in his own acne-ridden skin.

We'll have a teenager, and we haven't yet mastered the art of grade-school parenting.

Much to our surprise, our kids continue to move into the next phase of life when we really haven't passed the final exam for parenting them in the previous stage.

I'm going to be 40 soon. (I can't bring myself to italicize it.) If I'd been precocious enough to buy a house when I was ten, I'd be making my final mortgage payment this year.

Gus is ten. He could have paid off two car loans by now.

This unstoppable march of time is surreal to me. How in the world can we be nearing 40, our parents nearing their 70s and 80s? We were pretty good at being young. Can we handle middle age?

When I look at my mom now and see my grandma, it takes my breath away. And yet, there she is with her powder-soft hair and her wrinkled and spotted hands. When she was my age, my mom was beautiful beyond words. With her jet-black pixie cut and her mocha eyes, she turned heads everywhere she went and invited more marriage proposals than any one woman I know. She's still beautiful, but so fragile. So very different from that younger woman whom men adored and whose lap was my safe place to land.

We dropped the kids with Chris's parents while we visited our alma mater, and I was struck — as I often am — by their own dance with time. Still young at heart in so many ways, they're fast approaching 80. And always, I'm worried that our kids will wear them out, that we ask too much when we ask a day of them. And so we leave our own kids with strict instructions to be helpful, to be thoughtful, to bring joy to their grandparents instead of fatigue.

I wonder if the kids play on the family farm and dream away the days like I used to at their age. Do they lie in the grass and watch the clouds float by — pointing out elephants and airplanes and dog butts?

Does a single day feel like a year to them? That gloriously vast, endless stretch of unscheduled time? A year when you're young can stretch on forever. And then you turn around...and you're 40. From grass-stained knees and dirty toenails to bills and bank accounts and parent-teacher conferences.

It happens without warning.

Chris and I talked about a great deal of things during our drive on Saturday. We discussed our future, his career aspirations, the litany of novels waiting to move from my head to my paper. He recently read something indicating that with medical and technological advances, we could potentially live to be 118.

So we agreed to live to 118. And we promised to stay healthy. And we shook on it.

And we're making our kids agree to live to 150. Or else.

I mean, damn! We've got a lot of living yet to do. We've got kids to raise, future in-laws to disapprove of, grandkids to welcome, vacations to take, books to write, old farmhouses to remodel, friends to share good Cabernet with, libraries to explore, foreign countries that we've never set foot in. How can there possibly be enough time to accomplish everything we need to do?

118 years will help.

Now, I realize that if we both die at 118, I'll go a year before Chris. And that's okay. Because if he goes first and my Internet goes down, or the washing machine stops working, or a giant spider takes up residence in my bedroom, or George can't figure out how to properly position his protective cup, or grubs take over the lawn, or large birds need to be properly identified, or complex math problems need to be solved, well, then, I'm going to be in trouble.

But Chris will always have spellcheck. So, he'll be okay. And I'm guessing that he might even enjoy a well-deserved year of relative peace and quiet.

After 100 years with me, he'll probably have earned it.

"Flying"

Chris and I dropped the kids off with his parents and barricaded the basement stairs so Maggie couldn't venture down there to poop all over the floor in her separation anxiety-induced state. Early the next morning, we flew out of Indy for a long weekend of writing and re-connecting in Carrabelle, Florida.

Flying always makes me a bit edgy. I know in my head that it's a safer means of transportation than driving, but in my heart, it just seems so unnatural for us to be moving above the clouds in a giant, metal machine. My friend, Lynn, comforts herself by imagining God's hands lifting her up off the ground and carrying her to her destination. I found that image quite comforting as well.

And the Xanax didn't hurt, either.

My kids want more than anything to fly. With four kids, we've always driven on all of our vacations. We figured it was more fiscally prudent for us to invest in a giant Suburban with loads of cargo space than to fork out airfare for the six of us whenever we left home. And so far, it's worked well.

But the kids are antsy. They want to take a trip to California, to Hawaii, to someplace that requires us to fly. Two of them will vomit the entire way. One will be scared out of his gourd when he sees the houses below him turn into a scene straight out of Monopoly. Only one will appreciate the adventure. Only my brave girl.

And yet I'd like to grant them that wish soon.

Because flying is magical.

When I was a kid, flying took my breath away. The combination of fear and excitement and motion sickness kept me at the edge of my seat and glued to my tiny view of the disappearing world below. And despite what all the adults in my life said, I was convinced that those fluffy clouds surrounding me could hold me aloft like a giant bouncy house made of cotton candy. I defended my position with the annoying self-righteousness I used in my coyote pronunciation argument. (It can be pronounced "coyote" or "coy-oat." User preference. And now that I'm an English major grad, I continue to argue that I have the right to make up words and pronunciations as I see fit. This is one reason why Chris is so endeared to me. When I argue an indefensible point, he'll simply say two syllables, "Coy. Oat.")

Yesterday's flight was breathtaking. We took off into a misty, overcast gray sky. And I was white-knuckling my armrest and trying my damndest not to grab the hand of the unsuspecting stranger unlucky enough to be seated beside me.

But an hour or so into our flight, we rose above the storm clouds into the most beautiful sunrise imaginable. There was a distinct line between the dark clouds, the cotton candy clouds, and the blazing sunrise. Words are inadequate to describe the scene. (At least *my* words are inadequate. Julia Glass might not have the same issue.)

I never feel very far from the God who created and keeps us, but I have to admit that He felt much closer to me in that sunrise.

Looking down on the tiny forests and rivers and streams, the well-appointed and over-manicured neighborhood lawns, the bright blue swimming pools, the highways crawling with ant-cars, always makes me realize how small and insignificant I really am.

But.

I don't want to be insignificant. I don't want my kids' lives to be insignificant. We grapple so much with making the right decisions, moving to the right neighborhoods, taking the right jobs.

And there's so much world out there.

We've barely even scratched the surface.

I want my kids to fly because I want them to see the enormity of the life they've been blessed with. I want them to see that they can go anywhere, do anything, be anything. I want them to understand that not making the seventh grade basketball team isn't the end of the world. That losing a friend to a catty clique of girls won't change their existence. That not fitting in with their fifth grade peers doesn't mean they're not exceptionally unique with greater gifts to share with the world. Sure, every little thing that happens to us shapes who we are, helps define our path.

But the path is so limitless.

And too often, I'm afraid that I'll be the one to hold them back. That my fear of losing them to some unknown danger will force me into keeping them by my side where I foolishly believe I can protect them.

Because although I'm their temporary keeper on this earth, they all belong to a greater God who has bigger plans for them than I could ever imagine.

It's an interesting juxtaposition.

Those four little people are my life. They are the air that I breathe, the hope that I pin on this world. Losing one of them would cause my world to end in many significant ways. But if they lost me? They would still have this beautiful, wonderful gift of life. They would carry on. They would make their way.

My Dave's new song, "You and Me" has such a poignant line. "And when the kids are old enough, we're gonna teach them to fly."

There is no better gift we could offer them.

Bradley United Methodist Church
PENNSYLVANIA AND MAIN STREETS
GREENFIELD, INDIANA 46140